NEW ENGLISH FIRSTHAND

DEVELOPING COMMUNICATIVE LANGUAGE SKILLS

TEACHER'S MANUAL

Marc Helgesen
Steven Brown
Thomas Mandeville
Robin Jordan

development editor
Michael Rost

LINGUAL HOUSE

Teacher's Manual Contents

Teacher's Manual Page Reference

CONTENTS

INTRODUCTION

NEW ENGLISH FIRSTHAND is a functional course for elementary students of English as a Foreign or Second Language. As the title suggests, **NEW ENGLISH FIRSTHAND** gives the students direct experience with understanding and using English.

The syllabus of **NEW ENGLISH FIRSTHAND** is consistent with communicative teaching methodology in that it allows the students---as soon as possible--- to engage in meaningful interaction in English. The ideas, information, and choices for the main activities come directly from the participants---the textbook serves as a framework for preparation, organization, and evaluation.

The overall textbook design ensures that beginning students receive balanced practice with listening, speaking, reading, and writing skills. Each unit is based on a set of language functions and introduces grammatical patterns and lexical items that are most commonly used with the functions presented. A "classroom language" syllabus introduces and reviews expressions which allow students to clarify and understand things they hear.

Each of the twelve units consists of six separate sections: (1) **Listening** -- listening tasks, (2) **Conversation** -- conversation models, (3) **Duet** -- pair work, (4) **Solo** -- individual writing practice, (5) **Ensemble** -- group interaction, and (6) **Check Yourself** -- lesson review.

The book also provides integrated review activities to allow the students to practice what they are learning through PROJECT WORK. These activities, contained in the REVIEW SECTION, are best used after Units 6 and 12. Additionally, two vocabulary review activities -- SLAP!, a vocabulary game and LET'S TALK, a fluency game -- recycle what the students have learned.

A single unit in **ENGLISH FIRSTHAND** is designed to cover two to four class hours, depending on the extent to which each activity is used. Details and suggestions on using the text are provided on the pages of this manual that correspond to the pages in the student's book.

• LISTENING

The listening section is a very important part of the **English Firsthand** course. The first section of each unit -- the first two pages -- is the listening seciton; this section is linked with a taped extract from the **ENGLISH FIRSTHAND cassette**. The tape contains a narration of the introductiory Getting Ready section (see below) and all of the activity instructions, both of which are also printed in the student book. The extracts which are used in the exercises, however, are not printed in the student book. The TAPESCRIPT is contained only in this TEACHER'S MANUAL.

Each listening task corresponds to the unit theme and functions (meeting and introducing people, stating preferences, etc.). The ***Getting Ready*** section activates vocabulary, concepts, and expressions the students will need to perform the task successfully. This "schema building" (activation) helps students use their knowledge and experience to become more effective listeners. Written explanations have been kept to a minimum in order to keep the activity focused on listening rather than reading.

Following this brief preparation, the listening task is presented. The task generally calls for a simple selection from a series of photographs, illustrations, or brief written completion choices; occasionally the students are asked to write out a phrase or a sentence to complete the task.

Consistent with a natural acquisition approach to language learning, the listening "inputs" contain language which, in context, is understandable even though it may be beyond the production capacities of beginning and low-intermediate students. It is important for the teacher to encourage the students to focus on selecting parts of or clues from the input that help them perform the task.

Exposure to this higher level of language input in the context of a focused task will assist the students in developing their listening abilities and in dealing with English-speaking situations. Because the listening section is at a higher level than their productive abilities, many students will initially find this section difficult. The lesson plan pages of this TEACHER'S MANUAL provide techniques for making the listening more accessible for weaker students.

• CONVERSATION

The conversation section of each unit is important for introducing controlled speaking practice prior to the more open pair work (Duet) and group work (Ensemble) speaking tasks. A basic conversation model is given in each unit. It consists of approximately four A-B exchanges.

The conversation practice encourages the students to develop flexibility in using language patterns. Flexibility is encouraged through having the students select from a group of possible choices as they practice each conversation.

As the students work in pairs for this activity, it is important for them to realize that selection of one choice in any of the substitution slots inevitably changes the topic or theme of the planned conversation (just as speaker choices do in actual conversation). Therefore, it is important that students listen to the choice made by their partners before deciding what to say in their next speaking turn.

The use of choices directs the students to pay careful attention as they go through the dialogue, rather than leading them to recite lines quickly. Teachers should allow ample time for the students to perform the conversation. It is preferable for the student pairs to practice each convesation more than once so that they can switch roles, produce new combinations, and have fun as they practice, using the **Conversation Variations** given in this manual.

After the students have practiced the dialogue, they may add their own choices in the substitution slots, as well as expand on the basic dialogue. The conversations are kept open-ended so students can create their own continuations for the conversation.

One variation of the conversation is recorded on the **ENGLISH FIRSTHAND cassette tape**. It may be useful to allow the students to listen carefully to and repeat the taped conversation before they practice on their own. The tape can be also be used as a listening exercise (for example, by asking the students to recreate the gist of the dialogue after hearing it once) or as a memory aid for when they practice the conversation in pairs. Alternatively, the students may listen to the taped version after they have practiced in order to compare the taped version with their version.

This manual provides lesson-by-lesson notes on the special features of each dialogue, as well as additional suggestions for the classroom use of the conversations. Generally, the following procedure can be used:

1. Play the tape as the students read along silently. Answer questions about vocabulary.
2. (Optional) Play the tape again, one line at a time. Have students repeat.
3. Students work in pairs, practicing the conversation.
4. Students continue to practice, using the substitutions in the box at the bottom of the page.
5. Students insert substitutions of their own into the slots.

It is suggested that, after the initial introduction, the students spend a few minutes each class period practicing the dialogue.

• DUET

The DUET section is the crux of each unit. The DUET section is built around a PAIR WORK activity, which is designed on the basis of an information gap. For this activity it is essential that the students work in pairs. One student, who should refer only to the DUET A page during the exercise, has information unknown to his or her partner, who should refer only to the DUET B page throughout the activity.

Information gap tasks are well known for their communicative value: students ask each other for information they actually need to complete the task. A language reference box at the top of each DUET page ensures that students have access to language patterns and routines they need to collaborate on the DUET task.

In order to assure that all students are equipped to manage the activity, it may be useful to have the students listen to and repeat the sentences in the language reference box before doing the activity. This preparation helps ensure that they can focus on communication during the activity because they know where in the box to find forms they need. Also, they will have gone beyond the sheer physical difficulty that often accompanies saying something for the first time in a new language.

Each DUET activity is designed for a maximum of verbal interaction: the language box encourages accuracy, the communication task develops fluency. Before the students begin to work in pairs, the teacher should make sure that all students understand whatever background information has been given on the page as well as the task directions. During the pair activity itself, the teacher should circulate, answer questions for individual pairs and provide help to individuals as the need arises.

Detailed lessons plans for each acitivty are provided on the pages of this manual. Generally, the DUET tasks follow this procedure:

1. Divide the class into pairs (A and B). Have the students look at the appropriate page in their books.
2. Establish meaning for the information on the page and the task directions. Answer vocabulary questions.
3. Note the language box at the top of the page. Have the students practice the language in it.
4. Have the students do the activity. Circulate throughout the room, answering questions and noting areas for later work.
5. After the students have completed the activity, allow time for expansion and further correction (see information on corrections below).

If you have an odd number of students, it is suggested that you have one group of three (two people take part A) rather than joining a pair yourself. You will want to be free to help other students and make notes for later work during the activity time.

Some pairs inevitably complete the task before others. A BONUS! task is provided at the bottom of each DUET page. Students who finish the main task early should go one to the BONUS! for further, less controlled practice of the target functions and forms.

This TEACHER'S MANUAL provides a wide selection of **additional activities** and **expansion activities** that can be used after the DUET.

• SOLO

The SOLO section of each unit is useful for developing communicative skills in written English. In addition to their communication value, SOLO activities provide a tangible assignment for the teacher to collect, record, and comment on.

The SOLO section is built around short, focused writing activities that are done by students working individually. As such, the activities can be assigned as homework, or used as lead-in or follow-up activities at the beginning or end of a long class period.

Each SOLO activity is based on a written model (an announcement, a letter, etc.). Students provide their own information in completing the written task.

SOLO activities provide an excellent basis for informal peer interaction and evaluation. In peer evaluation, students read each other's writing and comment on or ask questions about what the other has written. This manual provides ideas in each unit for both an **in-class follow-up** and for **optional skill-building exercises**, which will allow your students to develop their reading and writing skills within the communicative goals of **ENGLISH FIRSTHAND.**

• ENSEMBLE

The ENSEMBLE section of each unit is extremely important for developing group cohesion and for establishing English as a means of communication among your students.

All of the ENSEMBLE activities are---in keeping with the orchestra metaphor---designed for groups of three or more. The suggested number for each group is given in the directions for each activity. The ENSEMBLE activities typically resemble games in that they have a purpose, reward quick thinking, and are entertaining.

Appearing near the end of each unit, ENSEMBLE activities allow the students to use language from all the preceding sections. The task given usually requires a student to interact verbally with several other students (for example, to plan a tour of their city or to make up and tell a story). During or at the end of the activity, the students produce something in writing as evidence of having performed the task successfully.

A specific plan is provided for each ENSEMBLE activity. The general procedure is as follows:

1. Have the students read the information on the page. Answer vocabulary questions.
2. Divide the class into groups based on the location of their desks,their ability levels (in which case generally students in the groups should be at roughly the same level to avoid having the stronger students monopolize), or random choice.
3. Note the language reference box. (Optional) Have the students practice saying the forms they are not familiar with.
4. If there is pre-activity work (for example, filling in a chart), allow time for the students to do it before the activity begins.
5. Have the students perform the activity. Circulate, answer questions and note areas for further work.

ENSEMBLES (except those whole class activities in which all students will finish at the same time) are followed by a **TRY THIS!** activity. Groups which finish the main task early should go on to the **TRY THIS!** for further, less controlled practice of the target functions and forms. Alternately, the **TRY THIS!** can be used as a separate activity during the following class.

• CHECK YOURSELF

CHECK YOURSELF is a useful section which appears at the end of each unit. The CHECK YOURSELF section allows students to review functional language, grammatical forms and vocabulary introduced in the unit.

Students work individually, or in pairs. Alternatively, the class as a whole may do the exercises orally, with the teacher moderating the activities. Each CHECK YOURSELF section has 20 items, so that a score can be kept, if desired.

Throughout **ENGLISH FIRSTHAND**, classroom language expressions (.e.g, "What does _____ mean?") appear in speech balloons. These are located in places that students are likely to need the given expression. A complete list appears on page 124 of the text for easy student reference. Students should be encouraged to make use of these phrases during classroom activities. Teachers and students should add to this list as the need for new classroom expressions arises.

• REVIEW ACTIVITIES

The APPENDIX CONTAINS four separate REVIEW ACTIVITIES:

(1) THE CLASS NEWSPAPER
(2) PROJECT FAIR
(3) SLAP!
(4) LET'S TALK!

THE CLASS NEWSPAPER and PROJECT FAIR are project work activities which call for students to direct their own learning. Projects, while demanding, are very rewarding in that students take on and accomplish a major task using English.

THE CLASS NEWSPAPER, recommended for use after Unit 6, recycles the language taught in the first half of the book. It guides student through the process of creating a newspaper.

PROJECT FAIR, which is recommended to be used after the text is completed, involves students -- usually in pairs -- in designing and carrying out their own projects. The results can be shared as a class or school event.

SLAP is a vocabulary review game, which can be utilized at different times during the course. SLAP 1 reviews vocabulary from Units 1-6. SLAP 2 covers Units 7-12.

LET'S TALK! is a fluency game. Students share their ideas and experiences while reviewing language taught throughout the course. LET'S TALK! can also be used as part of student evaluation in classes where grades are given. (See the special note along with the LET'S TALK! teaching notes.)

• EXTRA ACTIVITIES

In addition to the extra activities offered in the student textbook, his TEACHER'S MANUAL contains a rich storehouse of supplementary activities that can be used throughout the course. These varied activities, which are keyed in this manual to specific purposes in units and sections, will come under these names:

- **Optional warm-up activity**
  (a lead in to the LISTENING tasks)
- **Conversation variation**
  (an alternate way to practice the CONVERSATION)
- **Additional Activity**
  (a thematic activity linked to the DUET)
- **Expansion Activity**
  (a fluency activity linked to the DUET)

• **Optional Skill-Building Activity**
(a communicative writing exercise linked to the SOLO section)

These activities are intended to be used selectively by teachers in order to address particular student learning styles and to fill specific course goals.

• QUIZZES

In addition to the CHECK YOURSELF quizzes, which appear at the end of each unit, this manual provides separate supplementary quizzes. These quizzes appear at the back of the manual, along with an **answer key**.

Each quiz covers two units and has questions worth 20 points. The quizzes may be copied for distribution to the students. It is suggested that the quizzes be corrected in class either by the students themselves or with the students exchanging papers. In this way, students receive immediate feedback about their progress.

• Tips for teaching *ENGLISH FIRSTHAND*

•Large classes

ENGLISH FIRSTHAND was designed for and tested in large classes. The extensive use of pair work makes it possible to maximize the time students are actively using English. Since most students in large classes may not be accustomed to a communicative approach to language learning, the following procedures are recommended to make the material as effective as possible:

• Working in pairs

Once students are used to pair work, dividing the class will be no problem. At first you will probably need to arrange the class in pairs. Pair work is most effective when the students are looking at each other both so that they can make eye contact when they speak (rather than look down at their books) and because they are less likely to look at their partner's pages.

The easiest way to make this arrangement is by having the students in the row of desks closest to the front stand, turn their chairs around and sit looking at the students behind them.

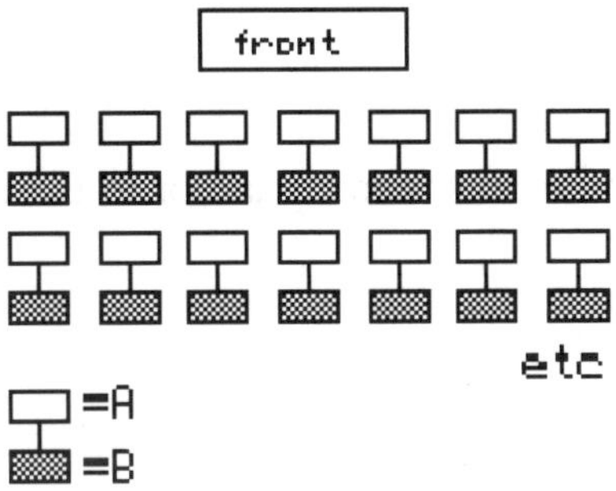

Students in all odd-numbered rows (3rd, 5th, etc. from the front) do the same. It is not necessary for them to move their desks.

If there is an odd number of students, one "pair" can consist of three students, with two students taking part as "A" and alternating turns during the activity.

• Giving instructions

Ways to give short, clear instructions are provided in the lesson plan sections of this manual. These instructions are indicated in *italic* type. One should remember, however, that explaining an activity is often the least effective way to get the students to understand what to do. Activities should be demonstrated:

-Do one or two examples with yourself "playing the role" of the student.
-Direct two students through the first part of an activity while the others watch.
-If an activity is somewhat complicated, teach it to 10-20% of the students while the others are working on something else. Have them teach the activity to the others in small groups.

If you feel it is necessary to give the instructions in the students' native language, this should be done only after they have heard the instructions in English.

• Teaching sequence

ENGLISH FIRSTHAND is usually taught in two or three class meetings (lessons) per unit. The following is a suggested lesson sequence:

Two lesson unit plan:

Class one:
1. (Warm-up) Optional activity listed in this manual and/or in-class follow-up for previous unit's *Check yourself*.
2. *Listening*
3. *Conversation*
4. *Duet*
Homework: *Solo*

Class two:
1. (Warm-up) In-class follow-up for *Solo*. and/or *Conversation* (short review/practice)
2. *Ensemble*
3. Optional activity listed in this manual
Homework: *Check yourself*

Three lesson unit plan:

Class one:
1. (Warm-up) Optional activity listed in this manual and/or in-class follow-up for previous unit's *Check yourself*.
2. *Listening*
3. *Conversation*

Class two:
1. (Warm-up) *Conversation* (short review/practice)
2. *Duet*
3. *Duet expansion* or *Solo*
Homework: *Solo* (of not done in class)

Class three:

1. (Warm-up) In-class follow-up for *Solo,* and/or *Conversation* (short review/practice)
2. *Ensemble*
3. One of the optional activities provided in this manual.

Homework: *Check yourself*

• Grading, checking homework

In many large class situations, the time required to check all student homework and classwork is not justified. With *Check yourself* material, go over the first few questions together, having several students either write their answers on the board or say their answers. Have them check their other answers for meaning using the "in-class follow-up" procedure listed in this manual. As they are checking their work, circulate and make a note of which students have not done the homework or who have only done part of it. Since regular study (rather than intensive cramming before tests) is necessary to learn to use English, consistency of homework should be a large part of the students' grades.

The quizzes should be corrected in class so the students get immediate feedback on their progress. The quizzes can then be collected and the scores recorded.

The LET'S TALK! and PROJECT FAIR review activities can be used as part of student assessment. Details are given along with the lesson notes.

Attendance and participation should also be considered when grading.

• Reluctant students

Change pair and group partners regularly so that even students who are reluctant to get involved are sometimes working with students who may encourage them to be more active.

Students in large classes are, understandably, often reluctant to answer questions in front of the entire class. This is caused not so much by shyness but by the fear of embarrassment if they are wrong. Minimize the questions students should answer in front of the entire group. When you need to ask questions to the whole group, limit them to "content" questions (where you are looking for real information, not just the correct use of a particular form). As the students answer, make no comment about the form. Simply restate the answer in the correct form if necessary.

One procedure that may be effective for encouraging reluctant students to answer questions is this: have all of the students stand. Each student can sit down after he or she has answered (right or wrong).

• Staying in English

Since students in EFL classes usually share the same native language, they have no real social need to use English as the common medium of communication. In order to encourage a gradual adoption of English as the medium of communication in your class, make sure they use the "classroom language" expressions that appear throughout the book. All of the expressions are listed at the end of the book for convenient student reference. You may wish to make a large wall chart with these expressions (writing in new expressions or routines that come up in your class) so you can point to the chart when the students need help staying in English.

In activities that can be done as games (for example, many of the *Duet* and *Ensemble* activities) students could get points for correct guesses (or similar answers), give counters (tokens, poker chips, etc.) for each point. Students may also take a point away from another student each time that person uses the native language. Once the students know the "chip game" it can be done with other activities by giving every student about 5 counters before the activity starts. If students are reluctant to take points from their partners, have them collect points for a team (e.g., All the A's in row one are a team. All the B's in row two are another team. etc.)

Another way to help them stay in English is to allow the students to use their native language only when they stand up. This type of procedure makes the students consciously think about when they wish to switch to their first language.

• **Corrections**

Making mistakes is a natural and important part of the language learning process. Students should not be made to feel self-conscious about making mistakes. You may find it useful to introduce techniques that can help the students become more accurate, without feeling the embarrassment that sometimes comes with teacher correction.

The purpose of corrections should always be to help the students find and correct their own mistakes. For that reason, corrections are more effective if the student, rather than the teacher, actually reformulates the mistake. The following are techniques that allow for student correction:

Language box. At the beginning of each *Duet* and *Ensemble*, have the students practice the language in the language box. This will ensure that that can find the forms when they are doing the activity. During the activity, circulate. When you hear a mistake, simply point to the place in the box that indicated the correct form. During the activities, limit corrections to mistakes in the form being taught. This allows the students to focus and organize the information.

Finger signals. When a student has left out a word, included an extra word or used the wrong word, have that student restate the sentence as you point to a finger for each word. Use your fingers to help the students identify the location of the mistakes.

Overall, **ENGLISH FIRSTHAND** is a lively, practical, personalized English course. It can be used effectively both by students with a strong personal interest in learning English and by those with less clear goals. When your students finish the course, they will have done more than merely study English. They'll have used -- and experienced -- English firsthand!

Unit 1 It's nice to meet you.

LISTENING Meeting new people

Getting ready

Here are some ways to ask a person's name.

What's your name?

I don't think we've met.

I don't think I know your name.

Hello. I'm Larry.

Sorry, I didn't catch your name.

Here are some ways to ask about someone's job.

What do you do?

Where do you work?

Are you a student?

Introduce yourself to three people.
Write their names.

Objective: The students will hear introductions and identify names and occupations.
Functions: introduce yourself, ask / tell about occupations, make an offer
Structures: WH-questions
Vocabulary Area: personal information, occupations

Procedure

1. Do the optional warm-up activity listed below.
2. (Optional) If your students find listening very difficult, do the "additional preparation" exercise below.
3. T: *Open your books to pages 10-11. Look at the pictures.*
4. T: *You will hear some people introducing themselves.*
5. T: *Look at "Getting Ready" on page 10. These are some ways to ask a person's name and job. Listen. Check the ones you know.* Play the first part of the tape.
6. T: *Introduce yourself to three people. Write their names on the cards on page 10.*
7. T: *Look at the "First Listening" on page 11. William is having a party. Some of the guests are meeting each other for the first time. Check the names you hear.* Play the "First Listening" segment of the tape. You may want students to do this in pairs so they can help each other. You may wish to stop after each item to check.
8. (Optional) T: *Work in pairs. Did you both get the same answers?*
9. Play the tape again if necessary.
10. Check by asking the students the questions (e.g., T: *Number one. What are their names?* A: John and Larry.) and eliciting their answers OR by having students work in groups of 2-4. They should compare answers and ask you about any they couldn't catch. (See the answer key on the next page.)
11. T: *Look at the "Second Listening." Listen again. What do they do? Write the jobs.* Play the "Second Listening."
12. Check the answers as in step 10. (See the answer key on the next page.)

Additional Preparation

Before they open their books, have the students listen to the First Listening one time. They should try to identify the following:

1. How many speakers?
2. How many males? How many females?
3. Where are the people?
   (Follow-up: How did you know?)
4. Is the situation formal or friendly?

General Notes

• In an informal conversation, an opening line such as offering a drink or making a comment about the setting (Nice party, isn't it?) is often used prior to a self introduction.
• A "homemaker" is someone who works full-time at home rather than having a job outside the home. "Housewife" is also used.
• An "accountant" is someone who keeps records of money in an office or company.

Optional Warm-up Activity

Circle game. On the chalkboard, write:

I'm _______. I like ______.
You're _______. You _______.

Work in groups of 8-10. Students stand in a circle. One begins by introducing herself and saying one thing she likes (e.g., I'm Emi. I like swimming.). The next student continues by repeating the information and adding his own (e.g., You're Emi. You like swimming. I'm Ken. I like ice cream.). The third student repeats the information about the first two and adds her own. The game continues until all students have added information. Variation: Instead of having them go in order, use a ball or similar object. Students throw the ball to whomever they want. That person takes the next turn. If your students have a variety of occupations, you may want to use, "I'm a (job)." for the second sentence.

Unit 1

First Listening

William is having a party.
Some of the guests are meeting each other for the first time.

Check the names you hear.

1. ☐ Jerry ☐ John ☐ Larry ☐ Gary
jobs ____________ ____________

2. ☐ Lisa ☐ Liz ☐ Jerry ☐ James
jobs ____________ ____________

3. ☐ Alison ☐ Aiice ☐ Jack ☐ Dick
jobs ____________ ____________

4. ☐ Brian ☐ Barry ☐ Yansu ☐ Young
jobs ____________ ____________

Second Listening

What do they do?
Write the jobs.

student, teacher, homemaker, mechanic, government worker, accountant, office worker

Tapescript

(Note that the *Getting Ready* sections and the activity directions are also narrated on the tape.)

Number 1.
John: Hi. Nice party.
Larry: Yeah. Really good. Great music.
J: My name's John.
L: Hi. It's nice to meet you. I'm Larry.
J: Nice to meet you, too.
L: What do you do, John?
J: Well, I'm a mechanic.
L: Oh really?
J: Yeah, I work at King Nissan Motors.
J: Hmm. A mechanic. How do you like that?
J: Oh, it's OK. The pay's good. What do you do?
L: Me? I'm a student.
J: Oh, a student?
L: Yeah, I'm studying at USC.
J: How do you know William then?
L: We met at a party a few months ago. How do you know him?
J: Well, we play baseball on the weekends.
L: Ah. Listen, can I get you something to drink?
J: Yeah...

Number 2.
Jerry: I don't think I know you. My name's Jerry.
Lisa: Hi, Jerry. My name's Lisa, Lisa Thompson.
J: Do you work with William?
L: No. I'm a teacher. I teach history at a high school in Monterey.
J: Oh, really. That sounds interesting.
L: It's fun. I like it. How about you?
J: Well, I work for a computer company.
L: Oh, for IBM or one of those big companies?
J: No, I work in the office at ArtScience Technologies.
L: Are you a computer programmer?
J: No, I work in the sales office. I'm just an office worker. Listen, how about a drink? Can I get you something?
L: Oh, yeah. Um, orange juice.
J: I'm sure they'll have it. Let me go and get it. By the way, how do you know William?
L: Well, we've been going out together for a few months.
J: Oh, really?

Number 3.
Alice: Hi. Did you just get here? I haven't seen you.
Jack: Yeah, I just got here a few minutes ago.
A: Well, can I get you something to drink?
J: Yeah, that'd be nice. Maybe a soft drink.
A: Here you are.
J: Oh, thanks. Are you a friend of William's?
A: Well, I just live next door and he told me there was going to be a party tonight and he invited me to come over. My name's Alice.
J: Oh, good to meet you, Alice. My name's Jack, Jack Sharp.
A: What do you do, Jack?
J: I'm an accountant.
A: An accountant? Really? So am I. I work at City Bank.
J: Oh, you do? ....

Number 4.
Barry: Hi. Would you like something to drink?
Young: Sure.
B: What would you like?
Y: Anything. Is that white wine?
B: Yes, would you like some?
Y: Um, please. [pause]
B: Here you are.
Y: Oh, thank you.
B: I'm Barry.
Y: I'm Young.
B: Young? Ah, where are you from?
Y: I'm from Japan.
B: Oh, really? Is Young a Japanese name?
Y: No. Actually, I'm Korean, but I grew up in Japan.
B: Oh. What are you doing here in Los Angeles?
Y: Um...I'm working for the government. I work in the visa section.
B: Oh, really. Then you work with William?
Y: That's right. We work in the same office. What about you?
B: Me? I'm a student. I'm majoring in Asian Studies.
Y: Oh, Asian Studies? I like that...

Answer Key

First/Second Listening:
1. John (mechanic) / Larry (student)
2. Lisa (teacher)/ Jerry (office worker)
3. Alice(accountant)/ Jack (accountant)
4. Barry (student) / Young (government worker)

CONVERSATION At a party

Lee is having a party. Two people introduce themselves.

★ Nice party, isn't it?

◆ Yes, it is.
By the way, I'm ______ (name).

★ Nice to meet you. I'm ______ (name).

◆ Would you like ___1___ ?

★ [Yes, please. / No, thank you.]

◆ What do you do, ______ (name)?

★ [I'm ___2___ . / I work ___3___ .]

◆ How do you know ___Lee___ ?

★ We play ___4___ together. Do you play?

◆ [Yes, I love ___4___ . / No, but I like ___5___ .]

★ How do you know ___Lee___ ?

◆ We ___6___ .

★ Oh.

1. a drink a sandwich some coffee	2. a student an office worker a homemaker	3. in a factory at a bank for a newspaper
4. tennis volleyball golf	5. running cycling swimming	6. work in the same office study English together go out together

Objective: The students will ask for and give personal information.
Functions: greet people, introduce yourself, ask/tell about likes/dislikes and occupations, offer/accept/refuse
Structures: WH- questions, present of *be* and other verbs, personal pronouns: *I, we, you*

Procedure

1. T: *Open your books to page 12. Look at the picture. Where are these people?* (A: At a party.) *Do you think they know each other?*
2. Play the tape. Have the students listen and read silently.
3. Answer questions about vocabulary and expressions.
4. (Optional) T: *Listen again. Repeat each line.* Play the conversation again. Pause after each sentence. Gesture for the students to repeat the sentences.
5. T: *Work in pairs.* (Gesture to show how you want the students paired.)
6. T: *Stand up. Practice the conversation.* Point out that the **[brackets]** indicate a forced choice. For example, with numbers 2 and 3, students can say "I'm a student." or "I work in a factory." but not both. (After a few minutes) T: *Change parts* (Point to your book to show that students who were playing the part on the left now do the part on the right.).
7. Encourage the students to substitute the words and phrases in the box at the bottom.
8. Encourage the students to make eye contact while they are practicing.
9. As the students work, circulate, answer questions and note areas for later work.
10. When students can do the conversation smoothly, encourage them to make changes other than those listed. This can be done by having them cover the substitution box with a piece of paper, a pencil case, etc. OR have them close their books and try to have similar conversations.

Conversation Variation

Have the students imagine that they are really at a party as they practice this conversation. They should stand and circulate. They practice the conversation with a partner, then move to a new partner to practice it again. They should do each part of the conversation at least four times.

General Notes

• These people are making "small talk." They are trying to find common interests, perhaps to be polite, perhaps to continue the conversation.
• "Go out together" (slot 6) refers to dating. "To go out with Lee" means to date Lee with some regularity.
• Make sure that students listen to each other so that their choices for slot 4 correspond.

Conversation Tapescript

Lee is having a party.
Two people introduce themselves.

Margie: Nice party, isn't it?
Gene: Yes, it is. By the way, I'm Gene.
Margie: Nice to meet you. I'm Margie.
G: Would you like a drink?
M: Yes, please.
G: What do you do, Margie?
M: I work at a bank.
G: How do you know Lee?
M: We play tennis together. Do you play?
G: No, but I like cycling.
M: How do you know Lee?
G: We work in the same office.
M: Oh.

DUET-A

Background information

Where	is	Lee	from?
	are	you	
What	does	he she	do?
	do	you	
Is	he she	married?	
Are	you		
How old	is	he?	
	are	you?	

He's She's I'm	from Chicago.	
He's She's I'm	a student. an office worker.	
Yes,	he she	is.
	I	am.
No,	he's she's I'm	not. single.
He's She's I'm	25.	

You are *A*. Fill in the chart.
Ask *B* for the information you need.

	Name	Hometown	Occupation	Marital status	Age
	Mari	San Francisco	teacher	single	
	Michael		student		19
	Kathy	Chicago		married	
	David		office worker		35
You					
Your Partner					

Bonus! Interview ***B***. Find out three more things.
Join another pair. Introduce ***B***.

Objective: The students will ask for and give personal information.
Function: ask for/ give personal information
Structures: present of *to be,*
WH- questions
personal pronouns: *I, you, he, she*
Vocabulary Area: personal information
Classroom language:
How do you spell it?

Procedure

1. Divide the class into pairs. One student in each pair is **A**. The other is **B.** T: *Row one, you are **A's*** (Point to row one). *Row two, you are **B's*** (Point to row two). *Row three, you are **A's*** (etc.).
2. T: *A's, look at page 13. **B's**, look at page 14.*
3. Point out the language box at the top of the page. T: *Look at the box.* (Optional) *Listen and say.* Say the sentences in the box. Have students practice by repeating after you.
4. T: *Look at the page. Are there any words you don't know?*
5. Introduce the task. T: *You will find out about these people and about your partner.*
6. While the other students watch, direct one pair through the first step of the exercise. T: (to any student **B**): *Ask **A**, "Where is Mari from?* Prompt **A** to answer. (She's from San Francisco.) T: *"San Francisco" is written in the space.*
7.*You know some of the information. Your partner knows the other information. Ask your partner. Write the information. After you ask about Mari, Michael, Kathy and David, you will ask about your partner.* When the students understand the task, have them do it in pairs.
8. As the students work, circulate, answer questions and note areas for later work.
9. As students finish the main task, have them continue by doing the *Bonus!* task. Have them find out three more things about their partners, then join another group and introduce their partners.
10. Do consolidation, correction and expansion as desired

Grammar and Usage

• Note the use of short responses such as "No, he's not." rather than "No, he is not married." Many students were taught in high school to give answers in only complete sentences. In conversation, it is perfectly normal to use short answers when the subject is known by all speakers.

General Notes

• If students tend to look at each other's books, have them sit face to face. It is nearly impossible for students at this level to read information from a partner's book when upside down. In large classes where it is impractical to move desks, have students work with the person behind of/in front of them. For example, students in odd-number rows (1,3,5, etc. counting from front to back) are **A**'s. Students in even-numbered rows are **B**'s. **A**'s stand up and turn around. It isn't necessary to move desks.
• Some students will not be used to the idea of information gap pair work and will take time to adjust to the idea of actually using English to exchange information rather than merely parroting known sentences. Allow them time to adjust.
• The language included here is for basic information exchange. Some of the questions (age and marital status) would most often be asked only in business situations (filling out forms, registering for school, etc.) You may wish to caution students against using these questions in social situations. The language in the conversation and ensemble are more appropriate for social situations.
• Depending on the situation, "Where are you from?" may be a question about one's hometown or one's nationality (or country). If asked in a person's native country, it usually concerns one's hometown. If asked in a non-native country, it usually means nationality.
• See the introduction (•Corrections) for suggestions on ways to correct during pair work.

Background information

DUET-B

Where	is	Lee	from?
	are	you	
What	does	he she	do?
	do	you	
Is	he she	married?	
Are	you		
How old	is	he?	
	are	you?	

He's She's I'm	from Chicago.	
He's She's I'm	a student. an office worker.	
Yes,	he she	is.
	I	am.
No,	he's she's I'm	not. single.
He's She's I'm	25.	

You are *B*. Fill in the chart.
Ask *A* for the information you need.

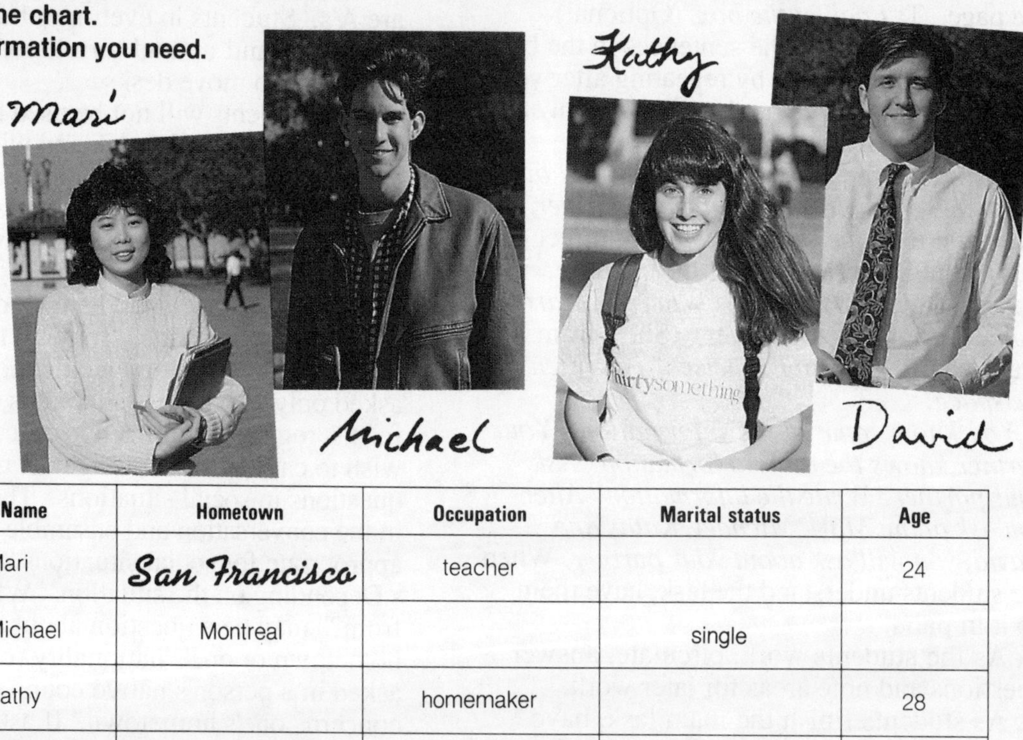

How do you spell it?

	Name	Hometown	Occupation	Marital status	Age
	Mari	San Francisco	teacher		24
	Michael	Montreal		single	
	Kathy		homemaker		28
	David	Atlanta		divorced	
You					
Your Partner					

Bonus! Interview ***A.*** Find out three more things.
Join another pair. Introduce ***A.***

Additional Activity

(This activity can be used anytime during this unit).

Names on their backs. Work as an entire group. Write the names of famous people (living) on sheets of paper. Tape one name on each student's back. The students must find out "their identities" by asking "yes/no" and the short (single-word answer) questions they have practiced in this unit. They can ask only one question before guessing their identities. If they are wrong, they must change partners.

To save time in thinking of and writing names, remind students of different types of famous people (actors, politicians, entertainers, writers, etc.) and have each student write two names on sheets of paper. Collect the papers and redistribute them. Students write two names to give you more choices and to avoid overlap.

Expansion Activity

Fluency Frames

Three "fluency frames" are introduced in the "extra activities" sections of Units 1, 2 and 3. They are not limited to the units in which they first appear. These are task-based activities which can be used with nearly any topic.

Fluency Frame #1:
Fluency Workshop.

Assign a topic. For this unit, the suggested topic is "introducing yourself."

Students work in pairs. One member of each pair speaks about the topic for exactly two minutes. The other member listens and, after the two minutes is over, asks questions to clarify. It is sometimes useful to specify the minimum number of questions that must be asked.

Then the the second student (the person who listened the first time) speaks for two minutes. The partner listens, then asks clarification questions.

Everyone changes partners to begin round two. This is most easily done by having the first speaker in each group stand and move to a new partner. If your students are sitting in rows, have everyone in the even-numbered rows move one seat forward (students at the front go to the back).

Round two is a repeat of the first round except that the speaking time is cut to 90 seconds. Students give the same "mini-speeches" they gave the first time, but a little more quickly.

Change partners again and do round three. In this round, cut the speaking time to 75 seconds.

The entire activity usually takes 25-30 minutes. The actual speaking time for each round can be changed to meet the needs and abilities of your students but we find the 120/90/75-second time ratio to work well with most students.

(This activity was suggested by K. Maurice in August, 1983 *TESOL Newsletter*.)

Answer Key

Checking answers as a whole class should not be necessary. You may wish to have each pair look at both books to make sure they have correctly filled in all blanks.

Answers for A's page are on page 14 and answers for B's page are on page 13 .

SOLO About you, about me

Read about Yoko.

Hello. My name is Yoko Takeda. I was born June 1, 1970. I'm from Hiroshima, Japan. I live at 4906 Astor in New York. My zip code is 10028. My phone number is 212-625-4288. I'm single. I'm a computer programmer. I work for IBM. I enjoy tennis and skiing. In my free time, I study art.

Fill in the form for Yoko.

STUDENT APPLICATION DATA SHEET

New Way School

989 West 7th St., New York, NY 10008

(212) 655-1370

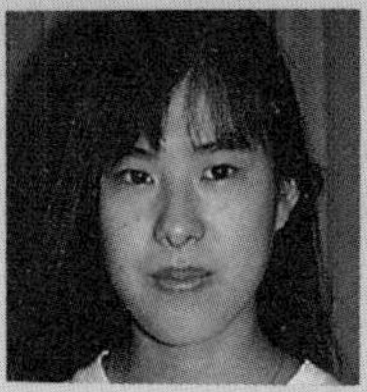

Date ______

Name Mr. Miss Ms. Mrs. ______ Last First Middle Initial

Address ______

______ ZIP ______

Telephone ( ) ______

Date of Birth ______

Marital Status ______ Nationality ______

Occupation ______

Interests ______

Fill in the form for yourself.

STUDENT APPLICATION DATA SHEET

New Way School

Put your photo here.

Date ______

Name Mr. Miss Ms. Mrs. ______ Last First Middle Initial

Address ______

______ ZIP ______

Telephone ( ) ______

Date of Birth ______

Marital Status ______ Nationality ______

Occupation ______

Interests ______

Write about yourself.
Use some of these words:

- ✓ name
- ___ born
- ___ live at
- ___ work for
- ___ study
- ___ enjoy

Hi. My name is

Objective: The students will identify personal information from a written text. They will fill out forms for themselves.
Function: giving personal information
Structures: Present of *be*, prepositions: *in, at, from, for*
enjoy + noun/gerund
Vocabulary Area: personal information

Procedure

1. T: *Open your books to page 15. Look at the picture. This is Yoko. You will read about her. Look at the form.* Answer any questions about the form.
2. *Read about Yoko. As you read, fill out the form for her.*
3. T: *Now, fill out the form for yourself. Then write about yourself. Use some of these words: name, born, live at, work for, study, enjoy.*

You may wish to assign this activity as homework.

In-class Follow-up

Have students make copies of the form. In pairs, students read their own paragraphs while their partners fill out the forms. If any information is missing, the partner may ask for it directly.

General Notes

• Point out that a title (Mr., Ms., etc.) may be used with the person's first and last name (Ms. Yoko Takeda), with a last name only (Ms. Takeda) but never with a first name only.
• In business situations in the U.S., "Ms." is generally used instead of "Miss" or "Mrs." Many women prefer it in all situations. If the student is unsure which title to use for a woman he or she is talking to, "Ms." is appropriate.
• Postal codes in the U.S. are called "zip codes."
• Yoko has no middle initial, so she has drawn a "---". The space on the form may be left blank or the student may draw a "---" instead of filling it in.
• On the form, the last (family) name precedes the first (given) name. While Western name normally follow a "first name, last name") order, forms often list the family name first to make putting them in alphabetical order easier.

Optional Skill-building Activity

Skill: speculating based on previously known information

Have the students write their paragraphs on separate pieces of paper. Collect the paragraphs. Delete or hide the names. Number the paragraphs and post them on the chalkboard using tape or magnets. Students go to the board, read as many paragraphs as possible in the allotted time and, on a separate piece of paper write the name of the person they think wrote each paragraph. At the end, announce the names that go with each paragraph number.

Note: If class size make it difficult for all students to look at the chalkboard at the same time, divide the class and the paragraphs in half. Put each set of paragraphs on a desk. Students pick up a paragraph, read it and guess who wrote it. They return it to the set and take another paragraph.

Answer Key

Task one:
for Yoko:
- Date: (today's date)
- Name: Ms. / Takeda, Yoko, --
- Address: 4906 Astor, New York, NY 10028
- Telephone: (212) 605- 4288
- Date of birth: June 1, 1970
- Marital status: single
- Nationality: Japanese
- Occupation: computer programmer
- Interests: tennis, skiing, studying art

Task two:
Answers will vary.
Example:
See Yoko's paragraph.

ENSEMBLE Find someone who...

Get to know the other people in your class.
Ask other students the questions. When someone says "yes", write the name on the line. Use a name only one time.

Are you	happy today? shy?	Yes, I am. No, I'm not.	Can you	use a computer? do 20 push-ups?	Yes, I can. No, I can't.
Do you	like spicy food? have a brother?	Yes, I do. No, I don't.	Were you	born in February? sick last week?	Yes, I was. No, I wasn't.

1. ...is happy today.
____
Are you...

2. ...likes spicy food.
____
Do you...

3. ...can use a computer.
____
Can you...

4. ...was born in February.
____
Were you...

5. ...likes to cook.
____
Do you...

6. ...can do 20 push-ups.
____
Can you...

7. ...often works or studies late.
____
Do you...

8. ...speaks two languages.
____
Can you...

9. ...has an interesting job.
____
Do you...

10. ...was sick last week.
____
Were you...

11. ...can play a musical instrument.
____
Can you...

12. ...is from a small town.
____
Are you...

13. ...has three brothers and sisters.
____
Do you...

14. ...is shy.
____
Are you...

15. ...likes to do housework.
____
Do you...

Try This! Interview a partner. Find three things that are the same about both of you. Find three things that are different.

Objective: The students will learn to ask for and give personal information.
Function: ask / tell about likes, abilities and personal information.
Structures: present and past of *to be,* modal auxiliary verb: *can,* passive voice as question routine
Vocabulary Area: personal information
Classroom language: *What does __ mean?*

Procedure

1. T: *Look at page 16. You will get to know other people in our class.*
2. T: *Look at the language box at the top of the page. Are there any words you don't know?* Answer questions about vocabulary.
3. (Optional) T: *Look at the box. Listen and say.* Say the sentences in the box. Have students practice by repeating after you.
4. Introduce the task. T: *You will try to find people who can say yes to the questions.*
5. T: *Look at the questions. The way to say it is written under the line. For example, Number one: "Find someone who is happy today." What's the question?* Point to "Are you..." under the line and encourage students to say, "Are you happy today?"
6. T: *Ask the questions to other people. When someone says, "yes" write the name on the line. Write only one name on each line. You can use each name only one time so you will have fifteen different partners.*
7. While other students watch, ask question one to any student. T: *Are you happy today?* If the student says, "yes," write that student's name on the first line and move to another student to ask the second question. If the first student says "no," ask another question. Continue until you get a "yes" answer. Then go to the next student.
8. When the students understand the task, have them begin.
9. As the students work, circulate, answer questions and note areas for later work.
10. As students finish the main task, have them continue by doing the *Try this!* task. Have them work in pairs. They try to find three things that are the same and three things that are different.
11. Do consolidation, correction and expansion as desired.

Grammar and Usage Notes

• Because the primary focus of this activity is to get the students interacting, don't do a major review of auxiliary verbs at this time. Students are given the forms under the question. Draw their attention to these forms.

General Notes

• "Can you speak two languages?" contains the possibility that the students may speak more than two languages. If a student speaks three or four languages (even if only enough to carry on a very basic conversation), the answer to this question is "Yes."
• Many students are unfamiliar with the word "push-up." Use this as an opportunity to teach the clarification phrase, "What does push-ups mean?" Point to the illustration of the person doing the exercise to help them understand.
• See the introduction section of this manual (• **corrections**) for suggestions on ways to correct student errors.

Answer Key

Answers will vary.
The correct questions are:

1. Are you happy today?
2. Do you like spicy food?
3. Can you use a computer?
4. Were you born in February?
5. Do you like to cook?
6. Can you speak two languages? ("Do you speak..." is also correct.)
7. Do you often work or study late?
8. Can you do 20 pushups?
9. Do you have an interesting job?
10. Were you sick last week?
11. Can you play a musical instrument? ("Do you play..." is also correct.)
12. Are you from a small town?
13. Do you have three brothers and sisters?
14. Are you shy?
15. Do you like to do housework?

CHECK YOURSELF

Match the sentences with the same meaning. (8 points)

d 1. I'm single.	a. Is he Chinese?
______ 2. Would you like a drink?	b. I don't think I know your name.
______ 3. Hi. I'm Kenji.	c. Where do you work?
______ 4. Where are you from?	d. I'm not married.
______ 5. Is he from China?	e. What country are you from?
______ 6. What do you do?	f. Can I get you something to drink?
______ 7. When were you born?	g. Hello. My name's Kenji.
______ 8. What's your nationality?	h. What's your date of birth?
______ 9. I don't think we've met.	i. Where were you born?

Fill in the blanks. Use words from the box. (12 points)

no	in	at	the	is	a	from	born	was
like	to	my	study	on	enjoy	work	in	not

Hello. ___My___ name is Peter Bron. I ______ born August 10, 1971. I'm ______ Germany but I live ______ New York ______ 549 West 112nd St. now. My phone number ______ 655-1012. I'm ______ student at Columbia University. I ______ English there. I ______ part-time at a department store. I'm ______ married. ______ my free time, I ______ to go to plays and art museums. I also ______ playing basketball.

Your score

Procedure

Exercise one.

1. T: *Look at page 17.* Point to the second exercise. T: *Look at the sentences. Match the sentences with the same meaning.*

2. (Optional). T: *Number one: I'm single. Which sentence on the right means "I'm single?"* Elicit "I'm not married." T: *"I'm not married." is letter "d" so "d" is written on the line. Match the other sentences.*

Exercise two.

1. Point to the second exercise. T: *Finish the sentences. Use words from the box.*

2. (Optional:) Point to item one. T: *Hello. My name is Peter Bron. I (blank) born August 10, 1971. What word goes in the blank?* Encourage the students to answer (A: was). Gesture for them to write the word in the space provided.

3. T: *Do the rest the same way.*

You may wish to assign the page as homework.

In-class Follow-up

• T: *Work in pairs. Did you both get the same answers?* As students compare their answers, circulate to make sure that all students have completed the homework. You may wish to have some students write their answers on the board.

General Notes

• The "Check yourself" pages are each worth 20 points. Each question and blank is worth one point. If you are giving grades, you may wish to keep track of student scores. Alternatively, if you have assigned the pages as homework and class size makes keeping track of individual points impractical, you may want to note which students have completed the assignment, those who did only part of it and those who didn't do it at all.

Answer Key

Exercise one:

1. d. I'm not married.
2. f. Can I get you something to drink?
3. g. Hello. My name's Kenji.
4. i. Where were you born?
5. a. Is he Chinese?
6. c. Where do you work?
7. h. What's your date of birth?
8. e. What country are you from?
9. b. I don't think I know your name.

Exercise two:

Hello. My name is Peter Bron. I was born August 10, 1971. I'm from Germany, but I live in New York at 549 West 112th St. now. My phone number is 655-1012. I'm a student at Columbia University. I study English there. I work part-time at a department store. I'm not married. In my free time, I like to go to plays and art museums. I also enjoy playing basketball.

Notes

Unit 2 Who are they talking about?

LISTENING Describing people

Getting ready

Here are some words that describe people.

Hair color	blond, brown, black, gray, red
Hair style	long, straight, curly, wavy, shoulder length, parted, pulled back
Face shape	long, oval, round
Body type	thin, slim, fat, heavy set, medium build, about 5 feet 7 inches, tall, short
Other	beard, moustache, glasses, wrinkles

Work with a partner. What does your partner look like? Circle the words above.

First Listening

Listen. What are the situations? Write the numbers.

☐ A party. They are describing a man.

☐ A police station. She is describing someone.

☐ An office. She is describing a skier.

☐ Someone's home. She is describing her sister.

☐ At work. He is describing his wife.

Objective: The students will identify pictures of people based on physical descriptions.
Function: describe people
Structures: descriptive adjectives, simple present, present continuous
Vocabulary Area: physical descriptions

Procedure

1. Do the optional warm-up activity listed below.
2. T: *Open your books to page 18. Look at the pictures.*
3. T: *You will hear some people talking about what other people look like.*
4. T: *Look at "Getting Ready" on page 18. These are some words that describe people. Do you know them?* Play the first part of the tape. Stop the tape at any words you don't think your students know. Point to a picture on page 19 to establish meaning.
5. T: *Work with a partner. What does your partner look like? Circle the words.*
6. (Optional) If your students find listening very difficult, do the "additional preparation" exercise below.
7. T: *Look at the "First Listening" on page 18. What are the situations? Write the numbers.* Play the "First Listening" segment of the tape. You may want students to do this in pairs so they can help each other. You may wish to stop after each item to check.
8. (Optional) T: *Work in pairs. Did you both get the same answers?*
9. Play the tape again if necessary.
10. Check by asking the students the questions (e.g., T: *What is situation number one?* A: A police station.) and eliciting their answers OR by having students work in groups of 2-4. They should compare answers and ask you about any they couldn't catch. (See the answer key on the next page.)
11. T: *Look at the "Second Listening." Listen again. Circle the person they are talking about.* Play the "Second Listening."
12. Check the answers as in step 10.
(See the answer key on the next page.)

Additional Preparation

Students work in pairs. They look at the pictures on page 19 and write the one or two things they notice most about each person (e.g., person 1-A: dark hair, sunglasses).

General Notes

• Terms that describe hair length are, of course, relative. Hair that covers the ears on a man may be considered "long" on a man but short on a woman.
• While "fat" is sometimes used to describe overweight people, it is more common and polite to use "heavy-set."

Optional Warm-up Activity

Physical description blackboard race. Work in teams (the number per team is the total number of students divided by the number of students you wish to have drawing on the blackboard at the same time). You or a student give a short physical description of a person (e.g., She's got long, wavy hair, parted on the left, and glasses.). A member of each team runs to the blackboard, draws a picture of the described person as quickly as possible, and runs back to her seat. The first person to draw a correct picture and sit down gets a point. Continue for at least ten rounds. The team with the most points is the winner. During the activity, team members are allowed to give hints and corrections in English.

Unit 2

Second Listening

Listen. Circle the person they are talking about.

	A	B	C	D
1				
2				
3				
4				

Tapescript

Number 1.

Police: OK, so you got a good look at this guy?
Witness: Uh-huh. I was standing outside the bank and he ran past me. He was running very fast.
P: OK. Could you tell me what you remember about him?
W: He was tall.
P: About how tall?
W: About this tall ...about six feet, two inches. (Uh-huh). And he was thin and he had dark hair.
P: Dark hair? About how long?
W: Let's see. It hung over his ears. And it was a little wavy. Yeah, dark, wavy hair.
P: I see. Anything else you remember? Beard?
W: Yes, he had a beard and moustache.
P: Beard and moustache. Long beard?
W: No, short beard, fairly well-trimmed.
P: OK. And do you remember anything about his clothing?
W: Gee, it happened so fast. Let me think. Um, he was wearing a jacket, like a sport coat, a blazer.
P: Do you remember the color?
W: Yeah, it was brown.
P: OK, thank you. That's a big help...

Number 2.

Friend: So I heard you got married recently.
Husband: Yeah. I got married last month.
Friend: Is she somebody I know? Have I ever met her?
H: Patricia Marsh. I think you met her once. Do you remember Jim's party last summer?
F: Yeah, I was there. But I don't remember meeting her.
H: Well, she's got brown hair, sort of short, and parted on one side... and dark eyes...
F: Oh, I think I remember her. Rather short, with short brown hair, and she wears glasses, right?
H: Umm, well, she has glasses, but she hardly ever wears them. She almost always wears contact lenses.
F: Hm, yeah. I think I remember her. Where did you meet her?
H: At college. We met about three years ago when we were at the University of Southern California. She was an education major and we met in a psychology class...

Number 3.

Woman: See that guy over there?
Friend: Which one?
W: The guy with the moustache.
F: Oh yeah. With the curly hair.
W: Right.
F: And the glasses.
W: No, not him. He isn't wearing glasses. The guy in the leather jacket.
F: Oh, I see him. The guy with the black leather jacket. The one without the beard.
W: That's right. No beard. He's the guy I was talking about. He's in my physics class. He's really smart. I want to introduce you to him later.
F: OK, sure. I'd like to meet him.

Number 4.

Friend: Bill, could you do me a huge favor?
Bill: Sure, if I can. What is it?
J: My sister's coming in from California tomorrow morning and I can't go meet her because I have a big business meeting. Could you possibly go out to the airport to meet her for me?
B: Tomorrow morning? Sure, I think so. What time?
J: It's at 11 o'clock. It's the United Air Lines flight from Los Angeles.
B: OK, fine.
J: Yeah. Her name is Heather.
B: Well, I've never met her. What does she look like?
J: Oh, she's 25 years old, she looks a lot like me, has a round face. She has kind of straight, shoulder-length blond hair.
B: Jan, there are a lot of people from California who are about 25 years old and have shoulder-length blond hair.
J: Well, she wears glasses and her hair is really, really blond, almost white.
B: OK, glasses, blond hair, I think I can find her.

Answer Key

First Listening

1. A police station **2.** At work
3. A party **4.** Someone's house

Second Listening

1. D **2.** C **3.** D **4.** A

CONVERSATION Do you want to see some pictures?

★ Do you want to see some pictures of my ___1___ ?

◆ Yeah, I'd love to. Who's that?

★ Which one?

◆ The ___2___ one with the ___3___

★ The [man / woman] wearing the ___4___? That's my ___5___ .

◆ What's [he / she] like?

★ [He's / She's] ___6___ .

◆ Oh, I see.

1. family / class / trip
2. tall / heavy set / short
3. brown hair / glasses / moustache
4. plaid shirt / long dress / shorts
5. boyfriend / sister, Maria / close friend
6. kind of shy / very outgoing / really nice

Objective: The students will describe people and relationships.
Functions: describe someone's appearance and character, describe family and personal relationships
Structures: descriptive adjectives, *WH* - questions

Procedure

1. T: *Open your books to page 20. Look at the picture. Where are these people?* (A: Probably on a college campus.) *They are looking at some pictures. What do you think the photographs are of?*
2. Play the tape. Have the students listen and read silently.
3. Answer questions about vocabulary and expressions.
4. (Optional) T: *Listen again. Repeat each line.* Play the conversation again. Pause after each sentence. Gesture for the students to repeat the sentences.
5. T: *Work in pairs.* (Gesture to show how you want the students paired.)
6. T: *Stand up. Practice the conversation.* (After a few minutes) T: *Change parts* (Point to your book to show that students who were playing the part on the left now do the part on the right.).
7. Encourage the students to substitute the words and phrases in the box at the bottom.
8. Encourage the students to make eye contact while they are practicing.
9. As the students work, circulate, answer questions and note areas for later work.
10. When students can do the conversation smoothly, encourage them to make changes other than those listed. This can be done by having them cover the substitution box with a piece of paper, a pencil case, etc. OR have them close their books and try to have similar conversations.

Conversation Variation

Have the student use a piece of paper to represent the photograph as they practice this dialogue. Each time they say a line, they pass the "photo" to their partner. This variation encourages students to look away from the text which helps to develop short-term memory.

General Notes

- If any of the vocabulary is unknown, encourage the students to ask, "What does ____ mean?" (which they learned in the Unit 1 Ensemble). Do this by pointing to the phrases on the "tool box" page (page 124) and having a student ask the question. This will help remind them that the tool box page is available for quick reference as well as encourage them to use English to understand more English.
- In North America, "boyfriend" and "girlfriend" usually refer to persons with whom one has a romantic relationship rather than simply referring to the sex of a friend.
- "Outgoing" refers to someone who is very friendly and talks to strangers easily.
- "What's he/she like?" means "What sort of person is he/she?" It refers to personality.
- Make sure that the students listen to each other so that their choices for slots 4, 5, and 6 correspond.

Conversation Tapescript

Woman: Do you want to see some pictures of my family?
Man: Yeah, I'd love to. Who's that?
W: Which one?
M: The tall one with the brown hair.
W: Oh, the woman wearing the plaid shirt? That's my sister, Maria.
M: What's she like?
W: She's really nice.
M: Oh, I see.

DUET-A

Who did it?

How old is	Luis? he? she?	He's She's	29.
How tall is			174 centimeters (tall). 5 feet 10 (inches).
How much does he weigh?		He weighs	65 kilograms. 135 pounds.
What is his hair like?		It's	short and curly.
		He has	long, black hair.
		He's	bald.
What color is his hair?		It's	blond.

Two people robbed a bank. Help the police find the criminals.
Fill in the charts.
Ask *B* for the information you need.
B will begin.

Clues:
The man is tall.
He has short, brown hair.
He's in his early or mid-30's.

Suspect	Height	Weight	Hair style	Hair color	Age
Luis Garcia	174 cm.	75 kg.	short	brown	29
Arthur Park	182 cm.	78 kg.	bald (no hair)	—	36
Jeff Elliot	185 cm.	80 kg.	long	black	32
Gary Lake	185 cm.	73 kg.	short, curly	light brown	33
Larry Baggs	168 cm.	77 kg.	short, straight	blond	34

Excuse me?

Suspect	Height	Weight	Hair style	Hair color	Age
Sarah Sawyer					
Paula Burns					
Lee Chen					
Rita Nelson					
Lisa Frank					

Clues:
The woman is in her late 30's or early 40's. She is rather short and heavy-set. She has short, black hair.

Who are the criminals?

Bonus! Look at page 19. ***B*** will think of a picture. Ask questions. Guess the picture.

Objective: The students will ask for and give information about physical description.
Function: describe someone's appearance.
Structures: *WH-questions,*
possessive pronouns: *his, her.*
descriptive adjectives
Vocabulary Area: physical appearance
Classroom language:
Excuse me?

Procedure

1. Divide the class into pairs. One student in each pair is **A**. The other is **B.** T: *Row one, you are **A's*** (Point to row one). *Row two, you are **B's*** (Point to row two). *Row three, you are **A's*** (etc.).

2. T: ***A's**, look at page 21. **B's**, look at page 22.*

3. Point out the language box at the top of the page. T: *Look at the box.* (Optional) *Listen and say.* Say the sentences in the box. Have students practice by repeating after you.

4. T: *Look at the page. Are there any words you don't know?*

5. Introduce the task. T: *Two people robbed a bank. You and your partner must help the police solve the crime.*

6. While the other students watch, direct one pair through the first step of the exercise. T: *The man is tall. He has short, brown hair. He's in his early or mid-30's.* (To any student **B**) ***A** knows about the men. Ask **A** about Luis.* Prompt **B** to ask, "How tall is Luis" by pointing to the language box in **B**'s book. Prompt **A** to answer. (He's 165 centimeters tall). Gesture for **B** to write the information on the chart.

7. T: *Find out about all the people. Who is the criminal?* When the students understand the task, have them do it in pairs.

8. As the students work, circulate, answer questions and note areas for later work.

9. As students finish the main task, have them continue by doing the *Bonus!* task. Have them look at page 19 and think of pictures. Partners ask questions and guess the pictures.

10. Do consolidation, correction and expansion as desired.

Grammar and Usage

• Note the difference between "It's curly." and "He has curly hair." The BE verb equates both parts of the sentence (His hair is curly. Her nose is big.) while "has" is used to show possession (He has curly hair. She has a big nose.)

• Students sometimes ask, "~~How much does he~~ weight?" Point out that they are confusing a noun (weight) and a verb (weigh). In this sentence, they should use "weigh."

General Notes

• Students should not be allowed to ask "Which suspects are tall?", etc. They should instead be encouraged to ask all the questions (as in the language box) so that they will have adequate practice.

• Arthur Park is completely bald and therefore has no hair color.

• See the introduction (•Corrections) for suggestions on ways to correct during pair work.

Additional Activity

(This activity can be used anytime during this unit).

Five pictures. Work in groups of 5-8. Give one student a set of five magazine photos of people. The other students cannot see the pictures. They ask questions about the physical descriptions of the people. They are allowed to take notes. When they have enough information about the first picture, they go on to picture two. This continues until they have asked about all five pictures. Then all the pictures are placed on a table. They must identify each picture by number along with their reasons (e.g., "This is number one because he has a beard."). The student who gave the descriptions may not speak until the other students have agreed on an order. If there are mistakes, that student may only tell how many. The other students will need to compare their information and change their guesses until they are correct.

Note: The more similar the pictures, the more specific the language used will need to be.

DUET-B

Who did it?

How old is	Luis? he? she?	He's She's	29.
How tall is			174 centimeters (tall). 5 feet 10 (inches).
How much does he weigh?		He weighs	65 kilograms. 135 pounds.
What is his hair like?		It's	short and curly.
		He has	long, black hair.
		He's	bald.
What color is his hair?		It's	blond.

Two people robbed a bank. Help the police find the criminals.
Fill in the charts.
Ask *A* for the information you need.
Begin by saying,
"Tell me about Luis Garcia.
How tall is he?"

Clues:
The man is tall.
He has short, brown hair.
He's in his early or mid-30's.

Suspect	Height	Weight	Hair style	Hair color	Age
Luis Garcia					
Arthur Park					
Jeff Elliot					
Gary Lake					
Larry Baggs					

Excuse me?

Suspect	Height	Weight	Hair style	Hair color	Age
Sarah Sawyer	165 cm.	58 kg.	short, straight	black	29
Paula Burns	167 cm.	53 kg.	shoulder length	dark brown	19
Lee Chen	170 cm.	63 kg.	long, wavy	black	34
Rita Nelson	165 cm.	61 kg.	short, curly	blond	23
Lisa Frank	155 cm.	67 kg.	short, wavy	black	39

Clues:
The woman is in her late 30's or early 40's. She is rather short and heavy-set. She has short, black hair.

Who are the criminals?

Bonus! Look at page 19. ***A*** will think of a picture.
Ask questions. Guess the picture.

Expansion Activity

Fluency Frames:
Three "fluency frames" are introduced in the "extra activities" sections of Units 1, 2 and 3. They are not limited to the units in which they first appear. These are task-based activities which can be used with nearly any topic.

Fluency Frame #2:
Mouth Marathon.
Write the suggested topic on the board. The topic for this unit is "my family."

Students work in pairs. Each member attempts to talk about the topic for as long as possible. The partner times the speaker. The speaker is stopped when one of three rules is broken:

- Do not pause for more than 5 seconds.
- Do not recite lists (numbers, days, etc.)
- Everything you say must be in English. If you say a word that is not English, you are out.

As partner listen and time, you may want them to count the second partners pause behind their backs. If the partner who has stopped can see the person counting, it is often difficult to get started again.

The winner is the student who goes for the longest time. Because of the five-second pause limit, it is rare for anyone to speak longer than three minutes. The activity usually takes about 10 minutes.

(This is based on an activity described by L.A.Meagher in the December, 1979 *TESOL Newsletter.*)

Answer Key

The criminals are Gary Lake and Lisa Frank.

Checking answers about each person as a whole class should not be necessary. You may wish to have the pair look at both books to make sure they have correctly filled in all blanks. Answers for A's page are on page 22, and answers for B's page are on page 21.

SOLO My family

Read about Ann's family. Write the names.

This is my family. I'm in the middle of the picture. The man wearing the glasses is my husband, Dave. We have three children. The oldest is Brian. He's the one in the solid red shirt. He's twelve and in seventh grade. The boy wearing glasses is Eric. He's eleven. He likes to play soccer. Joel is our youngest son. He's five. He's the one with the red and yellow striped shirt.

Find (or draw) a picture of your family. Write about it. Use some of these words:

- ____ father (or "dad")
- ____ mother (or "mom")
- ____ brother
- ____ sister
- ____ oldest
- ____ youngest
- ____ wearing

Objective: The students will read a paragraph describing a family. They will write paragraphs about their own families.
Function: identify and describe people and relationships
Structures: descriptive adjectives, simple present and present continuous tenses
Vocabulary Area: families

Procedure

1. T: *Open your books to page 23. Look at the picture. You will read about this family. As you read, write the people's names on the picture.*
2. T: *Now find or draw pictures of your family. Then write about your family. Use some of these words: father (or dad), mother (or mom), brother, sister, oldest, youngest, wearing.*

You may wish to assign this activity as homework.

In-class Follow-up

In pairs, students show their photographs and read their paragraphs. Students must learn and write at least five new things about their partner's family. Some of those items can be reported to the class.

General Notes

• If you are going to do this as an in-class activity, tell the students beforehand to bring photographs of their families.
• "The one in _____", "the one with ____" and "the one wearing___" are all ways to point out what someone is wearing.
• "Mom" and "dad" are very common, less formal terms for "mother" and "father."

Optional Skill-building Activity

Skill: associating written and visual information

Collect a large number of magazine pictures of people. This is easily done by asking each student to bring two or three pictures. Distribute the pictures so each student has one. Each student writes a short description of the one person in their picture. Collect the descriptions. Post the pictures on the walls along with some photographs that were not used. Redistribute the descriptions. Students must read the new paragraphs and try to find the picture it describes.

Answer Key

Task one:

Task two:
Answers will vary.
Example:
See Ann's paragraph.

Notes

ENSEMBLE

Family tree

Do you believe in ESP (Extra Sensory Perception)? Some people think that you can send messages just by thinking.

Is it	Gary's Joan's	nephew? sister-in-law?

- father
- mother
- wife
- husband
- son
- daughter
- brother
- sister
- child
- children

- uncle
- aunt
- grandfather
- grandmother
- grandson
- granddaughter
- niece
- nephew
- cousin
- mother-in-law
- father-in-law
- brother-in-law
- sister-in-law

Work in groups of 4. One person thinks of a picture.
Others ask questions to find out which picture.
Questions must have a family relationship word.
Count the questions. Each person takes three turns.

Add all the questions __________
Divide by pictures used ÷ ______
Your average __________

Try This!

Tell your partners about your family.
Ask two questions about each partner's family.

Objective: The students will learn to talk about family relationships.
Function: describe family relationships.
Structures: possessives with *'s* , pronoun *it* for a person
Vocabulary Area: families

Procedure

1. (Optional) T: Write "ESP" on the chalkboard. T: *Do you believe in ESP. Can people really send messages just by thinking?* Encourage students to respond. If they do not understand "ESP" (Extra Sensory Perception) encourage them to ask what it means (Point to the "What does ESP mean?" on the classroom language reference chart on p. 124). Use similar words (telepathy, mind-reading) or examples (Uri Geller) to help them understand.

2. T: *Look at page 24. This is an ESP test. We will find out who in class has the best ESP.*

3. T: *Look at the language box and the family relationship words. Are there any words you don't know?* Answer questions about vocabulary.

4. (Optional) T: *Look at the boxes. Listen and say.* Say the sentences and words in the boxes. Have students practice by repeating after you.

5. Divide the class into groups of 4.

6. Introduce the task. T: *Can you send messages just by thinking? You will test your ESP.*

7. While the students watch, do one example. T: *I am thinking of one person in this family. Who is it. You can not ask directly. You must use a "family relationship" word in your question. For example, you can't say, "Is it Larry?" You can say "Is it Joan's husband?" or "Is it Ann's father?"* Encourage students to guess. When students make wrong guesses, make a mark on the chalkboard. When someone guesses correctly, note the number of guesses it took.

8. When the students understand the task, have them begin.

9. Each student should take at least three turns. As the students work, circulate, answer questions and note areas for later work.

10. When groups finish, they should find their group average by dividing the number of pictures used by the total number of questions. Groups can compare averages. The groups with the lowest average has the best ESP.

11. As students finish the main task, have them continue by doing the *Try this!* task. Have them talk about their families. Each group member must ask two questions about each family described.

13. Do consolidation, correction and expansion as desired.

Grammar and Usage Notes

• In "Is it Gary's nephew?" (language box), the "it" refers to the choice the person who is guessing makes. One might also ask, "Are you thinking of (about) Gary's nephew?" or "Have you chosen Gary's nephew?"

General Notes

• "In-laws" are the family members of one's spouse. The use of " --in law" is usually confined to mother-in-law, father-in-law, brother-in-law, sister-in-law, daughter-in law and son-in-law.

• You may want to introduce the words "mom" and "dad" as informal (and very common) forms of "mother" and "father."

• The "ESP" test factor of this activity is simply used to make the drill aspect more interesting for the students. Since the comparison is based on group averages, you can have groups continue for the entire time available rather than stopping and moving on to the *Try this!* task.

• See the introduction (• **corrections**) for suggestions on ways to correct student errors.

Answer Key

Answers will vary.

CHECK YOURSELF

Fill in the blanks. Use the Family Tree ESP chart on page 24. (9 points)

Gary is Robert's oldest ___son___ .

Gary and Scott are ________s .

Ann is Gary's ________ .

Ann is David's ________ .

Beth is David and Ann's ________ .

Beth is Gary's ________ .

Jason is Larry's ________ .

Beth is Joan's ________ .

Scott is Jill's ________ .

Larry is Linda's ________ .

Find the conversation. Circle each choice. (5 points)

I'm looking for my brother.
Have you seen him?

(A.) I'm not sure.
What does he look like?

B. I'm not sure.
Who is he?

A. He's very intelligent.

B. He's really tall.

A. What color are his eyes?

B. What's his hair like?

A. He's got curly brown hair.

B. He's very friendly.

A. Is that him?
The man wearing the red shirt?

B. That isn't him...
The man wearing the red shirt.

A. Yes, I see him now.

B. No, I don't know him.

Read the answers. Check (✓) the correct questions. (6 points)

Q1. ✓ Does she have long hair?
____ Does she wear long hair?
____ Is her hair long?
A: Yes, she does.

Q2. ____ What's he like?
____ What does he look like?
____ What's his hair like?
A: He's tall and slim. He has short curly hair.

Q3. ____ What color is his shirt?
____ What color are his eyes?
____ What color is his hair?
A: It's blond.

Q4. ____ How old is she?
____ How tall is she?
____ How much does she weigh?
A: She's in her early 20's.

Q5. ____ Is she wearing a red coat?
____ What's she wearing?
____ Which one?
A: Jeans and a green shirt.

Q6. ____ What are you doing?
____ What do you do?
____ What are you?
A: I work at a hotel.

Q7. ____ Is that your brother?
____ Is he your uncle?
____ Is he wearing a suit?
A: Yes, it is.

Your score

#1

mind reader
to make you
smarter
growing hair
making energy
- lie detector

Procedure

Exercise one.

1. T: *Look at page 25.* Point to the first exercise. T: *Fill in the blanks. Use the "Family Tree ESP" chart on page 24.*

2. (Optional:) Point to item one. T: *Number one. Gary is Robert's oldest (blank)? What word goes in the blank?* Encourage the students to answer (A: son). Gesture for them to write "son" in the space provided.

3. T: *Do the others the same way.*

Exercise two.

1. Point to the second exercise. T: *Find the conversation. Circle each choice.*

2. (Optional:) Point to the first box. T: *I'm looking for my brother. Have you seen him? Which sentence comes next?* Encourage the students to answer (A: I'm not sure. What does he look like?). Gesture for them to circle "A."

3. T: *Find the rest of the conversation.*

Exercise three.

1. Point to the third exercise. T: *Read the answers. Check the correct questions.*

2. (Optional). T: *Number one: The answer is, "Yes, she does." What is the question?* Encourage the students to answer (A: Does she have long hair?).

You may wish to assign the page as homework.

In-class Follow-up

• T: *Work in pairs. Did you both get the same answers?* As students compare their answers, circulate to make sure that all students have completed the homework. You may wish to have some students write their answers on the board.

• T: *Work in pairs. Practice the conversations in part two.*

General Notes

• The "Check yourself" pages are each worth 20 points. Each item is worth one point.

Answer Key

Exercise one:

son	wife
brothers	nephew
niece	sister-in-law
sister	uncle
aunt	son-in-law

Exercise two:
A, B, B, A, A, A

Exercise three:

1. Does she have long hair?
2. What does he look like?
3. What color is his hair?
4. How old is she?
5. What's she wearing?
6. What do you do?
7. Is that your brother?

Notes

Unit 3 When do you start?

LISTENING Talking about daily activities

Getting ready

Here are some ways to ask people about their daily schedule.

How do you get to work?
What time do you start work?
What time is your first class?
What time do you finish?
Where do you usually eat lunch?
What do you usually do after school?

Work with a partner.
Ask your partner these questions.

What time do you get up? ______________________________

How do you get to school? ______________________________

Where do you eat lunch? ______________________________

What do you do after school? ______________________________

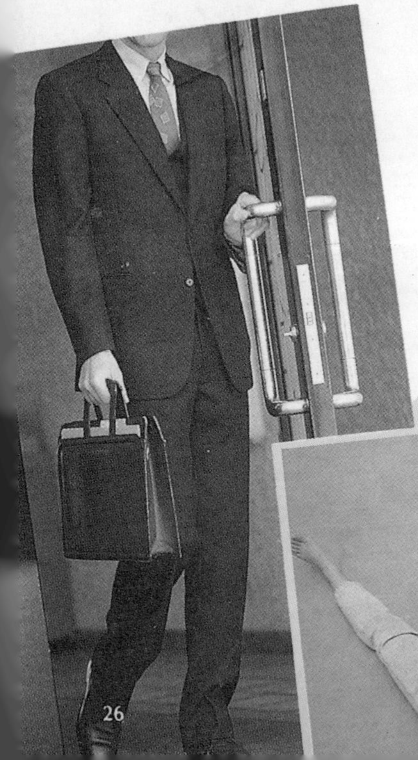

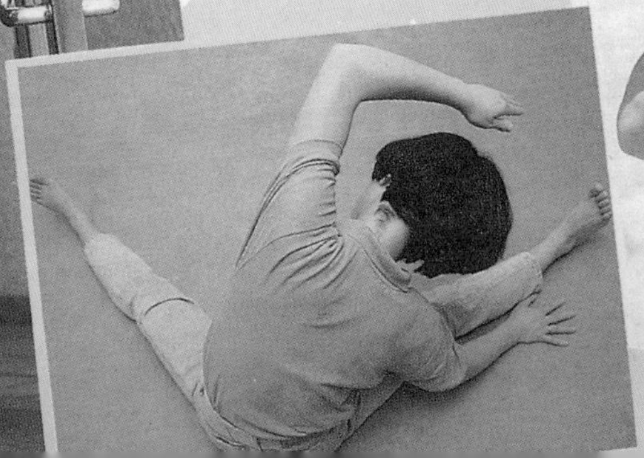

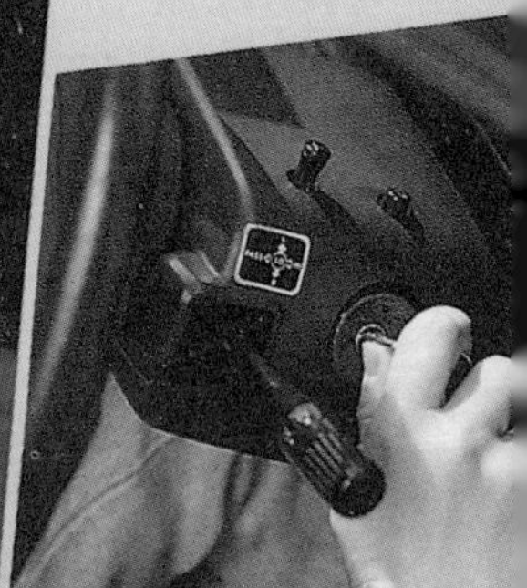

Objective: The students will identify and write information about people's daily routines.
Function: describe daily routines and habitual actions, talk about frequency
Structures: frequency adverbs, habitual present
Vocabulary Area: daily activities

Procedure

1. Do the optional warm-up activity listed below.
2. T: *Open your books to page 26. Look at the pictures.*
3. T: *You will hear some people talking about things they do every day.*
4. (Optional) If your students find listening very difficult, do the "additional preparation" exercise below.
5. T: *Look at "Getting Ready" on page 26. These are some ways to ask people about their daily schedule.* Play the first part of the tape.
6. T: *Work with a partner. Ask your partner these questions. Write the answers.*
7. T: *Look at the "First Listening" on page 27. People are talking about their daily schedules. Listen. Write the times. Check the other answers.* Play the "First Listening" segment of the tape. You may want students to do this in pairs so they can help each other. You may wish to stop after each item to check.
8. (Optional) T: *Work in pairs. Did you both get the same answers?*
9. Play the tape again if necessary.
10. Check by asking the students the questions (e.g., T: *What time does Alan start work?* A: 8:30. T: *What time does he finish?* A: 5:00.) and eliciting their answers OR by having students work in groups of 2-4. They should compare answers and ask you about any they couldn't catch. (See the answer key on the next page.)

Additional Preparation

Before the students open their books, play the "First Listening" one time. Students write down the sex of each speaker and any words they catch.

General Notes

• You may wish to include a "Second Listening" so students can confirm what they heard.
• Alan says, "On a good day it takes about a half hour to get home." He is talking about a day with little traffic. (segment 1)
• Lynn is a "single parent", which means that she is raising her children by herself. (segment 3)
• Luis says he usually watches the "late movie," a movie that is shown on television late at night or early in the morning - until about 2 or 3 a.m. (segment 4)

Optional Warm-up Activity

Frequency circle game. Give each student a piece of paper with one of the following written on it:

always, almost always, often, sometimes, hardly ever, never

On the chalkboard, write:

I always ____________.
almost always
often
sometimes
hardly ever
never

Tell the students to think of a true sentence about themselves that includes the word on their paper. Students work in groups of 8-10. They stand in a circle. One begins by saying his sentence (e.g., I hardly ever watch pro wrestling on TV.) The next student continues by repeating the information and adding her own (e.g., You hardly ever watch pro wrestling on TV. I almost always go to a disco on Saturday night.). The third student repeats the information about the first two and adds his own. The game continues until all students have added information.
Variation: Instead of having them go in order, use a pencil or another object as a pointer. Put it in the middle of the circle and spin it to decide who the next speaker will be.

First Listening

People are talking about their daily schedules.
Listen. Write the times.
Check (✓) the other answers.

Alan

starts work

8:30

finishes work

lunch
- ☐ eats in a restaurant
- ☐ goes swimming
- ☐ jogs

after work
- ☐ watches TV
- ☐ reads
- ☐ exercises

Naomi

starts class

finishes class

part-time job
- ☐ waitress
- ☐ office worker
- ☐ singer

after work
- ☐ exercises
- ☐ studies
- ☐ listens to music

Lynn

starts work

finishes work

lunch
- ☐ eats a sandwich
- ☐ doesn't eat lunch
- ☐ eats a big meal

after work
- ☐ goes shopping
- ☐ watches TV
- ☐ plays with her children

Luis

starts work

finishes work

lunch
- ☐ eats at 12:00
- ☐ eats between 1:00 and 2:00
- ☐ eats between 2:00 and 3:00

after work
- ☐ talks to his wife
- ☐ reads
- ☐ listens to music

Tapescript

This is Alan.
Interviewer: Alan, could you tell us something about what you do during
a typical day. You know, what time do you get up and so on?
Alan: Sure. I usually get up around six forty-five or seven and exercise for a while (uh-huh) and get to my office around eight thirty. I work in a law office so things are busy. I work from eight thirty to five. At lunch time I go swimming. (Swimming?) Yeah, there's a pool near the office. I usually finish work around five. On a good day it takes about a half hour to get home from the office, so I get home around five thirty. When I get home, I usually just fix dinner and eat by myself. And after dinner, I usually read. I like to read novels - detectives stories, that kind of thing. Mostly I relax in the evening...

This is Naomi.
Interviewer: Naomi, could you tell us little about what you do during a typical day?
Naomi: Well, I'm a student, and I sing in a band at night. (Um.) Yeah, and I really like it. I sing five nights a week and the band, of course, plays with me, of course. And, um, I don't like taking morning classes because it's awful for me to get up in the morning. So, my first class starts at one o'clock in the afternoon and my last class is finished at five. So, it's a great schedule. I really like it. And then after that I go home and pick up the rest of the guys. And we pack up the van with all of our equipment and we head on off to work. And we, basically, we start playing around eight and we're finished by eleven. So that's good. And the reason why is because we work at a hotel (Right) so we get out real early. And then after that we usually go out and have something to eat and then I go home and study for a couple of hours. And that's basically my day.
I: Oh, I see. So, thank you.

This is Lynn.
Interviewer: Lynn, can you tell us something about what you do during a typical day?
Lynn: Well, I start to work at the post office at six a.m. So I get up at five and have a quick breakfast and then I take the five-forty bus to the post office. It takes about ten or fifteen minutes. And I usually have my lunch break at about eleven a.m. and I eat a sandwich or a hamburger. I finish work at three in the afternoon. So I get home early -- a little after three. And when I get home I cook dinner and I play with the kids and then we all eat dinner together. And, well, that's a really important time of the day for me. And after dinner I help the kids with their homework and I get them ready for bed. And, since I'm alone, I'm pretty busy with three children in the evening, so I'm pretty tired and I usually go to bed around ten.

This is Luis.
Interviewer: Could you tell us what you do during a typical day.
Luis: Sure. I work at a small electronics parts factory. I work the late shift, in the evening. Actually four p.m. until midnight. So, I get up pretty late, about ten in the morning and eat breakfast and then, you know, do things around the house--wash dishes, that kind of thing. My wife works so we try to share the housework. (Right.) And then I eat lunch about two or three in the afternoon. And then go to work right away. And, uh, let's see. My dinner break is at, from seven-thirty to eight (Uh-huh) and I get off, as I said, at midnight (right) and get home about twelve-thirty. And them my wife and I talk for a while and she usually goes to sleep before I do. I watch the late movie, that kind of thing.

Answer Key

First Listening:

1. Alan:
- starts work: 8:30 a.m.
- finishes work: 5 p.m.
- lunch: goes swimming
- after work: reads

2. Naomi:
- starts class: 1 p.m.
- finishes class: 5 p.m.
- part -time job: singer
- after work: studies

3. Lynn:
- starts work: 6 a.m.
- finishes work: 3 p.m.
- lunch: eats a sandwich
- after work: plays with her children

4. Luis:
- starts work: 4 p.m.
- finishes work: midnight (12 o'clock at night)
- lunch: between 2:00 and 3:00
- after work: talks to his wife

CONVERSATION What are you doing tonight?

★ Hello.

◆ Hello, ________ (name). This is ________ (name).

★ Oh, hi ________ (name)

◆ What are you doing this Friday?

★ Friday? I have to work.
I ____1____ work on Friday night.

◆ Oh, ____2____.

★ I'm free Saturday.

◆ [Do you want to / Would you like to] ____3____?

★ That sounds good.
I ____4____ ____3____.
What time?

◆ Let's meet ____5____ at ____6____.

★ OK. I'm looking forward to it.

1. always / usually / almost always
2. I forgot / that's right / I didn't know that
3. go to the movies / go dancing / go out for pizza
4. hardly ever / never / almost never
5. in front of the theater / at the restaurant / at my place
6. 6:00 / 7:15 / 8:45

Objective: The students invite, and accept and refuse an invitation.
Functions: invite, accept/refuse an invitation and give a reason, suggest, thank
Structures: frequency adverbs: *always, almost always, usually, hardly ever, almost never, never*
present continuous as future:
I'm looking forward to it.

Procedure

1. T: *Open your books to page 28. Look at the picture. Where are these people?* (A: At their homes, talking on the phone.)*What do you think they are talking about?*
2. Play the tape. Have the students listen and read silently.
3. Answer questions about vocabulary and expressions.
4. (Optional) T: *Listen again. Repeat each line.* Play the conversation again. Pause after each sentence. Gesture for the students to repeat the sentences.
5. T: *Work in pairs.* (Gesture to show how you want the students paired.)
6. T: *Stand up. Practice the conversation.* Optional: Since the conversation is on the phone, have students stand back to back so they can't see their partners.
(After a few minutes) T: *Change parts* (Point to your book to show that students who were playing the part on the left now do the part on the right.).
7. Encourage the students to substitute the words and phrases in the box at the bottom.
8. As the students work, circulate, answer questions and note areas for later work.
9. When students can do the conversation smoothly, encourage them to make changes other than those listed. This can be done by having them cover the substitution box with a piece of paper, a pencil case, etc. OR have them close their books and try to have similar conversations.

Conversation Variation

Because the conversation takes place on the telephone, have the students stand back to back. As with real telephone conversations, they can not see the person they are speaking with.

General Notes

• You may wish to point out that
1. "go to a (the) ____" is used with a place or an event (go to the movies, a concert, etc.).
2. "go _____ing" (go + gerund) is used with an activity (go dancing, go shopping).
3. "go _____" is used with a place (go home, go downtown).
• Make sure that students listen to each other so that their choices for slot 3 correspond.
• "What are you doing this Friday?" is a common way to ask "What are you going to do this Friday?"
• "Rarely" and "seldom" are often taught with the other frequency adverbs. While they are used, "hardly ever" is much more common in spoken American English.

Conversation Tapescript

Paul: Hello.
Naomi: Hello, Paul. This is Naomi.
N: Oh, hi, Naomi.
P: What are you doing this Friday?
N: Friday? I have to work. I always work on Friday night.
P: Oh, that's right.
N: I'm free Saturday.
P: Do you want to go to the movies?
N: That sounds good. I almost never go to the movies. What time?
P: Let's meet in front of the theater at 7:15.
N: OK. I'm looking forward to it.

DUET-A

How often?

How often do you Do you ever	get up before 8:00? take a taxi to work? go shopping on Saturday?	I	always almost always often sometimes hardly ever never	get up before 8:00. do.

Read each question. Check (✓) your answers.
What do you think ***B*** will say? **GUESS *B*'s answers. Check (✓) them.**

I don't understand.

How often do you…	Always	Almost always	Often	Sometimes	Hardly ever	Never	Always	Almost always	Often	Sometimes	Hardly ever	Never	The same	Almost the same	Different
	How often do you…						***How often does B…***								
get up before 7:00?															
go shopping on Saturday?															
get to school or work late?															
eat bread for breakfast?															
go to bed before 10:00?															
go to the movies on the weekend?															

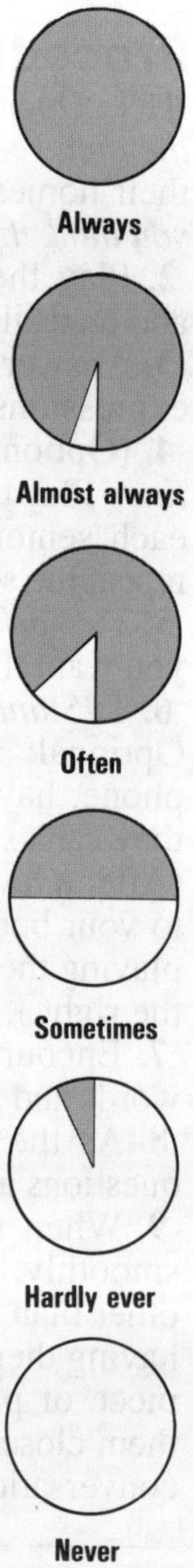

Write two more questions.

Ask *B*. Are ***B***'s answers **THE SAME, ALMOST THE SAME,** or **DIFFERENT**?
Check (✓) the gray boxes.

How many times did you guess ***B***'s answer? ____

Bonus! Find three things you and ***B*** do that are the same.
Find three differences.

Objective: The students will talk about frequency and routine behaviors.
Function: ask / tell about frequency and routine
Structures: simple present, frequency adverbs: *always, almost always, often , sometimes, hardly ever, never*
Vocabulary Area: daily routine
Classroom language: *I don't understand.*

Procedure

1. Divide the class into pairs. One student in each pair is **A**. The other is **B.** T: *Row one, you are **A's*** (Point to row one). *Row two, you are **B's*** (Point to row two). *Row three, you are **A's*** (etc.).
2. T: *A's, look at page 29. **B's**, look at page 30.*
3. Point out the language box at the top of the page. T: *Look at the box.* (Optional) *Listen and say.* Say the sentences in the box. Have students practice by repeating after you.
4. T: *Look at the page. Are there any words you don't know?*
5. Introduce the task. T: *You will find out how often your partner does things.*
6. While the other students watch, direct one pair through the first step of the exercise. T: (to any student **A**): *Look at question one. How often do you get up before 7:00? Check your answer. How often do you think **B** gets up before 7:00? You don't know. Guess what **B** will say. Check you answer. Now, ask **B**.* Prompt **A** to say, "How often do you get up before 7:00?" Prompt **B** to answer. Gesture for **A** T: (to **A**) *Was **B's** answer the same, almost the same, or different? Check the gray box.*
7. *Do the rest the same way. You will need to think of your own questions for the last two.* When the students understand the task, have them do it in pairs.
8. As the students work, circulate, answer questions and note areas for later work.
9. As students finish the main task, have them continue by doing the *Bonus!* task. Have them find three things they do at the same time and three things that are different.
10. Do consolidation, correction and expansion as desired.

Grammar and Usage

- Refer to the graphs on the students' pages for information about frequency adverbs (always, almost always,often, sometimes, hardly ever, never) .
- In a sentence, the adverbs of frequency usually follow "can", "do", "have" or "be" when these verbs are in the sentence. They usually come before any other verbs.
- "Often" and "sometimes" can come at the end of a clause or sentence.
- "Hardly ever" and "never" are negative, so they cannot be in the same clause as another negative.

General Notes

- Since the information changes completely when different people are partners, students who wish or need extra practice can repeat the activity with another partner using the other duet page.
- Students need not feel that they "should" know how their partners will respond. They guess before asking to make the task more interesting.
- See the introduction (•Corrections) for suggestions on ways to correct during pair work.

Additional Activity

(This activity can be used anytime during this unit).
Frequency "find someone who...". Work as a whole class. Make a copy of the frequency "find someone who" (next page) for each student. Students circulate and ask the questions. They try to find one person for each. They can use a name only one time (i.e., if someone says no, they can ask another question. If the person says yes, they need to find another partner for the next question). See Unit 1, Ensemble for a more complete explanation of "Find someone who" instructions. Students may want to refer to the language boxes on pages 29-30 for support.

DUET-B

How often?

How often do you Do you ever	get up before 8:00? take a taxi to work? go shopping on Saturday?	I	always almost always often sometimes hardly ever never	get up before 8:00. do.

Read each question. Check (✓) your answers.
What do you think ***A*** will say? **GUESS *A*'s answers. Check (✓) them.**

I don't understand.

How often do you...	*How often do you...* Always	Almost always	Often	Sometimes	Hardly ever	Never	*How often does A...* Always	Almost always	Often	Sometimes	Hardly ever	Never	The same	Almost the same	Different
sleep late on weekends?															
go to a restaurant on Saturday?															
take a bus to work or school?															
work on Sunday?															
watch the evening news?															
visit relatives (aunts, uncles, etc.) during New Year's?															

Write two more questions.

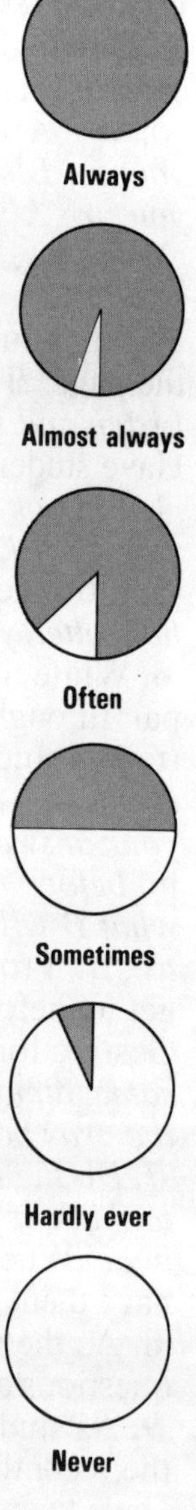

Ask *A*. Are ***A***'s answers **THE SAME, ALMOST THE SAME,** or **DIFFERENT** ?
Check (✓) the gray boxes.

How many times did you guess ***A***'s answer? ______

Bonus! Find three things you and ***A*** do that are the same.
Find three differences.

Find someone who...

1. often falls asleep watching TV.

____

2. usually gets up late.

____

3. sometimes cries at sad movies.

____

4. never eats breakfast.

____

5. is almost always late for class.

____

6. always does the homework (all of it).

____

7. hardly ever listens to music.

____

8. usually works on Friday night.

____

9. hardly ever gets nervous before a test.

____

10. never goes dancing.

____

Expansion Activity

Fluency Frames:
Three "fluency frames" are introduced in the "extra activities" sections of Units 1, 2 and 3. They are not limited to the units in which they first appear. These are task-based activities which can be used with nearly any topic.

Fluency Frame #3:
Line up.
Write the topic on the chalkboard. For this unit, the suggested topic is "my daily schedule."

Students stand in parallel lines. Each student should be facing another. Facing students are partners for the first round. On the teacher's signal, the students talk about the topic for exactly one minute.

After one minute, have the students change partners. This is easily done by having each member of the first line move one person to the right. The first person goes to the back of the line. When students are facing their new partners, have them discuss the topic, again for one minutes.

This process continues as long as time and interest permits. It should be done at least five times.

(We learned "Line up" from Carl Adams.)

Answer Key

Because the students are exchanging personal information, answers will vary. They may wish to look at each other's pages after completing the exercise to make sure they have accurately recorded the information.

SOLO

Read about Erika's schedule. Write the verbs:

drive eat fix ~~get up~~ go have is leave read watch work

Write about your schedule. Use some of these words:

____ drive	____ go	____ study
____ eat	____ have	____ take
____ fix	____ leave	____ watch
____ get up	____ read	____ work

Objective: The students will read about a person's daily routine. They will write about their own schedules.
Function: talk about daily routine
Structures: frequency adverbs: *always, usually*
prepositions of time: *until, from, to, at about, by*
Vocabulary Area: daily routine

Procedure

1. T: *Open your books to page 31. Look at the pictures. This is Erika. As you read, finish the sentences about her.*
2. T: *Now write about your schedule. Use some of these words: drive, eat, fix, get up, go, have, leave, read, study, take, watch, work.*

You may wish to assign this activity as homework.

In-class Follow-up

Students work in pairs. They read their paragraphs to each other and see how many things they do that are the same or that they do at the same time. They can continue until they find at least three things they do at the same time.

General Notes

• "Eat" and "have", in the context of meals, mean the same thing. To "take" a meal is unusual in American English. It is used in British English.
• At this time, you may want to teach students different ways to read the time in English. This can be done by drawing a clock on the chalkboard and eliciting those ways students know. If they are unable to suggest all the ways, write the first letter of each phrase on the board to help them.

3:30
Three thirty
Half past three

3:15
Three fifteen
A quarter after three
A quarter past three
Fifteen after three

3:45
Three forty-five
A quarter to four
A quarter of four
Fifteen to four

Optional Skill-building Activity

Skill: reading for details

Tell the students that you are going to read the information about Erika. You will make some mistakes. They should read along silently and, when they hear a mistake, circle it in their books. After you read the script (below), have them tell you the mistakes they found. (Note: the "mistakes" are underline in the following script. However, as you read, do not stress the mistakes.)
Script:
I get up at 6:45. Then I eat breakfast and <u>watch TV</u> until 8:30. I always drive to work. I usually leave for work at 8:<u>15</u>. I work from 9:00 to 5:00. I usually each lunch in <u>a cafe</u>. My break is from 12:00 to 1:00. I fix dinner at <u>exactly</u> 6:00. I usually watch TV <u>after</u> 10:30. I go to bed by <u>7:00</u>.

Answer Key

Task one:
1. I <u>get up</u> at 6:45.
2. Then, I <u>eat (have)</u> breakfast and <u>read</u> the newspaper until 8:30.
3. I always <u>drive</u> to work. I usually <u>leave</u> for work at 8:30.
4. I <u>work</u> from 9:00 to 5:00.
5. I usually <u>eat (have)</u> lunch in the cafeteria. My break <u>is</u> from 12:00 to 1:00.
6. I <u>fix</u> dinner at about 6:00.
7. I usually <u>watch</u> TV until 10:30.
8. I <u>go</u> to bed by 11:00.

Task two:
Answers will vary.
Example:
I get up at 7:00. I eat breakfast and read the newspaper. I leave for school at about 8:30. I go to school from 9:00 to 3:00. I usually have lunch in the cafeteria. I go home at 3:00 and fix dinner at about 6:30. Then I study. I go to bed around 12:00.

What do they like to do?

What's her name? How old is she? What does she do?	Her name's Paula. She's 25. She's a computer programmer.		
What does she like to do in her free time?	She	likes	to swim. playing volleyball. reading.
Is there anything she doesn't like?		doesn't like	baseball.

Work in groups of three. As a group, choose one picture.
Think of a story about the picture. Write the information on the chart.

I don't know.

PICTURE 1

Name ______________ Age ______

Occupation ______________

Something that she *LIKES* to do

____

Something that she *DOESN'T LIKE* to do

____

Other information ______________

____

PICTURE 2

Name ______________ Age ______

Occupation ______________

Something that she *LIKES* to do

____

Something that she *DOESN'T LIKE* to do

____

Other information ______________

____

PICTURE 3

Name ______________ Age ______

Occupation ______________

Something that she *LIKES* to do

____

Something that she *DOESN'T LIKE* to do

____

Other information ______________

____

I don't understand.

After you finish, change groups. Ask other students about the information in their charts.

Try This! Think of stories for the other pictures.
Which person would you like to know? Why?

Objective: The students will learn to talk about personal information, likes and dislikes. They will recycle language from previous units.
Function: ask for / give information about names, ages, occupations and preferences.
Structures: Wh-questions, possessive pronouns: *her, his*
likes/doesn't like + infinitive, gerund, noun
Classroom language:
I don't know.
I don't understand.

Procedure

1. T: *Look at page 32. You will think of a story about one of these people.*
2. T: *Look at the language box at the top of the page. Are there any words you don't know?* Answer questions about vocabulary.
3. (Optional) T: *Look at the box. Listen and say.* Say the sentences in the box. Have students practice by repeating after you.
4. Divide the class into groups of 3.
5. Introduce the task. T: *You will think of a story about one of these people.*
6. While the other students watch, direct one group through the first step of the exercise. T: *Which picture do you want to use?* Encourage them to select one picture. T: *What do you think her name is?* When they select a name, gesture for them to write it on the line. T: *Answer the other questions about her. Think of a story about her.*
7. When the students understand the task, have them begin.
8. As the students work, circulate, answer questions and note areas for later work.
9. When students have finished thinking of their stories, begin the next step. T: *Change groups. Tell your story to your new group. Ask about their stories.*
10. As groups finish the main task, have them continue by doing the *Try this!* task. Have them think of stories about the other pictures.
11. Do consolidation, correction and expansion as desired.

Grammar and Usage Notes

• Words such as *like, love, hate. etc.* can take either the infinitive (*to* + verb: *I like to swim*) or the gerund (verb+*ing* : *I like swimming.*) The meanings are practically identical, but many speakers feel that the infinitive sounds slightly more hypothetical than the gerund.
• When talking about sports, *play* + gerund (*She likes playing volleyball.*) or the infinitive (*She likes to play volleyball.*) can be used. Generally, sports which require more than one person (soccer, tennis, baseball, etc.) use *play.* Sports which are possible to do alone (swimming, jogging, skiing, bowling, etc.) do not use *play.* The exceptions are golf (which can be used either way), western fighting sports (boxing, fencing, wrestling, etc.) which do not use *play* and martial arts (karate, judo, etc.) which usually use *practice.*

General Notes

• If students have difficulty with the second stage of the activity (think of a story), remind them that most stories have a problem. Ask what they think the person's problem might be.
• If your students find changing groups confusing, have the group members number off (1-2-3). Have the 1's move one group forward or to the right. The 2's move one group back or to the left. The 3's remain where they are.
• Since this activity is designed to encourage fluency, corrections are not recommended at this time.

Answer Key

Answers will vary.
Example:
Picture 1:
Name: Paula Age: 23
Occupation: Legal secretary
Something that she LIKES to do
go to classical music concerts
Something she DOESN'T LIKE to do
go hiking
Other information: She plays the violin. She's going to get married next year.

CHECK YOURSELF

Circle the word that give a similar meaning. (5 points)

1. I get up at 7:30 every day. — I [**always** (circled) / sometimes / never] get up at 7:30.
2. John goes to the movies every week. — He [sometimes / hardly ever / often] goes to the movies.
3. Maria takes the train about once a month. — She [never / hardly ever / often] takes the train.
4. I try to go to bed early every night, but sometimes I go to bed late. — I [always / never / often] go to bed early.
5. William has a date every weekend. — He [always / sometimes / often] has a date on the weekend.
6. I ate squid once. It was terrible! I won't eat it again. — I'll [sometimes / never / hardly ever] try it again.

Find the mistakes. Cross out the sentences that are wrong. (5 points)

1. • ~~I almost get up at 7:00.~~
   • I almost always get up at 7:00.
2. • What do you do tonight?
   • What are you doing tonight?
3. • I usually sleep at 11:30 p.m.
   • I usually go to bed at 11:30 p.m.
4. • Do you like to go to a movie?
   • Would you like to go to a movie?
5. • How often do you play tennis?
   • How many times do you play tennis?
6. • I often go to shopping.
   • I often go shopping.

Fill in the blanks. Use words from the box. (10 points)

from	at	then	after	watches	looks	until	~~gets~~	
by	takes	to	leaves	goes	for	gets	in	on

Bill usually *gets* up at about 7:00. ________ he gets dressed and eats breakfast. He ________ for work at 7:45. He drives ________ work. It ________ about 20 minutes. He works ________ 8:30 until 4:30. He usually ________ home at 5:00. ________ the evening he ________ TV and reads ________ 11:00. He usually ________ to bed at 11:30.

Your score

Procedure

Exercise one.

1. T: *Look at page 33.* Point to the first exercise. T: *Look at the sentences. Circle the word on the right that gives the sentence the same meaning as the sentence on the left.*

2. (Optional). T: *Number one: I get up at 7:30 every day. I (blank) get up at 7:30. Which word goes in the blank?* Encourage the students to answer (A: always). Gesture for them to circle the word.

3. T: *Do 2-6 the same way.*

Exercise two.

1. Point to exercise two. T: *Some of these sentences have mistakes. Find the mistakes. Cross out those sentences.*

2. (Optional). T: *Number one. Which sentence is wrong?* Encourage the students to answer (A: I almost get up at 7:00.). Gesture for them to cross out the sentence.

3. T: *Do 2-6 the same way.*

Exercise three.

1. Point to the third exercise. T: *Finish the sentences. Use words from the box.*

2. (Optional:) Point to item one. T: *Bill (blank) up at about 7:00. What word goes in the blank?* Encourage the students to answer (A: gets). Gesture for them to write "gets" in the space provided.

3. T: *Do the rest the same way.* (Explanations of the reasons why the sentences are wrong are included in the "General Notes.")

You may wish to assign the page as homework.

In-class Follow-up

• T: *Work in pairs. Did you both get the same answers?* As students compare their answers, circulate to make sure that all students have completed the homework. You may wish to have some students write their answers on the board.

General Notes

•Explanations of mistakes in part two:

1. The sentence needs a frequency adverb. "Almost" is used to modify words like "always," but by itself tells nothing about frequency.

2. "What do you do..." is used to talk about habits and repeated actions like work. Since the sentence includes "tonight," it refers to a specific time in the future.

3. "I usually go to bed at 11:30." is usual. One might say, "I'm usually sleeping at 11:30." Since it is difficult to know exactly when one falls asleep, "go to bed" is used.

4. While one might say, "Do you like to go to movies." when asking about a person's habits and interests, "Would you like..." is used when inviting or suggesting.

5. If asking about frequency, use "How often...?" "How many times" refers to a specific period of time (e.g., How many times do you play tennis in a week/month/year?).

6. "To" is used for places, not activities (e.g., I often go to that store.).

Answer Key

Exercise one:

1. I always get up at 7:30.
2. He often goes to the movies.
3. She hardly ever takes the train.
4. I often go to bed early.
5. He always has a date on the weekend.
6. I'll never try it again.

Exercise two:

The following sentences are ***WRONG****.*
(Explanations included in "General Notes," above.)

~~1. I almost get up at 7:00.~~
~~2. What do you do tonight?~~
~~3. I usually sleep at 11:30 p.m.~~
~~4. Do you like to go to a movie?~~
~~5. How many times do you play tennis?~~
~~6. I often go to shopping.~~

Exercise three:

Bill usually gets up at about 7:00. Then he gets dressed and eats breakfast. He leaves for work at 7:45. He drives to work. It takes about 20 minutes. He works from 8:30 until 4:30. He usually gets home at 5:00. In the evening he watches TV and reads until 11:00. He usually goes to bed at 11:30.

Unit 4 Where does this go?

LISTENING Describing locations

Getting ready

Here are some ways to describe locations.

Work with a partner. Describe your room.

Objective: The students will identify the locations of objects.
Function: describe locations
Structures: prepositions of location, imperative mood
Vocabulary Area: rooms and furnishings

Procedure

1. Do the optional warm-up activity listed below.
2. T: *Open your books to page 34. Look at the pictures.*
3. T: *You will hear some people deciding where to put things in a new apartment.*
4. T: *Look at "Getting Ready" on page 34. These are some ways to describe location.* Play the first part of the tape.
5. T: *Work with a partner. Describe your room.* Optional: Have the partners make a quick drawing of the room described.
6. T: *Look at the "First Listening" on page 35. Margie is moving into a new apartment. Her friend is helping her.*
7. (Optional) If your students find listening very difficult, do the "additional preparation" exercise below.
8. *Listen. Where do they put things? Write the letters in the right locations.* Play the "First Listening" segment of the tape. You may want students to do this in pairs so they can help each other. You may wish to stop after each item to check.
9. (Optional) T: *Work in pairs. Did you both get the same answers?*
10. Play the tape again if necessary.
11. Check by asking the students the questions (e.g., T: *Where did they put the plant?* A: In the corner to the right of the desk.) and eliciting their answers OR by having students work in groups of 2-4. They should compare answers and ask you about any they couldn't catch. (See the answer key on the next page.)

Additional Preparation

Students work in pairs. They decide where they would put the items if it were their apartment. As they are deciding, they should not touch the book. This will ensure that they use the prepositions they will be hearing on the tape rather than simply pointing and saying, "The plant goes here."

General Notes

• Many North Americans choose to move to a new house or apartment without the help of professional moving companies. They carry their possessions in their car or in a rental truck. Friends often help them with the task.

Optional Warm-up Activity

Split pictures. Work as an entire class. Get magazine pictures of the insides of several rooms. Rooms with a lot of furniture are best. You will need one picture per 5 students. Cut each picture into five sections. Mix all the picture pieces together and randomly distribute one to each student. Students try to find all the people who have other parts of their pictures. The circulate and describe their pictures. They can ask questions about other students' pictures. No one is allowed to look at anyone else's picture until they think they have found all the other members of their group.

Unit 4

First Listening

Margie is moving into a new apartment. Her friend, Daniel, is helping her.
Listen. Write the letters (a-f) in the right locations.

1. The living room

a. a plant

b. a television

c. a picture

2. The kitchen

d. dishes

e. a microwave oven

f. pots and pans

Tapescript

Number 1, the living room.
Daniel: Ah, what about this plant?
Margie: Let's see, the plant? Uh, I think maybe in the corner there behind the desk.
D: Behind the desk?
M: Yeah, to the right of the desk.
D: OK. That looks good.
M: OK
D: Over here?
M: Yeah, just a little bit farther back into the corner. OK. That looks good, doesn't it?
D: Yeah, I think so. That's a good place for it.

M: Would you mind helping me with the TV now?
D: OK. Sure. Where would you like to put it?
M: OK, why don't we put it, let's see, on the top of the cabinet there, to the right, on the right hand side of the cabinet.. Hm, maybe a little bit more to the right would be better.
D: OK. But not too close to the edge.
M: Well, yeah, but slide it down a little bit more. OK? Yeah, that looks good.

M: OK, now just the picture. Where do you think would be a good spot for the picture?
D: How about over here?
M: Right on that wall?
D: Above the cabinet, in the middle here?
M: OK. Yeah, I think, yeah, make it a little left, not right over the TV...no...A little bit
more to the left.
D: How's this?
M: Yeah, make it more toward the center of the cabinet, I think.
D: How does that look? Is it straight?

Number 2, the kitchen.
Daniel: What about...these dishes? Where do you want to put these dishes?
Margie: Those can go in the sink. They're dirty now so I have to wash them before I put them away.
D: Do you want me to wash them for you?
M: No, no. Just put them in the sink, just leave them in the sink.

M: Do you want to help me with this microwave oven?
D: All right.
M: OK, let's see. I think, um, maybe in the corner along the right wall.
D: On that counter there?
M: Yeah, yeah. Put it on the counter in the corner. OK.

M: Ah, now these pots and pans, could you put them on the shelf for me there?
D: OK, sure.
M: Put them on the top shelf. Yeah. OK, yeah, that looks fine.

Answer Key

First/Second Listening:
1.

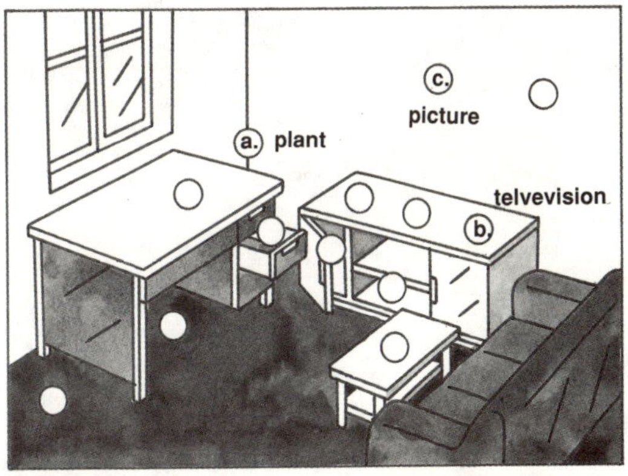

2.

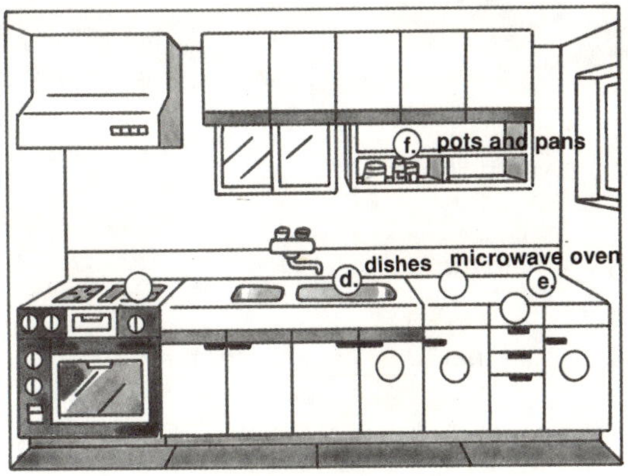

CONVERSATION Could you help me?

★ What are you doing?

◆ I'm ___1___ .

★ Could you help me?

◆ Sure. What do you want?

★ Could you get that ___2___ for me?

◆ Which one?

★ The ___3___ one ___4___ .

◆ OK. Where do you want it?

★ Put it ___5___ .

◆ Oops!

1. watching TV
   reading the newspaper
   writing a letter

2. bowl
   plate
   vase

3. glass
   yellow
   large

4. on the top shelf
   next to the TV
   on the table

5. on this counter
   in the cabinet
   under the sink

Objective: The students will talk about locations and descriptions of objects.
Functions: ask for/agree to help, describe objects and locations
Structures: *WH*-questions, prepositions of place; *in, on, next to, under*
present continuous:
I'm watching TV.

Procedure

1. T: *Open your books to page 36. Look at the picture. Where are these people?* (A: At home, in the kitchen.) *What is the man doing?*
2. Play the tape. Have the students listen and read silently.
3. Answer questions about vocabulary and expressions.
4. (Optional) T: *Listen again. Repeat each line.* Play the conversation again. Pause after each sentence. Gesture for the students to repeat the sentences.
5. T: *Work in pairs.* (Gesture to show how you want the students paired.)
6. T: *Stand up. Practice the conversation.* Optional: Have the students use a book, notebook or other object to represent the bowl.
(After a few minutes) T: *Change parts* (Point to your book to show that students who were playing the part on the left now do the part on the right.).
7. Encourage the students to substitute the words and phrases in the box at the bottom.
8. Encourage the students to make eye contact while they are practicing.
9. As the students work, circulate, answer questions and note areas for later work.
10. When students can do the conversation smoothly, encourage them to make changes other than those listed. This can be done by having them cover the substitution box with a piece of paper, a pencil case, etc. OR have them close their books and try to have similar conversations.

Conversation Variation

At the beginning on the conversation students should stand about 2 meters (6-7 feet) apart. This will encourage them to speak loudly. As they progress through the conversation, they can move closer together. They should use a book or another object to represent the item in slot 5.

General Notes

• "Could you...?" is a way to ask for a favor. As used here, it has nothing to do with asking about ability.
• "Sure" is an informal way of saying"Yes." The nuance is "Of course."
• "Oops!" is an informal American English expression indicating that a mistake has been made.

Conversation Tapescript

Husband: What are you doing?
Wife: I'm watching TV.
H: Could you help me?
W: Sure, what do you want?
H: Could you get that bowl for me?
W: Which one?
H: The large one on the table.
W: OK. Where do you want it?
H: Put it on this counter.
W: (sound of dish breaking) Oops!

DUET-A

What's the difference?

Is	there	a	coffee mug? telephone?	Yes,	there is. there are two.
Are		any	pictures?	No,	there isn't. there aren't.
What	color shape pattern		is it? are they?	It's They're	black. square. striped.
What	does it do they		look like?		
What's the		man	doing?	He's	reading a magazine.

How do you say ____ in English ?

You and **B** have pictures of rooms that are almost the same.
Find out what is different. Ask about *color, location, style* and *actions*.
Use the clues. You do not need every clue.

Clues

sofa	picture
coffee table	telephone
magazine	dial
cushion	push button
ashtray	on
shirt	off
antenna	newspaper
coffee mug	book
reading	watching TV

Item	What is different?
1. *coffee mug*	
2.	
3.	
4.	
5.	
6.	
7.	

Bonus! Look at the picture on page 39 for one minute.
Close your book. Describe the room to **B**.

Objective: The students will ask for and give descriptions of objects.
Function: describe rooms and furnishings
Structures: descriptive adjectives, *There is / isn't / are / aren't... any* in interrogative / negative sentences
Vocabulary Area: rooms and furnishings
Classroom language: *How do you say _____ in English?*

Procedure

1. Divide the class into pairs. One student in each pair is **A**. The other is **B.** T: *Row one, you are **A's*** (Point to row one). *Row two, you are **B's*** (Point to row two). *Row three, you are **A's*** (etc.).
2. T: *A's, look at page 37. **B's**, look at page 38.*
3. Point out the language box at the top of the page. T: *Look at the box.* (Optional) *Listen and say.* Say the sentences in the box. Have students practice by repeating after you.
4. T: *Look at the page. Are there any words you don't know?*
5. Introduce the task. T: *You and your partner have pictures that are almost the same. You need to find the differences.*
6. While the other students watch, direct one pair through the first step of the exercise. T: (to any student **A**): *What do you think will be different in **B's** picture?* If necessary, prompt **A** by pointing to the words "coffee mug" on the chart. Prompt **A** to ask, "Is there a coffee mug?" and "What color is it?" Prompt **B** to answer (It's white [with pictures of animals].) Gesture for **A** and **B** to write the difference on their chart.
7. T: *Find at least seven things that are different.* When the students understand the task, have them do it in pairs.
8. As the students work, circulate, answer questions and note areas for later work.
9. As students finish the main task, have them continue by doing the *Bonus!* task. Have **A** look at page 39 for one minute. **A** then closes the book and describes the room to **B**. **B** can have the book open and can ask questions. They repeat the process with **B** looking at page 34.
10. Do consolidation, correction and expansion as desired.

Grammar and Usage

• Students frequently forget to include the *be* verb when using the present continuous. You may want to call their attention to the last line in the box and point out that the "'s" stands for "is."
• Students often confuse "see" and "watch." "Watch" , rather than "see", is the verb used for viewing television.

General Notes

• The students will not need to use all the clues.
• See the introduction (•Corrections) for suggestions on ways to correct during pair work.

Additional Activity

(This activity can be used anytime during this unit).
Rod pictures. Work in pairs. If possible, have them use Cuisenaire rods (Algebricks), small wooden rods. If these are not available, have them draw or use toothpicks. One student thinks of a picture and tells the other how to make or draw it. (e.g., Take a blue rod. Put it on the table. Put an orange rod to the right of the blue rod. etc.).
Variation 1: Students from Asian countries that use character-based writing systems (e.g., Japan, Taiwan, mainland China) can think of a character instead of a picture. Students tell partners how to make the character using the rods. The partner tries to guess the meaning before the figure is completely finished. (Note: Tell the students that they do not have to follow the stroke order they use when writing. It is helpful to teach them the following words: horizontally, vertically, diagonally. They may want to refer to the language box on page 40 for support.)
Variation 2: Have them work in groups of three. One person explains while two build. They compete to be the first to recognize what they are making.

DUET-B

What's the difference?

Is	there	a	coffee mug? telephone?	Yes,	there is. there are two.
Are		any	pictures?	No,	there isn't. there aren't.
What	color shape pattern		is it? are they?	It's They're	black. square. striped.
What	does it do they		look like?		
What's the		man	doing?	He's	reading a magazine.

How do you say ___ in English?

You and ***A*** have pictures of rooms that are almost the same.

Find out what is different. Ask about *color, location, style* and *actions*.
Use the clues. You do not need every clue.

Clues

sofa	picture
coffee table	telephone
magazine	dial
cushion	push button
ashtray	on
shirt	off
antenna	newspaper
coffee mug	book
reading	watching TV

Item	What is different?
1. *coffee mug*	
2.	
3.	
4.	
5.	
6.	
7.	

Bonus! Look at the picture on page 34 for one minute.
Close your book. Describe the room to ***A***.

Expansion Activity

Who is it?
Students work in pairs. One partner closes his or her eyes while the other describe a person in the room, using locations as well as physical descriptions practiced in Unit 2. The other student guesses the identity of the person being described.

Fluency Frames:
Three "fluency frames" are introduced in the "extra activities" sections of Units 1, 2 and 3. Use any one of the "frames" with this topic for Unit 4:
• *My bedroom* or *My living room*

Answer Key

Differences:
1. Animal poster (Cincinnati Zoo poster) / picture of car
2. TV is off/on.
3. The man is wearing/not wearing a jacket.
4. The sofa has no cover/ has a green cover.
5. The man is reading a magazine/ watching television.
6. There is a magazine / newspaper on the table.
7. The cup is black / white (with pictures of animals).
8. There is a white (push-button) phone/ green (dial) phone.

Phrasing of the answers may vary.

SOLO There's no place like home.

Read about Lee's apartment.

My apartment is very small. There is only one room. I don't have a lot of furniture. There are a lot of books in the bookcase between the windows. There is a desk and chair against the left wall. My TV is on the floor to the left of the desk. There are some plants on it. In the back right corner there is a chest of drawers. My stereo is next to the chest.

Draw a picture of your room. Write about it.
Use some of these words:

____ to the left of	____ between	____ against
____ to the right of	____ in front of	____ on
____ next to	____ in back of	____ in

Objective: The students will read a description of an apartment. They will write about their own apartments and houses.
Function: describing rooms and furnishings
Structures: prepositions of place: *on, against, next to, in, between*
prepositional phrases: *to the right/left of, in front/back of*
There is(n't) / are(n't)
Vocabulary Area: furniture

Procedure

1. T: *Open your books to page 39. You will read about this room. If you find any words you don't know, guess what they mean from the picture and the location words: on, to the left of, etc.*

2. T: *Now, draw a picture of your room. Write about it. Use some of these words: in the center, to the right of, to the left of, against, next to, on, in.*

You may wish to assign this activity as homework.

In-class Follow-up

Students work in pairs. They read their room descriptions while their partners draw the room. Partners may ask questions to clarify. When they finish, they compare the drawings to those they did in the book.

General Notes

- A one-room apartment is called a "studio apartment" in the U.S.
- A "chest of drawers" is also simply called a "chest."
- Describing one room in detail will generate more of the target language than a limited description of an entire apartment. You may wish to ask the students to describe their living rooms, bedrooms, or the largest room in their house.

Optional Skill-building Activity

Skill: predicting

Before the students read the paragraph at the top of the page, have them look at the pictures. Have them write five sentences describing the room, working individually or in pairs. As they read the textbook paragraph, they circle the sentences with the same meaning as the sentences they wrote.

Answer Key

Answers will vary.
Example: See the paragraph about Lee's apartment.

Notes

It was on the book.

The eraser The stapler	was	in on under in front of in back of to the right of to the left of	the book. the ruler. the stapler. the eraser.
Now it's			
		between	the pen and the key.

Step one:

Work in groups of three.
Each person puts five things (a pen, a coin, an eraser, etc.) **on the desk.**
Arrange them to show these locations:

- in
- on
- under
- in front of
- in back of
- to the right of
- to the left of
- between

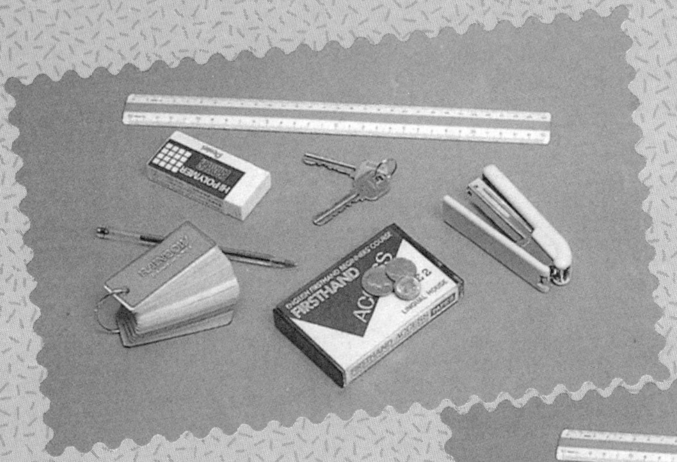

I don't know.

Step two:

Two people close their eyes.
The other person changes three things.

Try to find the changes.
Continue.

How many changes did you find? ________
In your group, who found the most? ________

Try This! Draw a "modern art" picture. Use circles, squares, rectangles, etc.
Don't let your partners see it. Tell them how to draw it.

Objective: The students will learn to describe the location of objects.
Function: describe location
Structures: simple past, simple present, prepositions of location: *in, on, under, between*
prepositional phrases:
in front / back of,
to the right / left of
Vocabulary Area: classroom objects
Classroom language: *I don't know.*

Procedure

1. (Optional) T: *Close your eyes. Think about this room. Where is the* *light switch?* Encourage students to answer. Continue with several other objects in the classroom that are slightly difficult to remember.

2. *Look at page 40. This is a memory activity.*

3. T: *Look at the language box at the top of the page. Are there any words you don't know?* Answer questions about vocabulary.

4. (Optional) T: *Look at the box. Listen and say.* Say the sentences in the box. Have students practice by repeating after you.

5. Divide the class into groups of 3.

6. Introduce the task. T: *You will test your memory. Each person in your group will put five things on the desk. Use things like pens, coins, rulers and erasers. Mix them together. Arrange them to show "in, on, under, in front of, in back of, to the right of, to the left of and between."*

7. While the other students watch, direct one group through the first step of the exercise. T: (to two students): *Close your eyes.* (gesture if necessary) T: (to the other student): *Change three things. Open your eyes. What was moved?* Encourage them to answer. Guide them through the language box if necessary.

8. When the students understand the task, have them begin.

9. As the students work, circulate, answer questions and note areas for later work.

10. As students finish the main task, have them continue by doing the *Try this!* task. Have them draw "modern art" pictures consisting of circles, squares, triangles, etc. Partners can not see them. They tell each other how to draw each picture, then compare it to the original.

11. Do consolidation, correction and expansion as desired.

Grammar and Usage Notes

- You may wish to very briefly review the meanings of the prepositions before beginning this activity. You can do this by using objects similar to those in the picture and eliciting the words from the students.

General Notes

- Prepositions of location *by* and *near* are excluded from this activity because they indicate general, rather than specific, location.
- If any groups are smaller than three, they should use more objects per person to make the activity challenging.
- See the introduction section of this manual (• **corrections**) for suggestions on ways to correct student errors.

Answer Key

Answers will vary. Students should use forms like those in the language box.

Notes

CHECK YOURSELF

Look at the picture. Circle the correct choice. (6 points)

1. The large plant is [in back of / to the left of / to the right of] the sofa.
2. There is a glass [on / beside / under] the book.
3. The bottle is [on / in / under] the ice bucket.
4. The cat is sleeping [on top of / under / next to] the coffee table.
5. There is a coffee table [to the right of / in back of / in front of] the large sofa.
6. There is a lamp [between / next to / in front of] the sofas.

Finish the conversation. Put the words in order.
There is one extra word in each group. (2 points each = 14 points)

- *What are you doing?* [you, do, what, doing, are]
  - ☐ ______________________ . [to, listening, radio, I'm, on, the]
- ______________________ ? [you, could, to, me, help]
  - ☐ Sure. ______________________ ? [want, like, you, do, what]
- ______________________ ? [bowl, you, could, that, me, for, those, get]
  - ☐ Which one?
- ______________________ . [one, a, table, big, the, on, the]
  - ☐ ______________________ ? [it, what, you, where, do, want]
- ______________________ . [it, to, put, next, oven, an, the]

Your score

Procedure

Exercise one.

1. T: *Look at page 41* Point to the first exercise. T: *Look at the picture. Circle the words in each sentence that are correct.*

2. (Optional). T: *Number one: The large plant is (blank) the sofa. Which words go in the blank?* Encourage the students to answer (A: in back of). Gesture for them to circle the words.

3. T: *Do 2-6 the same way.*

Exercise two.

1. Point to the second exercise. T: *This is a conversation. Put the words in the right order. There is one extra word in each group.*

2. (Optional). T: *The conversation starts like this:*
The first sentence is, "What are you doing?" The extra word is "do." What is the second sentence? Elicit answers (A: I'm listening to the radio. Extra word: on).

3. T: *Find the rest of the dialogue.*

You may wish to assign the page as homework.

In-class Follow-up

- T: *Work in pairs. Did you both get the same answers?* As students compare their answers, circulate to make sure that all students have completed the homework. You may wish to have some students write their answers on the board.
- T: *Work in pairs. Practice the conversations in Part Two.*

General Notes

- The "Check yourself" pages are each worth 20 points. The items in the first activity are worth one point each. Each sentence in the second activity is worth two points. If you are giving grades, you may wish to keep track of student scores. Alternatively, if you have assigned the pages as homework and class size makes keeping track of individual points impractical, you may want to note which students have completed the assignment, those who did only part of it and those who didn't do it.

Answer Key

Exercise one:

1. The large plant is in back of the sofa.
2. There is a glass on the book.
3. The bottle is in the ice bucket.
4. The cat is sleeping under the coffee table.
5. There is a coffee table in front of the large sofa.
6. There is a lamp between the sofas.

Exercise two:

What are you doing?
I'm listening to the radio.
Could you help me?
(Sure.) What do you want?
Could you get that bowl for me?
(Which one?)
The big one on the table.
Where do you want it?
Put it next to the oven.

Unit 5 Where is it?

LISTENING Giving directions

Getting ready

Match these sentences with the pictures.

1. It's next to the hotel.
2. Turn right.
3. Go straight.
4. It's across from the hotel.
5. Turn left.
6. It's between the hotel and the drug store.
7. It's past the hotel, on the right.
8. It's on the corner.

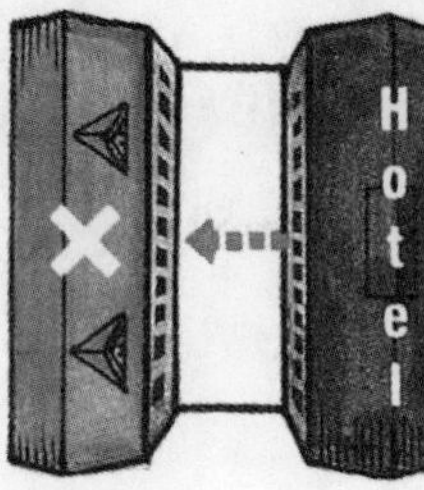

____

____

____

____

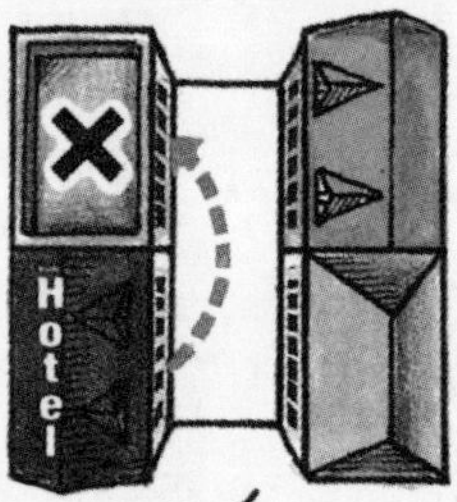

1

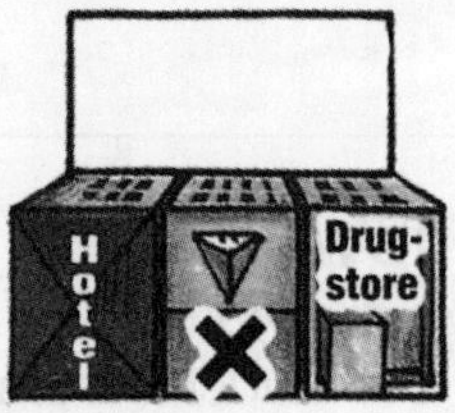

____

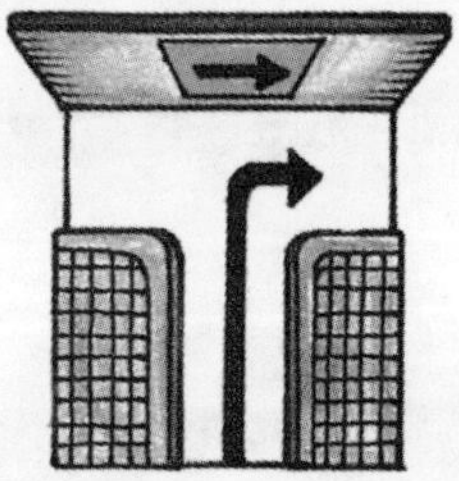

____

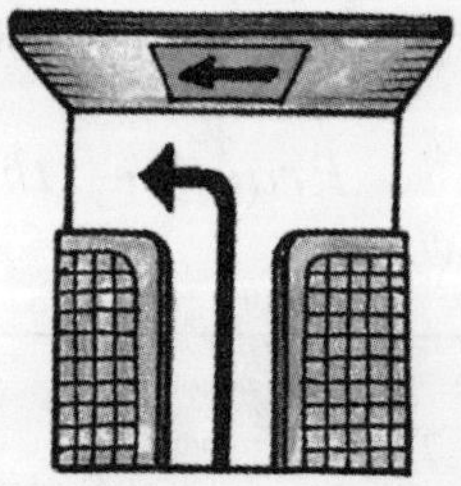

____

Where is your school?
Write three sentences.

near

across from

next to

Objective: The students will follow directions and identify locations.
Function: ask for/ give directions
Structures: prepositions of location, *imperative mood*
Vocabulary Area: stores, buildings and shops

Procedure

1. Do the optional warm-up activity listed below.
2. T: *Open your books to pages 42-43. Look at the maps.*
3. T: *You will hear some people giving directions.*
4. T: *Look at "Getting Ready" on page 42. These are some ways to give directions and say where something is. Listen. Match the sentences with the pictures.* Play the first part of the tape. You may want students to do this in pairs so they can help each other.
5. Check by asking the students the questions (e.g., T: *Where is number one?* A: In the middle.) and eliciting their answers OR by having students work in groups of 2-4. They should compare answers and ask you about any they couldn't catch. (See the answer key on the next page.)
6. (Optional) If your students find listening very difficult, do the "additional preparation" exercise below.
7. T: *Look at the "First Listening"on page 43. Listen. Follow the directions. Write the places on the map.* Play the "First Listening" segment of the tape. You may want students to do this in pairs so they can help each other. You may wish to stop after each item to check.
8. (Optional) T: *Work in pairs. Did you both get the same answers?*
9. Play the tape again if necessary.
10. Check the answers as in step 5. (See the answer key on the next page.)

Additional Preparation

Students look at page 43. Think of a building that is labeled on the map. Give the students directions from the bus stop to that place. Students follow the directions and tell you which shop it is. Do this 3-4 times or, after 1 example, have the student do it in pairs.

General Notes

• One of the speakers in segment 1 wants to find a "video shop", a store that rents video tapes.
• The words "signal", "traffic light", and "light" are interchangeable in American English.
• Streets are not named on this map to encourage students to use landmarks --well-known or easy to notice places, buildings or objects -- as reference points for giving directions.

Optional Warm-up Activity

Blindfolded directions. Work as an entire class. If possible, move the desks out of the center of the room. Leave a few obstacles (such as chairs or umbrellas) scattered randomly. Blindfold one student. Place a marker (a coin or piece of chalk works well) on the floor on the opposite side of the room. The other students give the blindfolded student directions to the marker. The blindfolded student follows the directions until he finds the marker.

Note: To increase the amount of language used, have the students work in pairs after they understand the activity. In each pair, one student is blindfolded. Scatter a lot of markers around the room. The blindfolded students try to collect as many as possible. During the activity, circulate and scatter more markers.

Tapescript

Number 1: a video shop
A: Excuse me. Is there a video shop around here?
B: Oh, sure. It's called Video Forum. It's just on the next block.
A: How do I get there?
B: Go down to the corner. You see that gas station?
A: Um-hmm.
B: Turn right there. Go one block and then turn right again. It's between the McDonald's and Tower Records.
A: OK. I see. Thanks.

Number 2: a shoe store
C: While I'm downtown, I want to buy some boots.
D: Well, there's a shoe store one street over.
C: Where?

First Listening

You are at the bus stop.
Follow the directions. Write the places on the map.

1. a video shop
2. a shoe store
3. a post office
4. an appliance store
5. a stationery store
6. a supermarket

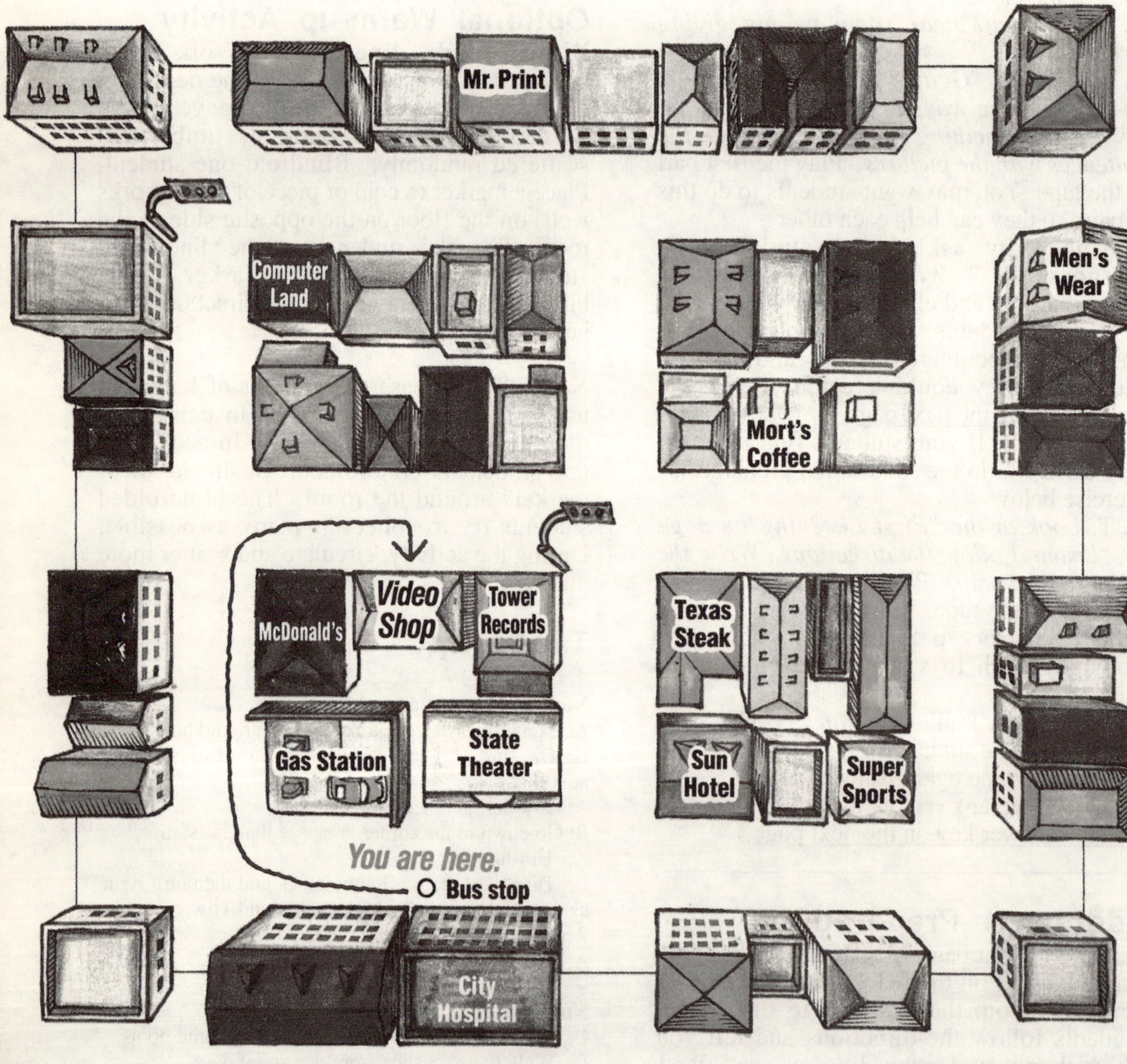

D: Go to the corner. Turn left by the theater. On the next corner, you'll see a steak restaurant. I think it's Texas Steak. Anyway, turn right. The shoe store is next to the steak place. It's across from a coffee shop.
C: Wait. Wait. I go to the steak restaurant, then turn right. Across from a coffee shop?
D: That's right. It's a big shoe store. You can't miss it.

Number 3: a post office
E. Oh. I almost forgot. I need to get some stamps.
F: Let's stop at the post office.
E: Is there a post office around here?
F: Yeah, it's on our way. We go on this street to the second corner. You know that sports store? We turn left there. Then we go straight two blocks. It's on the left just before we cross the street.
E: Wait, I don't understand.
F: Left at the sports store. Straight for two blocks. It's on the corner just before we cross that big street. It's across from a men's clothing store.
E: Oh, across from the men's wear store. I know where it is now.
F: It doesn't matter, I'm coming with you.

Number 4: an appliance store
G: I really want to look for a CD player today. Do you know of a cheap appliance store?
H: A cheap appliance store? I've heard that Rocket Electric is good.
G: Rocket Electric. Where's that?
H: Oh, it's easy to get to. You go down to the corner and, let's see, turn left at the theater. And then go straight for two blocks. Cross that big street. And it's right in front of you.
G: Left at the theater, straight for two blocks, cross the street. It will be in front of me
H: That's right. It's next to a print shop.
G: Great. Thanks.

Number 5: a stationery store
I: Excuse me. Is there a stationery store near here?
J: A stationery store? Yeah, there's a stationery store on the next block. Just go straight past the Sun Hotel. It's between the hotel and Super Sports.
I: Between the Sun Hotel and Super Sports. I see. Thanks.

Number 6: a supermarket
K: Oh, I need to buy some food. I want to stop by a supermarket before I go home.
L: Well, Sunshine Supermarket is near here.
K: Where?
L: You go to the corner and turn right.
K: By the theater?
L: No. The other way. You go to the gas station. Then turn right.
K: Right at the gas station?
L: Right. Then you go to the first traffic light. And there's a computer store on the corner.
K: Straight to the first signal...
L: Yeah. Then you turn right at the computer shop and it's the third store on your right. It's across from Mr. Print.
K: Two shops past the computer store. Across from Mr. Print.
L: Right.

Answer Key

Getting Ready:

first row: 4 3 7

second row: 8 1 6

third row: 2 5

First Listening:

1. video shop **2.** shoe store **3.** post office
4. appliance store **5.** stationery store
6. supermarket)

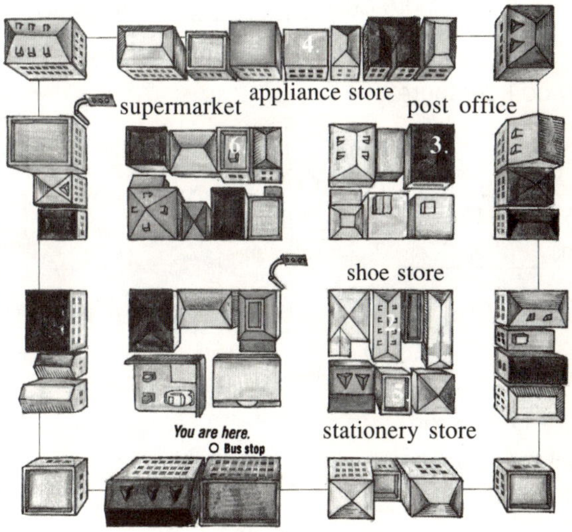

CONVERSATION How do I get there?

★ Excuse me. Is there a(n) ___1___ near here?

◆ Yes. There's one ___2___ the post office.

★ How do I get there?

◆ Go down this street to ___3___.
Then turn ___4___.

★ This street to ___3___,
then ___4___?

◆ Yeah. Then go straight about three blocks.
You'll see it on the ___5___.

★ On the ___5___. I see.

◆ It's ___6___ the park.

★ Thanks. Oh, yeah.
And where's ___7___?

◆ We're standing in front of it.

★ Oh. Thanks.

1. bookstore stationery shop appliance store	2. across from next to just past	3. the signal the corner Third Street	4. right left
5. right left southwest corner	6. next to past across from	7. Stewart's Department Store the Grand Hotel the art museum	

Objective: The students will ask for and give directions.
Functions: get someone's attention, ask for/give directions, thank
Structures: prepositions of location: *across from, next to, past,*
imperative mood
Go straight. Turn right.

Procedure

1. T: *Open your books to page 44. Look at the picture. Where are these people?* (A: On the street.) *What do you think they are talking about?*
2. Play the tape. Have the students listen and read silently.
3. Answer questions about vocabulary and expressions.
4. (Optional) T: *Listen again. Repeat each line.* Play the conversation again. Pause after each sentence. Gesture for the students to repeat the sentences.
5. T: *Work in pairs.* (Gesture to show how you want the students paired.)
6. T: *Stand up. Practice the conversation.* (After a few minutes) T: *Change parts* (Point to your book to show that students who were playing the part on the left now do the part on the right.).
7. Encourage the students to substitute the words and phrases in the box at the bottom.
8. Encourage the students to make eye contact while they are practicing.
9. As the students work, circulate, answer questions and note areas for later work.
10. When students can do the conversation smoothly, encourage them to make changes other than those listed. This can be done by having them cover the substitution box with a piece of paper, a pencil case, etc. OR have them close their books and try to have similar conversations. The should give directions to places near their school.

Conversation Variation

Write "Excuse me?" on the chalkboard. As the students practice the conversation, have them imagine that they are on a busy, noisy city street. It is hard to hear. When a partner says a line, they must respond with "Excuse me?" The partner repeats the line, then they say their next line. The partner also asks for repetition. In addition to "Excuse me?" you may want to include other ways of asking for repetition such as "Could you repeat that?", "I'm sorry?" and "Pardon?"

General Notes

• This is a conversation between strangers on a street.
• An "appliance store" sells electric machines for household use like irons and coffee makers. It may also sell stereos, TVs, etc.
• A "stationery store" sells items you need for deskwork -- notebooks, pens, envelopes, etc. ("Stationer" is an old English word for "shopkeeper".)
• Many students do not know how to give directions using the points of the compass(southwest corner, etc.). You may want to give extra practice by drawing a map of the neighborhood and asking the students to tell you locations of landmarks such as stores.

Conversation Tapescript

Man: Excuse me. Is there an appliance store near here?
Woman: Yes. There's one next to the post office.
M: How do I get there?
W: Go down this street to the signal. Then turn right.
M: This street to the signal, then right?
W: Yeah. Then go straight about three blocks. You'll see it on the right.
M: On the right. I see.
W: It's across from the park.
M: Thanks. Oh, yeah. And where's the Grand Hotel?
W: We're standing in front of it.
M: Oh. Thanks.

DUET-A

How do I get to...?

Excuse me.	Is there a stationery store near here?		Yes, there is. No, there isn't.
	How do I get to Where's		the First National Bank? Uno's Pizza?
Go down Take	this street that street River Road	to across past	Second Street. the river. Fourth Street.
Go straight two blocks.			
Turn	right (at the station). left (at the second street).		
It's	on the (northeast) corner. the second building on the left. next to the bank.		

Choose the buildings for these places. Write the numbers in the bottom area. (Do not write in the top area.)

1. the TBS Building 2. Anton's Bakery 3. Uno's Pizza 4. ABC Video 5. a post office

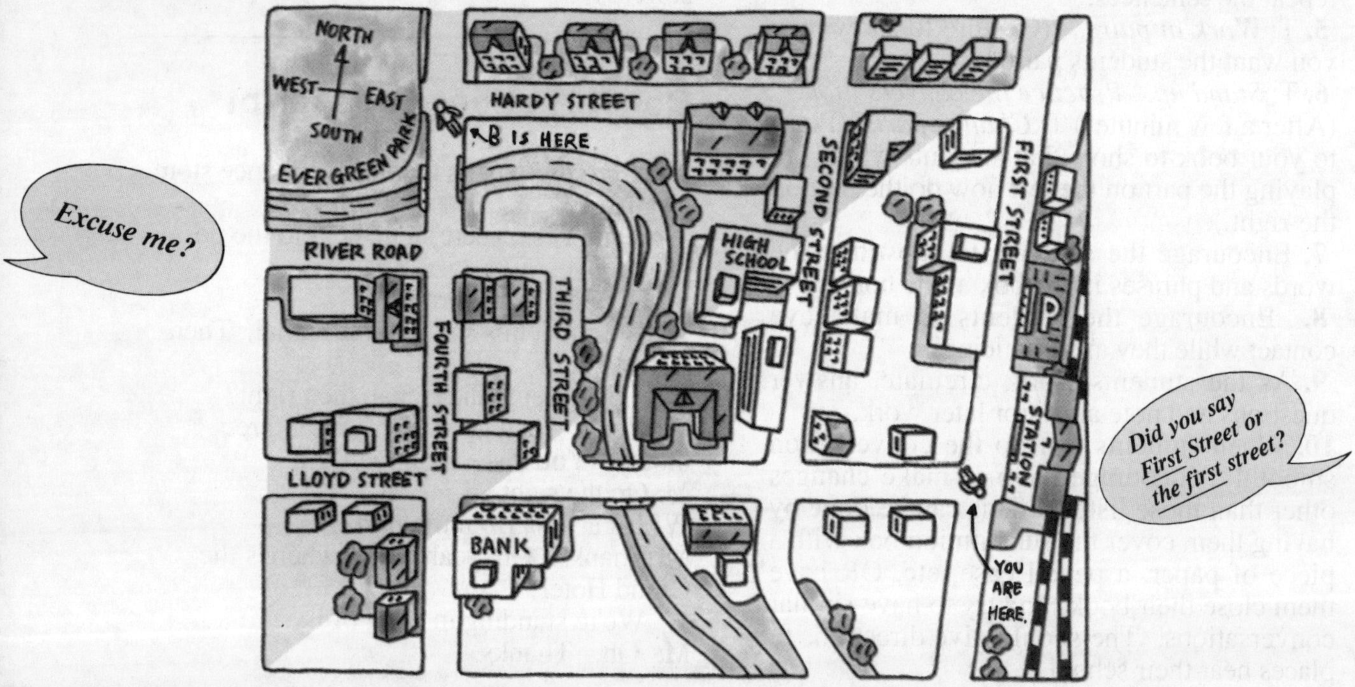

You are in front of the station.

Ask *B* how to get to these places. Write the letters on the buildings.

A. a stationery store B. Stewarts Department Store C. New Town Cinema
D. Waldo Books E. a sporting goods shop

Bonus! Tell ***B*** how to get to places in this city. ***B*** will guess the places.

Objective: The students will ask for and give directions.
Function: ask about existence and location of places and shops, get someone's attention, ask for and give directions
Structures: imperative mood, preposition of place and direction: *on, at, next, across, past,*
Vocabulary Area: places and shops
Classroom language: *Did you say ___ or ___?*

Procedure

1. Divide the class into pairs. One student in each pair is **A**. The other is **B**. T: *Row one, you are **A's*** (Point to row one). *Row two, you are **B's*** (Point to row two). *Row three, you are **A's*** (etc.).
2. T: *A's, look at page 45. **B's**, look at page 46.*
3. Point out the language box at the top of the page. T: *Look at the box.* (Optional) *Listen and say.* Say the sentences in the box. Have students practice by repeating after you.
4. T: *Look at the page. Are there any words you don't know?*
5. Introduce the task. T: *You will give directions and find out where things are.*
6. Point to the places listed above the map. T: *Choose buildings for these places. Write them in the white area. Do not write in the pink area.*
7. Point to the places listed under the map. T: *You need to go to these places. **A**, you are in front of the station. **B**, you are in front of the park.* While the other students watch, direct one pair through the first step of the exercise. T: (to any student **A**): *Ask **B** how to get to a stationery store.* Prompt **B** to answer. Gesture for **A** to follow the directions and write the place on the map.
8. T: *Ask your partner how to get to the places. Tell your partern how to get to the other places.* When the students understand the task, have them do it in pairs.
9. As the students work, circulate, answer questions and note areas for later work.
10. As students finish the main task, have them continue by doing the *Bonus!* task. Have them give directions to places in their city. They should not tell their partners the places. Partners follow the directions (in their heads or on a paper or map) and guess where they are.
11. Do consolidation, correction and expansion as desired.

Grammar and Usage

• Students often confuse "the third street" and "Third Street." They should use the first when counting streets and the second for names of streets. Names of numbered streets do not include "the."

General Notes

• Since the information changes completely when different people are partners, students who wish or need extra practice can repeat the activity with a new partner using the other duet page.
• If you students live in a country where many streets do not have names, encourage them to use landmarks (well-known or easy to find locations) rather than street names.

Additional Activity

(This activity can be used anytime during this unit).

"Where's the bank" jazz chant. This is a jazz chant -- a rhythm pronunciation exercise. (See next page.) Make copies of the chant for each student. Read it rhythmically. Then have the students read it along with you. There are two parts. **A**'s part starts at the left margin. **B**'s part is indented. You may want to have the students clap or snap their fingers in rhythm as they are chanting. This will help in learning stress and intonation.

Underlined words may be substituted with other directions and locations.

DUET-B

How do I get to...?

Excuse me.	Is there a stationery store near here?		Yes, there is. No, there isn't.
	How do I get to Where's		the First National Bank? Uno's Pizza?
Go down Take	this street that street River Road	to across past	Second Street. the river. Fourth Street.
Go straight two blocks.			
Turn	right (at the station). left (at the second street).		
It's	on the (northeast) corner. the second building on the left. next to the bank.		

Choose the buildings for these places. Write the letters in the top area.
(Do not write in the bottom area.)

A. Softwrite Stationery Store
B. Stewarts Department Store
C. New Town Cinema
D. Waldo Books
E. Ace Sports Shop

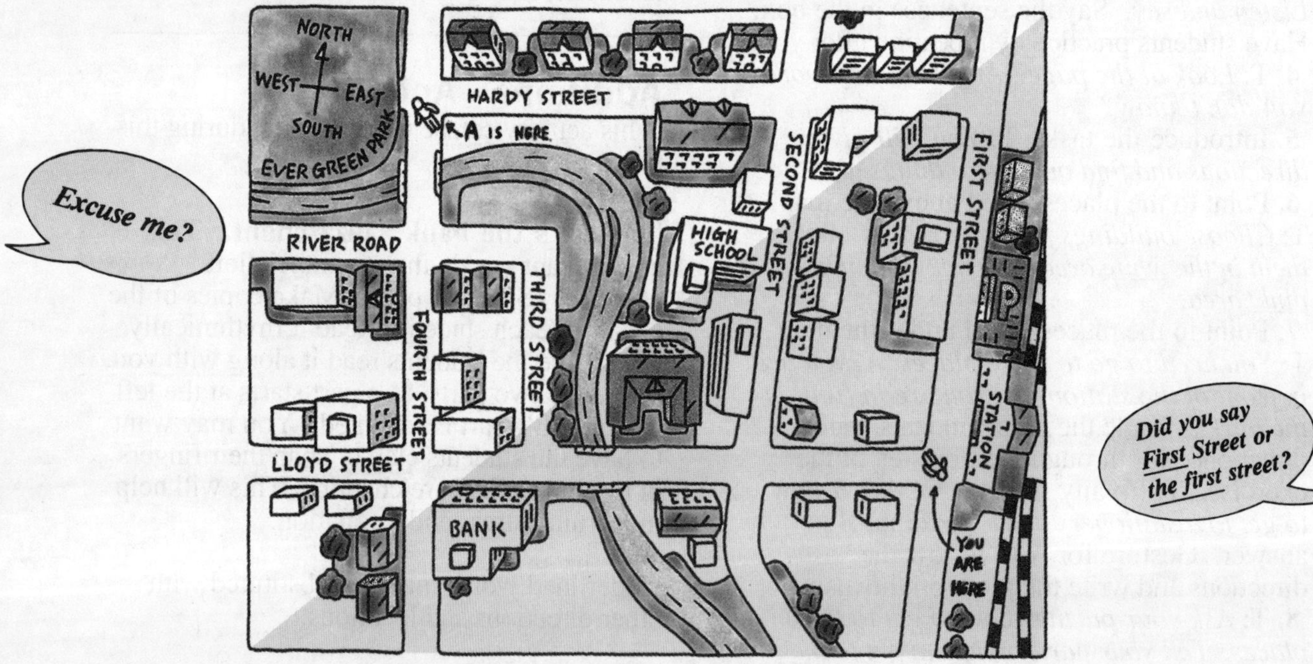

You are in front of Evergreen Park.
Ask *A* how to get to these places. Write the numbers on the buildings.

1. the TBS building
2. a bakery
3. Uno's Pizza
4. a video shop
5. a post office

Bonus! Tell ***A*** how to get to places in this city. ***A*** will guess the places.

Where's the bank?

Excuse me. Where's the bank?

Go down this street to the corner and then turn right.
Go down that street to Main Street and then turn left.
When you get to the park, you'll see it on the right.

Did you say...
I go down this street to the corner and then turn right?
I go down that street to Main Street and then turn left?
When I get to the park, I'll see it on the left?

Right.

Left ?

No, right!

Not left ?

Go right!

Oh, right!

Yeah.

This jazz chant was inspired by the work of Carolyn Graham, author of several books of jazz chants (Oxford University Press).

Answer Key

Since the students are exchanging information that they have produced, they should look at each other's pages after the activity to check if their communication was successful.

Expansion Activity

Make a copy of the "Ten words" worksheet for each student. Have them follow the instructions. (Note: You may wish to have them fill in the worksheet as homework before the class in which would will do the activity.) This vocabulary review activity can be used at any time, not just during unit 5.

Ten words

This is a vocabulary review game.
Write a word in each box. Use words that you know but that are a little difficult.

Work with a partner.
Show your words to your partner.
Tell your partner what each word means.
You can give the **real** meaning or a **false** meaning. Your partner must decide if your meaning is true or false. If it is false, your partner must say the real meaning.
Look at your partner's words.
Listen to the meanings. Are they true or false.
You get one point every time you are correct.

SOLO Directions

Look at the map and read the description.

It is easy to find my house. When you leave the school, turn left. Turn left again and go to Highway 42. Turn right at the highway. Go straight to Hill Street. Then turn right again. Turn left at the park. Go past the railroad tracks. My house is on the right.

Draw a map from a well-known place (a school, large store, bus stop, etc.) **to your house.**
Then write the directions.
Use some of these words:

____ turn	____ straight	____ across from
____ left	____ past	____ next to
____ right	____ go past the	

map

directions

Objective: The students will read directions to someone's house. They will write directions to their own houses.
Function: giving directions
Structures: imperative mood, prepositions of direction: *to, past*

Procedure

1. T: *Open your books to page 47. Look at the map. Read the directions.*
2. (Optional) T: *As you read, draw a line from the school to the house.*
3. T: *Draw a map from a well-known place -- this school, a large store, a bus stop -- to your house. Then write the directions. Use some of these words: turn, left, right, straight, past, go past the, across from, next to.*

You may wish to assign this activity as homework.

In-class Follow-up

Students work in pairs. They show their maps to each other. They read their own directions while their partners follow on the maps.

General Notes

• If students' houses are too near well-known places (e.g., across the street from the school), have them write the directions between two well-known places that you know are some distance apart.
• Students often confuse "past" and "passed." "Passed" is a verb. It means "went beyond a given point" (I passed the station on my way.) or "succeeded" (I passed the test.). "Past" shows the place or time that is being referred to (Go past the railroad tracks. He's been here for the past month.).

Optional Skill-building Activity

Skill: predicting

Before the students read the paragraph at the top of the page, have them look at the map. Have them list all the prepositions they would use if they were giving directions from the school to the house. They may do this individually or in pairs. As they read the paragraph, they circle each preposition in the paragraph that they listed.

Answer Key

Answers will vary.
Example:
My house is near the train station. Go out the south exit of the station and turn left. Cross the street. Turn right at the next corner and go straight for two blocks. Turn left. My house is the third building on the left.

Notes

Welcome to my city!

What should a visitor see in your city?

Step one:

Work in groups of 3.
What are your favorite places? **Write them.**

Famous/interesting/important places:	Restaurants:	Entertainment places:
■ ■	■	■
■	■	■

Step two:

Decide the 4 best places for a visitor to go. Draw a map of your city.
Label the places. Write about them.

My city!

Point of interest

Be sure to see ______________ (name).
It's famous because ______________
______________.
When you go there, you will see ______________
______________.
Location: It's in the ______________ (north, south, etc.) part of town.

Point of interest

Don't miss the ______________.
It's well-known because ______________
______________.
You can see ______________
______________.
Location: It is near the ______________.

N

Restaurant

For dinner, try ______________ (restaurant name).
They make very good ______________ (kind of food).
The prices are ______________ (cheap/moderate/expensive).
Location: ______________
______________.

Entertainment

Go to ______________
______________ for an entertaining time.
It's great because ______________
______________.
Location: ______________
______________.

Step three:

Change groups.
Tell your partners about your choices. Listen to their ideas. How many were the same?

Try This!
Work as a group.
What are the 10 most interesting places in your city for a visitor?
Join another group. Combine lists. Decide on the 8 most interesting places.

Objective: The students will learn to describe important and interesting places in their city.
Function: describe places, state location, give reasons,
Structures: clauses of reason, prepositions of location
Vocabulary Area: sightseeing and other places

Procedure

1. T: *Look at page 48. You will make a guide map for this city.*
2. T: *When visitors come to our city, what should they see?* Encourage students to give ideas.
Write them on the chalkboard.
3. Divide the class into groups of 3.
4. T: *What are your favorite places?*
5. While the other students watch, direct one group through the first step of the exercise. T: (to any student): *What's one place you like to go?* When that student gives an idea, gesture for the student to write the suggestion. T: *Write at least four famous, interesting or important places, two restaurants and two entertainments places.* They may include some of the places they suggested in step two, above.
6. When the students understand the task, have them begin.
8. When they have listed places, introduce Step two. T: *Decide the four best places for a visitor to go. Draw a map of this city. Label the places. Write about them.*
9. As the students work, circulate, answer questions and note areas for later work.
11. As groups finish the main task, have them continue by doing the *Try this!* task. Have them list the ten most interesting places for a visitor. They then join another group, combine lists and decide on the eight most interesting.
13. Do consolidation, correction and expansion as desired.

Grammar and Usage Notes

• Students sometimes confuse "famous" and "popular." A "famous" place is well-known. "Famous" does not imply people like or dislike it, only that they know about it. "Popular" means the place is well-liked.

General Notes

• Let the students decide the definitions of terms like "cheap" and the relative fame of the points of interest they pick. There are no correct answers.
• It time permits, you may want to have them write about one or two more places in each category.
• No language box appears at the top of this page because the forms are included in the place description spaces.
• Since this activity is designed to encourage fluency, corrections are not recommended at this time.

Answer Key

Answers will vary.

Example:
For dinner, try the Green Street Grill.
They make very good beef stew.
The prices are moderate.
Location: the corner of Green Street and 15th Avenue.

Notes

CHECK YOURSELF

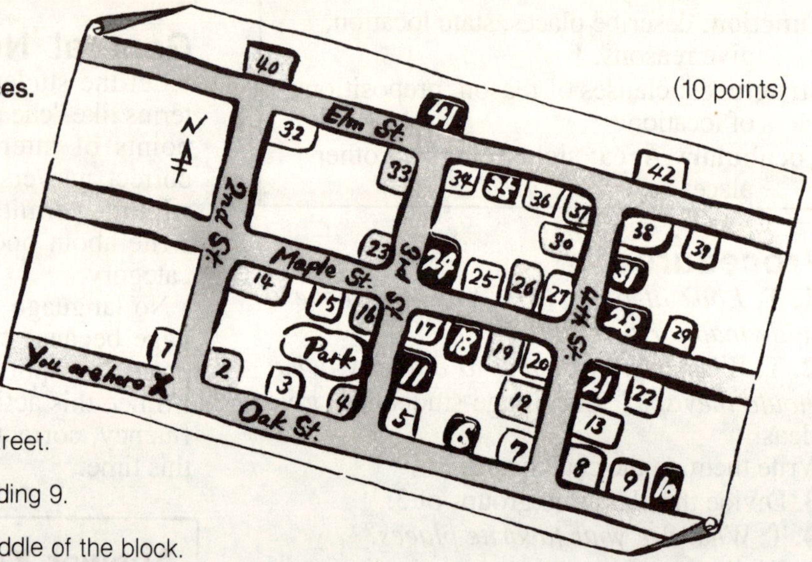

Look at the map. Finish the sentences. (10 points)

1. Building 35 is ________ Elm Street.
2. Building 10 is ________ to building 9.
3. Building 31 is ________ the middle of the block.
4. Building 11 is across ________ the park.
5. Building 18 is ________ buildings 17 and 19.
6. Building 24 is on the northeast ________ of Maple St. and 3rd St.
7. Building 21 is ________ the corner ________ 4th St. and Maple.
8. Building 41 is on Elm St. ________ the north end of 3rd St.
9. As you walk along Oak St., you'll see building 6 ________ the left.
10. Building 28 is on the ________ corner of Maple St. and 4th St.

Follow the directions. Write the building numbers. (2 points each = 10 points)

__7__ 1. Go straight ahead two blocks. You'll see it on your left on the corner before you cross the street.

______ 2. Go up 2nd St. to Maple St. and turn right. Go two blocks and turn left at 4th St. You'll see it on your right in the middle of the block.

______ 3. Go along this street to the next corner and turn left. Go straight to Elm St. It's on the right.

______ 4. Go up 2nd St. to Elm St. and take a right. Go two blocks to 4th St. It's on the southwest corner.

______ 5. Go to 3rd St. and turn left. It's the second building on the right, across from the park.

______ 6. Go up 2nd St. to Maple St. and turn right. After you cross Third St., it's the third building on the right.

Your score

Procedure

Exercise one.

1. T: *Look at page 49.* Point to the first exercise. T: *Look at the map. Where are the buildings? Write your answers in the blanks.*

2. (Optional). T: *Number one: Building 35 is* *(blank)* *Elm Street. Which word goes in the blank?* Encourage the students to answer (A: on). Gesture for them to write the word.

3. T: *Do 2-10 the same way.*

Exercise two.

1. Point to the second exercise two. T: *Follow the directions. Write the building numbers.*

2. (Optional) As you read the first example, encourage students to follow the directions on the map with their fingers. T: *Go straight ahead two blocks. You'll see it on your left on the corner before you cross the street. Where are you?* Encourage the students to answer (A: Building 7).

3. Do 2-7 the same way.

You may wish to assign the page as homework.

In-class Follow-up

• T: *Work in pairs. Did you both get the same answers?* As students compare their answers, circulate to make sure that all students have completed the homework. You may wish to have some students write their answers on the board.

General Notes

• The "Check yourself" pages are each worth 20 points. The items in the first activity are worth one point each. Each item in the second activity is worth two points. If you are giving grades, you may wish to keep track of student scores. Alternatively, if you have assigned the pages as homework and class size makes keeping track of individual points impractical, you may want to note which students have completed the assignment, those who did only part of it and those who didn't do it.

Answer Key

Exercise one:

1. Building 35 is on Elm Street.
2. Building 10 is next to building 9.
3. Building 31 is in the middle of the block.
4. Building 11 is across from the park.
5. Building 18 is between buildings 17 and 19.
6. Building 24 is on the northeast corner of Maple St. and 3rd St.
7. Building 21 is on the corner of 4th St. and Maple.
8. Building 41 is on Elm St. at the north end of 3rd St.
9. As you walk along Oak St., you'll see building 6 on the left.
10. Building 28 is on the northeast corner of Maple St. and 4th St.

Exercise two:

1. 7
2. 31
3. 34
4. 37
5. 11
6. 19

Notes

Unit 6 Tell me what happened.

LISTENING Talking about past activities

Getting ready

Here are some ways people talk about the past.

I was born in Illinois.

I started school when I was six.

She got married last year.

His grandmother died last week.

He graduated from college in 1991.

She changed jobs two years ago.

She worked as a teacher for three years.

Answer these questions.

Where were you born? ____________________

When did you start school? ____________________

When did you graduate from high school? ____________________

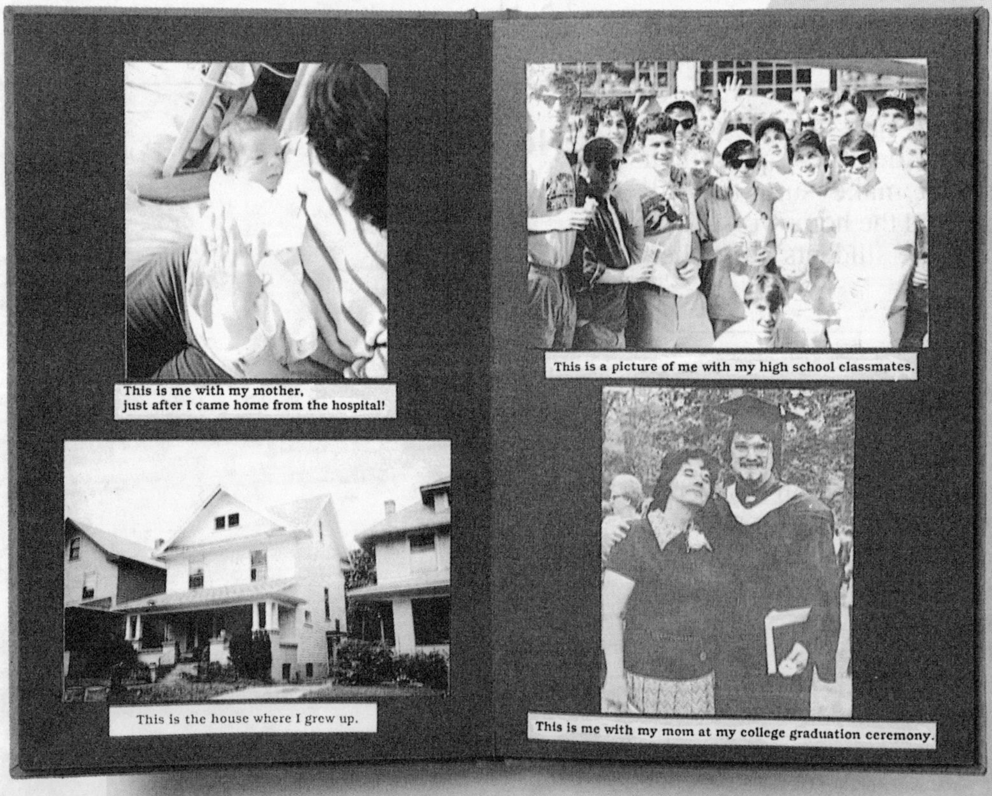

Objective: The students will identify past events in people's lives.
Function: talk about the past
Structures: simple and habitual past
Vocabulary Area: personal information

Procedure

1. Do the optional warm-up activity listed below.
2. T: *Open your books to page 50. Look at the pictures.*
3. T: *You will hear some people talking about the past.*
4. T: *Look at "Getting Ready" on page 50. These are some ways to talk about the past.* Play the first part of the tape.
5. T: *Answer the questions about yourself: Where were you born? When did you start school? When did you graduate from high school?*
6. (Optional) If your students find listening very difficult, do the "additional preparation" exercise below.
7. T: *Look at the "First Listening" on page 51. Sue, Jeff and Lynn are talking about their pasts. Listen. Write the names on the lines.* Play the "First Listening" segment of the tape. You may want students to do this in pairs so they can help each other. You may wish to stop after each item to check.
8. (Optional) T: *Work in pairs. Did you both get the same answers?*
9. Play the tape again if necessary.
10. Check by asking the students the questions (e.g., T: *What did she say?* A: She was born in Chicago in 1965.) and eliciting their answers OR by having students work in groups of 2-4. They should compare answers and ask you about any they couldn't catch. (See the answer key on the next page.)

Additional Preparation

Students work in pairs. They look at the sentences in sections 1-4 on page 51. Each student writes or says one sentence about himself. The sentences should be similar to those in each section.

General Notes

• "Started school" usually refers to the time someone began kindergarten or first grade, the first school experience in their life.
• Jeff refers to his job at a "gas station." This is a common American expression for "service station." Others call the place where gasoline is sold a "filling station." (segment 2)
• Lynn refers to her "English name." It is the name she is known by to her English-speaking friends. (segment 4)

Optional Warm-up Activity

Four events. Work in groups of 6-10. Each student takes a sheet of paper and folds it into four squares. In each square, the students write an interesting or important event from their lives (like the events in the listening activity). They should not show their papers to anyone. The four sections are torn apart and each group's squares are mixed and shuffled. Students take turns selecting a square and reading it aloud. The other students guess who wrote the sentence. The writers confirm correct guesses. The person who makes the most correct guesses is the winner.

Unit 6

First Listening

Three people are talking about past events.
Write the names on the correct lines.

come from

_______ I was born in Dallas in 1967.
_______ I was born in Hong Kong in 1972.
_______ I was born in Osaka in 1974.
__Sue__ I was born in Chicago in 1965.

first

_______ I moved to a small town when I was ten years old.
_______ I moved into my own apartment when I was twenty.
_______ I got my first job just after high school. I worked at a gas station.
_______ I moved to the U.S. when I was eight years old.

then

_______ I graduated from high school in 1990.
_______ I got married in 1987.
_______ School was difficult at first.
_______ I graduated from the University of Illinois.

and then

_______ I changed my major last year.
_______ I taught in a small high school for two years.
_______ I changed jobs last year. Now I work for an electronics company.
_______ I started working last year.

Sue

Jeff

Lynn

Tapescript

This is Sue.

Interviewer: Sue, could you tell us something about your past. Say, two or three important events.
Sue: Yeah, I was born in Chicago in 1965, (Uh-huh). When I was ten, we moved to a small town in Indiana.
I: How did you like that?
S: I hated it. I had to leave all my friends behind. So I had to make new ones. And then I went off to college and I graduated when I was 21 from the University of Illinois. (Um) And the same year I started to teach. And I was trained as a high school teacher and I taught math for two years in a school in a real small town before I moved here.
I: Oh, I see.

This is Jeff.

Interviewer: Jeff, could you tell us something about your life. Say, just two or three main events, important events?
Jeff: Well, I was born in Dallas, Texas in 1967. (Um-hmm) I think that was important, and well, I got out of high school and started working for a gas station. That was my first real job. Then I got married in 1987. I was 20 years old then. And last year I changed jobs. I started working for an electronics company. And we make things like calculators and things like that .
I: Computers. Stuff like that?
J: Yeah.

This is Lynn.

Interviewer: Ah, so, Lynn, could you tell us something about your past, say two or three interesting or important events.
Lynn: Well, I was born in Hong Kong in 1972.
I: In Hong Kong?
L: Yeah. Lynn is my English name. Then we moved to the U.S. when I was about eight.
I: So how was that? Getting used to America and all?
L: School was really hard for me in the beginning.
I: I imagine. But you must have done all right?
L: Yeah, well, I graduated. And now I'm at the University of California. I changed my major just last year and now I'm studying business.
I: Oh, you changed your major to business?
L: Right.

Answer Key

First Listening:

1. Sue:
- I was born in Chicago in 1965.
- I moved to a small town when I was ten years old.
- I graduated from the University of Illinois.
- I taught in a small high school for two years.

2. Jeff:
- I was born in Dallas in 1967.
- I got my first job just after high school. I worked at a gas station.
- I got married in 1987.
- I changed jobs last year. Now I work for an electronics company.

3. Lynn:
- I was born in Hong Kong in 1972.
- I moved to the U.S. when I was eight years old.
- School was difficult at first.
- I changed my major last year.

CONVERSATION How was your weekend?

★ Hi. How was your weekend?

◆ ___1___. I went ___2___ with some friends.

★ Oh, really? That sounds ___3___.

◆ How about you?

★ On Saturday I had to ___4___, and on Sunday I ___5___.

◆ What? I didn't know you ___6___.

★ Uh...I ___7___.

1. Great. Pretty good. So-so.	2. camping sailing hiking	3. like fun interesting exciting	4. help a friend do some shopping work
5. went skiing drove to San Francisco got married	6. could ski had a driver's license were engaged	7. can't, really don't wasn't	

Objective: The students will talk about the past.
Functions: talk about past activities, express surprise
Structures: simple past, *went* + gerund: *I went hiking.*
present participles as adjectives: *exciting, interesting*

Procedure

1. T: *Open your books to page 52. Look at the picture. Where are these people?* (A: At an office.) *Look at the man's leg. What do you think happened?*
2. Play the tape. Have the students listen and read silently.
3. Answer questions about vocabulary and expressions.
4. (Optional) T: *Listen again. Repeat each line.* Play the conversation again. Pause after each sentence. Gesture for the students to repeat the sentences.
5. T: *Work in pairs.* (Gesture to show how you want the students paired.)
6. T: *Stand up. Practice the conversation.* (After a few minutes) T: *Change parts* (Point to your book to show that students who were playing the part on the left now do the part on the right.).
7. Encourage the students to substitute the words and phrases in the box at the bottom.
8. Encourage the students to make eye contact while they are practicing.
9. As the students work, circulate, answer questions and note areas for later work.
10. When students can do the conversation smoothly, encourage them to make changes other than those listed. This can be done by having them cover the substitution box with a piece of paper, a pencil case, etc. OR have them close their books and try to have similar conversations.

Conversation Variation

Have the students playing the part on the left imagine that they are shy and a little embarrassed about what happened on Sunday. They speak softly and try to avoid eye contact. Students playing the part on the right are outgoing. They speak loudly and try to make strong eye contact.

General Notes

• This conversation takes place at a company. The speakers are talking before work on a Monday morning.
• In this conversation, it is essential that the students listen to each other so that slot 6 corresponds to slot 5 and slot 7 to slots 5 and 6.

Conversation Tapescript

Man: Hi. How was your weekend?
Woman: Great. I went camping with some friends.
M: Oh, really? That sounds like fun.
W: How about you?
M: On Saturday I had to help a friend and on Sunday I went skiing.
W: What? I didn't know you could ski.
M: Uh...I can't, really.

DUET-A

What did she do there?

What did	she you	do in Los Angeles? do there?	She I	went to a museum. watched a football game. ate at a Mexican restaurant.
How did	she you	get there?	She I	went by bus (plane, car) drove. flew.
Where did	she you	go (next) ?	She I	went to Los Angeles.

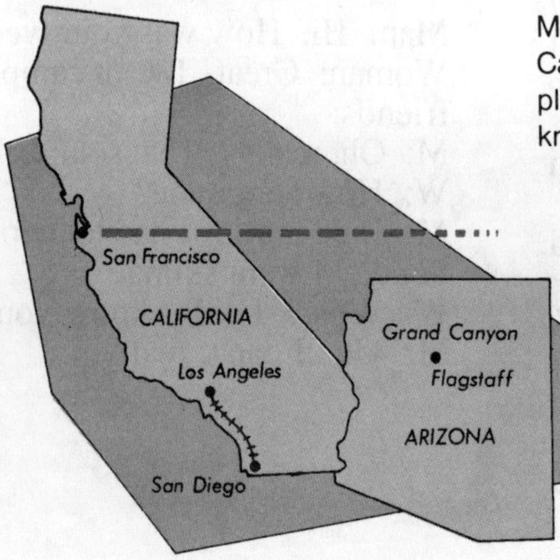

Margie just got back from a vacation in California and Arizona. You know some of the places she went and things she did. Your partner knows the rest.

How she traveled:

- Airplane
- Bus
- Car
- Train

Step one:

Find out where she went, how she got to each place and what she did. Fill in the chart.

Place	How she got there	What she did
San Francisco	Flew.	*Went to...*
Los Angeles		Visited a friend at UCLA.
San Diego	Took a train.	
Flagstaff, Arizona		Hiked in the Grand Canyon.

Step two:

Ask about *B*'s most interesting vacation. Write the information.

Place	How **B** got there	What **B** did

Bonus! What did people do 100 years ago that you don't do? How many things can you and **B** list?

Objective: The students will ask about recent event.
Function: ask / tell about past activities
Structures: simple past (regular and irregular)
WH- questions
prepositions of place and direction: *in, at, to, by*
Vocabulary Area: travel
Classroom language:
How do you spell it?

Procedure

1. Divide the class into pairs. One student in each pair is **A**. The other is **B**. T: *Row one, you are **A's*** (Point to row one). *Row two, you are **B's*** (Point to row two). *Row three, you are **A's*** (etc.).
2. T: *A's, look at page 53. **B's**, look at page 54.*
3. Point out the language box at the top of the page. T: *Look at the box.* (Optional) *Listen and say.* Say the sentences in the box. Have students practice by repeating after you.
4. T: *Look at the page. Are there any words you don't know?*
5. Introduce the task. T: *Margie just got back from a vacation in California and Arizona. You will find out about her trip. Then, you'll find out about a vacation your partner took.*
6. While the other students watch, direct one pair through the first step of the exercise. T: *First she went to San Francisco.* (To any student **A**): *Ask **B**, "What did she do in San Francisco ?* Prompt **B** to answer (She went to Fisherman's Wharf. She ate at a great crab restaurant). Gesture for **A** to take notes.
7. T: *Find out how she traveled and what she did.* When the students understand the task, have them do it in pairs.
8. When students begin finishing Step one, introduce Step two. T: *Ask about a vacation your partner took. Where did your partner go? How did he/she get there? What did he/she do? Write the information on the chart.*
9. As the students work, circulate, answer questions and note areas for later work.
10. As students finish the main task, have them continue by doing the *Bonus!* task. Have them list things people did 100 years ago that they don't do now.
11. Do consolidation, correction and expansion as desired.

Grammar and Usage

• You may want to point out the irregular past forms of "go (went)", "eat (ate)","drive (drove)", "fly (flew)", "swim (swam)", and "take (took)."
• You may want to teach the students pronunciation rules for ed. The rules are as follows:
The "ed"
- sounds like /t/ when it follows a voiceless consonant sound (except /t/):

[f, k, p, s, ʃ, tʃ]

- sounds like /d/ when it follows a vowel sounds or a voiced consonant sound (except /d/):

[b, g, l, m, n, r, v, z, ŋ, dʒ]

-sounds like /ɪd/ when it follows /t/ or /d/.

The phonetic transcriptions above are from the International Phonetic Alphabet (IPA). Most consonant symbols are the same as the usual sound of the letters. Those which are different are as follows:

[ʃ] wi<u>sh</u> [tʃ] wat<u>ch</u> [ŋ] ga<u>ng</u> [dʒ] e<u>dge</u>

General Notes

• "UCLA" is a common abbreviation for "the University of California at Los Angeles."
• "Flagstaff, Arizona" is the city closest to a popular entrance to the Grand Canyon, a U.S. National Park.
• "Fisherman's Wharf" is a famous sight-seeing spot in San Francisco, an area with lots of seafood restaurants and small shops.
• "Highway 1" refers to California Highway 1, a scenic route that follows the coast along the length of the state.
• See the introduction (•Corrections) for suggestions on ways to correct during pair work.

What did she do there?

DUET-B

What did	she you	do in Los Angeles? do there?		She I	went to a museum. watched a football game. ate at a Mexican restaurant.
How did	she you	get there?		She I	went by bus (plane, car) drove. flew.
Where did	she you	go (next) ?		She I	went to Los Angeles.

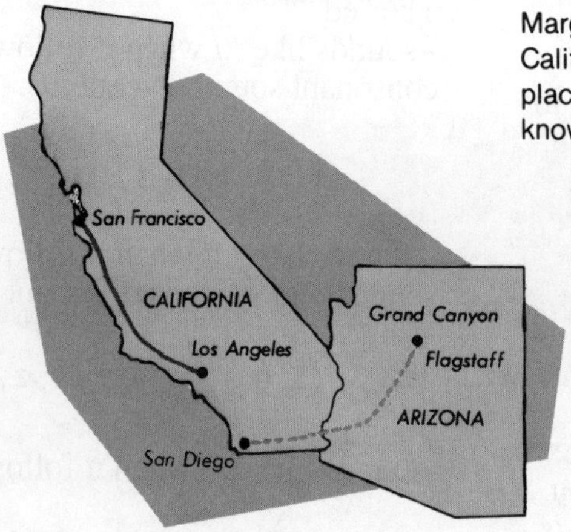

Margie just got back from a vacation in California and Arizona. You know some of the places she went and things she did. Your partner knows the rest.

How she traveled:

Airplane
Bus
Car
Train

Step one:

Find out where she went, how she got to each place and what she did. Fill in the chart.

Place	How she got there	What she did
San Francisco	*Flew.*	Went to Fisherman's Wharf. Ate at a great crab restaurant.
Los Angeles	Rented a car and drove down Highway 1.	
San Diego		Swam at the beach.
Flagstaff, Arizona	Took the bus.	

Step two:

Ask about *A*'s most interesting vacation. Write the information.

Place	How A got there	What A did

Bonus! What did people do 100 years ago that you don't do?
How many things can you and **A** list?

Additional Activity

(This activity can be used anytime during this unit).

To tell the truth. Students work in groups of three. They each tell about something interesting that they have done. The choose the most interesting or unusual story. They get as much information about it as possible. Each group joins with another group. Each person from the first group pretends that the event is really about him or her. Students from the other group ask each person questions about the event to try to decide who is telling the truth.

Answer Key

Checking answers as a whole class should not be necessary. You may wish to have the pair look at both books to make sure they have correctly filled in all blanks. Answers for A's page are on page 54 and answers for B's page are on page 53 .

Expansion Activity

Pantomime the past.
Make one copy of the "pantomime the past" worksheet for each 10 students. Cut the sheets into strips. Students work in groups of 10. Give one strip to each student.

Tell students to imagine that the sentence on the sheet really happened to them. They must pantomime the action as their partners guess.

Variation: Have student think of the most unusual thing they have ever done. They pantomime the action while others guess.

Pantomime the past

You ate 15 dishes of spaghetti.

You flew in a hang glider.

You went camping and in rained a lot.

You climbed a mountain in January.

You ate in a very nice restaurant and didn't have enough money to pay.

You rode an elephant.

You went to a zoo. A lion escaped.

You put too much soap in a washing machine.

You went hiking in a forest and got lost.

You went to a party and met a movie star.

SOLO

Yesterday was a terrible day for Erika.

A bad day

1

She _get_ _up_ at 9:20.

2

She didn't have time for breakfast so she ______ an apple in the car.

3

On her way to work, she ______ another car.

4

She finally ______ to the office at 10:45.

5

During lunch she ______ soup on her dress.

6

Later, when she was fixing dinner, she ______ it.

7

She ______ asleep watching TV.

8

Finally, she ______ to bed at 10:00.

Look at the pictures. Finish each sentence.
Write the past forms of these verbs:

burn   eat   fall   get

~~get up~~   go   hit   spill

Was yesterday good or bad for you? ______
Write about your day.
Use some of these words:

____ drove	____ left	____ went
____ ate	____ read	____ had
____ fixed	____ studied	____ watched
____ got up	____ took	____ worked

Objective: The students will read about a person's day. They will identify the past form of regular and irregular verbs.
Function: talk about the past
Structures: simple past (regular and irregular),
time clause with *when*
too + adjective

Procedure

1. T: *Open your books to page 55. Look at the pictures. Do you remember Erika? You met her in Unit 3* (page 31). *Yesterday, she had a very bad day. Read about Erika. As you read, finish the sentences. Use the past form of the verbs.*

2. T: *Was yesterday good or bad for you? Write about your day. Use some of these words: drove, ate, fixed, got up, left, read, studied, took, went, had, watched, worked.*

You may wish to assign this activity as homework.

In-class Follow-up

Students work in pairs. Each student reads the paragraph while the partner listens. The partner can not take notes. After listening, the partner tries to remember as many facts as possible.

General Notes

• Instead of writing about yesterday, you may want the students to write about a day that was particularly good or bad for them.

Optional Skill-building Activity

Skill: speculating based on previously known information

Have the students write their paragraphs on separate pieces of paper. Collect all of the paragraphs. Delete or hide the names. Number the paragraphs and post them on the chalkboard using tape or magnets. Students go to the board, read as many paragraphs as possible in the allotted time and, on a separate piece of paper write the name of the person they think wrote each paragraph. At the end, announce the names that go with each paragraph number.

Note: If class size make it difficult for all students to circulate and look at the chalkboard at the same time, divide the class and the paragraphs in half. Put each set of paragraphs on a desk. Students pick up a paragraph, read it and guess who wrote it. They return it to the set and take another paragraph.

Answer Key

Task one:

1. She <u>got up</u> at 9:20.
2. She didn't have time for breakfast, so she <u>ate</u> an apple in the car.
3. On her way to work, she <u>hit</u> another car.
4. She finally <u>got</u> to the office at 10:45.
5. During lunch she <u>spilled</u> soup on her dress.
6. Later, when she was fixing dinner, she <u>burned</u> it.
7. She <u>fell</u> asleep watching TV.
8. Finally, she <u>went</u> to bed at 10:00.

Task two:
Answers will vary.
Example:
Yesterday was a good day for me. I got up early and had a lot of time for breakfast. I fixed my favorite breakfast. Then I read the newspaper and left for work at my usual time. I drove to work. The streets were not very crowded. After work, I had dinner with my friends . I went to bed about 11:00.

Notes

What happened?

What do you think	she he they	did?
Do you think	she he they	went to a concert? went swimming? had a fight?

Maybe I think	she he they	heard some good news. went to a movie. played soccer.
Yes, I do.		
I don't think so.		
I'm not sure.		

Work in groups of three.
Look at each picture. What did the people just do?
Give your ideas. Listen to your partners' ideas.
When you agree, WRITE THE ACTION ON THE LINES.

How do you say ____ in English?

Everyone changes groups.
Tell them your ideas.

How many times did your new partners give the same answer? ____

Try This!

Tell your partners five interesting things you did last year.
Four are true. One is not true.
Your partners must guess which is not true.

Objective: The students will learn to speculate about recent events.
Function: talk about past actions, speculate about what someone did, agree/ disagree
Structures: simple past (regular and irregular verbs).
Classroom language:
How do you say ____ in English?

Procedure

1. T: *Look at page 56. You will decide what these people did.*
2. T: *Look at the language box at the top of the page. Are there any words you don't know?* Answer questions about vocabulary.
3. (Optional) T: *Look at the box. Listen and say.* Say the sentences in the box. Have students practice by repeating after you.
4. Divide the class into groups of 4.
5. Introduce the task. T: *You will look at the pictures and decide what the people did. When you agree, write the actions.*
6. While the other students watch, direct one group through the first step of the exercise. T: *Look at the first picture. What did she just do?* Elicit answers from all four students. T: *Which of the answers do you like the best?* When they decide, gesture for them to write their answer on the line. T: *Do this for each picture.*
7. When the students understand the task, have them begin.
8. As the students work, circulate, answer questions and note areas for later work.
9. When students have written their answers, introduce Step two. T: *Everyone change groups. Tell your new group your ideas. Listen to their ideas. How many times did you get the same answer?*
11. As students finish the main task, have them continue by doing the *Try this!* task. Students each say five things they did last year. Four things are true and one is not. Partners must guess which is not true.
12. Do consolidation, correction and expansion as desired.

General Notes

• If your students find changing groups confusing, have the group members number off (1-2-3-4). Have the 1's move one group forward or to the right, the 2's move two groups away, the 3's move three groups away. The 4's remain where they are.
• The pictures in this activity are deliberately vague. The students should be encouraged to use their imaginations. There are no correct answers.
• If certain students tend to monopolize discussions, consider (a) putting them in the same group or (b) assigning them the task of "discussion controller." This means that they make sure each member of the group offers at least one suggestion for each picture.
• To turn this activity into a game, award one point for each answer that is suggested by only person per group during Step two. Points are given for all "unique" answers so more than one student can get a point for the same picture.
• See the introduction (• **corrections**) for suggestions on ways to correct student errors.

Answer Key

Answers will vary.

Examples:
She went shopping.
He won some money.
He had a fight with his boss.
She lost the key to the apartment.
They got engaged.
Their friend died.

Notes

CHECK YOURSELF

Read the story. Change the words in (parentheses). (10 points)

Last year, I *went* (go) to Chicago during Christmas break. I *visited* (visit) some old college friends. I ________ (stay) at a very nice hotel. Chicago restaurants are great. My friends and I ________ (eat) Chinese, Greek, and Italian food. They also ________ (take) me to a huge bookstore on Michigan Avenue and I ________ (buy) some magazines. I ________ (see) the Sears Tower, the world's tallest building. It ________ (is) foggy that day so I ________ (don't) go to the top. The only thing I didn't like about the trip was the weather. The first couple of days ________ (are) sunny, but after that it ________ (get) cold and windy. I ________ (have) a good time but I was glad to get back to Los Angeles.

Finish the conversation. Put the words in order.
There is one extra word in each group. (2 points each = 10 points)

- *How* ________________? [was, weekend, ~~how~~, your, did]
  - ☐ Great. I went skiing.
- Oh, really? ________________. [fun, that, like, is, sounds]
  ________________? [go, where, you, went, did]
  - ☐ To Pine Mountain. The snow was really good.
- ________________? [go, you, bus, did, by, take]
  - ☐ No, Jan drove.
- ________________? [long, how, get, did, far, there, to, take, it]
  - ☐ About an hour.
- That's not bad.

Your score

This is the end of the first half of *NEW ENGLISH FIRSTHAND!* Now is a good time to review what you have learned.

Try: *THE CLASS NEWSPAPER* project........page 108
and
SLAP!........page 113

Procedure

Exercise one.
1. T: *Look at page 57.* Point to the first exercise. T: *Read the story. Change the words in parentheses to the past.*
2. (Optional:) Point to item one. T: *Last year, I (blank) to Chicago... What is the past of "go"?* Encourage the students to answer (A: went). Gesture for them to write "went" in the space provided.
3. T: *Do the rest the same way.*

Exercise two.
1. Point to the second exercise. T: *This is a conversation. Put the words in the right order. There is one extra word in each group.*
2. (Optional). T: *The conversation starts with "How." The next sentence is "Great. I went skiing." What is the rest of the first sentence?* Encourage students to answer (A: was your weekend?). Gesture for students to write the sentence. T: *The extra word is "did."*
3. T: *Find the rest of the dialogue.*

You may wish to assign the page as homework.

In-class Follow-up

• T: *Work in pairs. Did you both get the same answers?* As students compare their answers, circulate to make sure that all students have completed the homework. You may wish to have some students write their answers on the board.

• T: *Work in pairs. Practice the conversations in Part Two.*

General Notes

• The "Check yourself" pages are each worth 20 points. The items in the first activity are worth one point each. Each sentence in the second activity is worth two points. If you are giving grades, you may wish to keep track of student scores. Alternatively, if you have assigned the pages as homework and class size makes keeping track of individual points impractical, you may want to note which students have completed the assignment, those who did only part of it and those who didn't do it.

Answer Key

Exercise one:
Last year, I went to Chicago during Christmas break. I visited some old college friends. I stayed at a very nice hotel. Chicago restaurants are great. My friends and I ate Chinese, Greek, and Italian food. They also took me to a huge bookstore on Michigan Avenue and I bought some magazines. I saw the Sears Tower, the world's tallest building. It was foggy that day so I didn't go to the top. The only thing I didn't like about the trip was the weather. The first couple of days were sunny, but after that it got cold and windy. I had a good time but I was glad to get back to Los Angeles.

Exercise two:
How was your weekend?
Great. I went skiing.
Oh , really ? That sounds like fun.
Where did you go?
To Pine Mountain. The snow was really good.
Did you go by bus?
No, Jan drove.
How long did it take to get there?
About an hour.
That's not bad.

Notes

Unit 7 I think I'd like that.

LISTENING Who's talking?

Getting ready

Do you know these occupations?

a. teacher b. hairdresser c. postal clerk d. police officer e. doctor f. dentist
g. clothing store clerk h. mechanic i. supermarket clerk j. bank teller

Who is talking? Write the letters.

______ I need to check the X-rays, but I think your wisdom teeth will need to come out.

______ The apples are $2.45, the stew is $1.13. That comes to $3.58.

__a__ Hand in your homework tomorrow.

______ I think your engine needs some major repairs.

______ I think it's too long in front. Let's cut it there.

______ It will cost $7.50 to send this airmail.

______ Someone stole your money?

______ What kind of traveler's checks would you like?

______ You need to take this medicine and get some rest.

______ What size?

Which of the jobs would you like the most?
Which one would you like least?

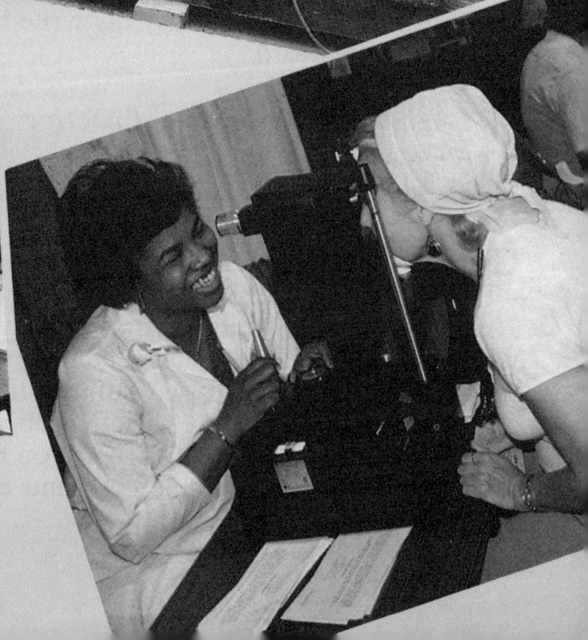

Objective: The students will identify the occupations of speakers and identify summaries of what they say.
Function: talk about occupations
Structures: mixed
Vocabulary Area: occupations

Procedure

1. Do the optional warm-up activity listed below.
2. T: *Open your books to page 59. Look at the pictures.*
3. T: *You will hear some people talking at work.*
4. T: *Look at "Getting Ready" on page 58. Do you know these occupations? Who is talking? Write the letters.* Play the first part of the tape.
5. Check by asking the students the questions (e.g., T: *Who said, "I need to check the X-rays...?"* Student: A dentist.) and eliciting their answers OR by having students work in groups of 2-4. They should compare answers and ask you about any they couldn't catch. (See the answer key on the next page.)
6. (Optional) If your students find listening very difficult, do the "additional preparation" exercise below.
7. T: *Look at the "First Listening"on page 59. Listen. Write the number of the speaker next to the correct picture.* Play the "First Listening" segment of the tape. You may want students to do this in pairs so they can help each other. You may wish to stop after each item to check.
8. (Optional) T: *Work in pairs. Did you both get the same answers?*
9. Play the tape again if necessary.
10. Check as in step 5. (See the answer key on the next page.)
11. T: *Look at the "Second Listening." Listen again. Check the sentences that mean the same things as what the speakers say.* Play the "Second Listening."
12. Check the answers as in step 5.
(See the answer key on the next page.)

Additional Preparation

Write the names of the occupations from page 59 on the chalkboard: teacher, postal clerk, doctor, hairdresser, police officer, store clerk, mechanic. Ask the students what words they associate with each person. Begin with "teacher." As students suggest words such as "book," "homework," "chalkboard, " etc. write them on the board. Continue with the other occupations.
Variation: After doing the first one together, have them work in pairs or small groups.

General Notes

• To help the students build anticipation skills, have them read the summary sentences before they listen to each segment. Remind them that the correct answer is one of the three given so they should focus on clues to those specific answers rather than trying to understand the entire meaning.
• Many occupation names are changing in American English to make them less associated with a particular sex. Words such as "police officer," "postal clerk," "flight attendant" and "fire fighter" are replacing their earlier forms ("policeman," "postman," "stewardess," "fireman").
•"Check O.K. on seven." (segment 2): many North American supermarket customers pay for their purchases with a check. This clerk is asking for approval to accept the check; he must get this approval from the manager.

Optional Warm-up Activity

Occupations and tools. Work as an entire class. Make copies of the occupation pictures from the Listening and Ensemble pages of this unit and put them on index cards or write the names of occupations on cards. Have the students think of equipment that is used in each occupation (e.g., doctor - stethoscope, teacher - textbooks, etc.). List their ideas on the board. Give an occupation card to each student. Have them find out each other's "occupation" by asking questions about the equipment (e.g., Do you use a wrench? Yes, I'm a mechanic./ No, I'm not a mechanic.). Each time a student receives a "yes" answer, that student collects the card. The student who gives up the card gets a new one from the teacher. The student who collects the most cards is the winner.

Unit 7

First Listening

Listen to each speaker.
Write the number of the speaker next to the correct picture.

☐

______ You have a test on Friday.
______ Read the homework assignment.
______ There is no class on Friday.

☐

______ It's too big to mail.
______ This package is for you.
______ It will cost $5.50 to send this.

☐

______ You need a lot of rest.
______ We have to operate immediately.
______ There's nothing you can do about it.

☐

______ You don't really need a haircut.
______ I'll cut some off the front and back.
______ You should shampoo your hair more often.

☐

______ Come with me. You're under arrest.
______ Tell him to come inside and wait.
______ We'll send someone to your house.

☐

______ The store is closed now.
______ We're out of onions.
______ The total is $4.34.

☐

______ Your car needs major repairs.
______ This car is in perfect condition.
______ Pick up your car at 5:00.

Second Listening

Listen again.
Check (✓) the sentences that *SUMMARIZE* what the speakers say.

Tapescript

Number 1.
Mechanic: Well, I hate to tell you this, but it's probably a broken camshaft. We'll have to tear the engine completely apart. I'm not sure what else is damaged, but repairs could run into hundreds of dollars.
Customer: How much?
Mechanic: We're talking lots of money here. We can give you a rough estimate before we begin work, but it's going to take a lot of work. Frankly, I don't know if you want to spend so much repairing this car.

Number 2.
Supermarket clerk: OK, that's onions, a dollar twenty-five...soup are three for one seventy...the spaghetti is eighty-nine. Anything else?
Customer: No, that's it.
S: That's $4.34.
C: OK. Can I write a check for twenty?
S: You got a check cashing card?
C: Yes.
S: OK, fine. Check OK on seven!

Number 3.
Hairdresser: You know you have really beautiful hair, with just... the curl's great. It looks really nice. But, you know, I think it's way too long in the back. I think maybe I'll cut a little off in the front here. Yeah, that looks good. And I'll take a bit off the back and cut it a little bit shorter in the front. Is it OK?

Number 4.
Customer: Ah, yeah, I'd like to mail this to Japan.
Postal Clerk: Do you want it to go air mail or sea mail?
C: Air mail, please.
P: What's in it?
C: Well, let's see. There's a book and some other things. Some photographs.
P: Is there a letter in it?
C: No. No letter.
P: OK. That can go book rate then. That'll be $5.50.
C: Oh, five-fifty? Cheaper than I thought.

Number 5.
Doctor: Well, Mr. Andrews, the results of your tests have come back and there's nothing serious, you don't need to worry too much, but you are going to have to start taking it easier. OK?
Patient: OK. I guess I have been working too hard.
D: Yes, you'll have to work less. If you continue at the pace you've been working, it's just going to get worse.
Patient: OK. Anything else?
D: I'd like you to take this medication three times a day. And rest!

Number 6.
Police officer: Third precinct. Sergeant Rose.
Smith: Is this the police station?
P: Yes, it is, sir.
S: This is Bill Smith at 121 Spring Street. Can you send somebody over here right away?
P: OK, Mr. Smith. What seems to be the problem?
S: I think there's somebody outside my window. I can, I can see a shadow or something near my front window.
P: OK, OK, well stay calm. Don't hang up the phone. Check that your doors are locked and we'll send somebody over right away. OK?
S: OK.

Number 7.
Teacher: OK, that just about wraps it up today. Ah, before next class, read chapter seven and go over the questions on page one eighty-five...that's one eighty-five. Uh, we'll discuss them next time. Do you have any questions now? Yeah.
Student: Do you want us to write out the answers to those questions?
T: You can take notes on them. You don't have to write them out for me, but it might be a good idea to write notes for yourself, yeah.

Answer Key

Getting Ready:
f. dentist
i. supermarket clerk
a. teacher
h. mechanic
b. hairdresser
c. postal clerk
d. police officer
j. bank teller
e. doctor
g. clothing store clerk

First/Second Listening:
1. mechanic
(Your car needs major repairs.)
2. supermarket clerk
(The total is $4.34.)
3. hairdresser
(I'll cut some off the front and back.)
4. postal clerk
(It will cost $5.50 to send this.)
5. doctor (You need a lot of rest.)
6. police officer
(We'll send someone to your house.)
7. teacher (Read the homework assignment.)

CONVERSATION

Can you use a computer?

★ Please have a seat, ________
name

◆ Thank you.

★ Now, what kind of job are you interested in?

◆ Well, I enjoy ___1___ and I'm good at ___2___ .

★ Can you ___3___ ?

◆ Yes, I can.

★ How about a job as a ___4___ ?

◆ Well, that doesn't sound very ___5___ . Is there anything else?

★ Would you like to be a ___6___ ?

◆ A ___6___ ? Yes, I think I'd like that.

★ OK. Let's think about that...

1. helping people typing meeting people	2. languages office work sales	3. speak Japanese use a computer do math well (mathematics)
4. hotel clerk secretary clerk	5. interesting exciting challenging	6. tour guide computer operator sales rep. (representative)

Objective: The students will talk about abilities and preferences.
Functions: offer a seat, ask/tell about abilities/preferences, make a suggestion
Structures: *enjoy* + gerund:
I enjoy typing.
modal auxiliary verb: *can*
participles as adjectives:
interested / interesting, challenging, exciting

Procedure

1. T: *Open your books to page 60. Look at the picture. Where are these people?* (A: an employment agency). *Have you ever been to an employment agency? What questions did they ask you?*
2. Play the tape. Have the students listen and read silently.
3. Answer questions about vocabulary and expressions.
4. (Optional) T: *Listen again. Repeat each line.* Play the conversation again. Pause after each sentence. Gesture for the students to repeat the sentences.
5. T: *Work in pairs.* (Gesture to show how you want the students paired.)
6. T: *Stand up. Practice the conversation.* Optional: Have the students begin by standing and sit down after the seat is offered.
(After a few minutes) T: *Change parts* (Point to your book to show that students who were playing the part on the left now do the part on the right.).
7. Encourage the students to substitute the words and phrases in the box at the bottom.
8. Encourage the students to make eye contact while they are practicing.
9. As the students work, circulate, answer questions and note areas for later work.
10. When students can do the conversation smoothly, encourage them to make changes other than those listed. This can be done by having them cover the substitution box with a piece of paper, a pencil case, etc. OR have them close their books and try to have similar conversations.

Conversation Variation

Have the students playing the part of the employment service worker imagine that they are bored and even sleepy. They speak slowly and with very little interest or emotion. Occasionally, they yawn. Students playing the part of the person looking for a job are nervous and excited. They speak quickly.

General Notes

• Students often confuse words like "interested" and "interesting." The "-ed" ending is used for a person's feeling. The "-ing" ending is used for the person or thing that creates that feeling. You may want the students to remember the story of Ed (a man's name). Draw a picture of a man on the chalkboard. Say: *This is Ed. Ed is interested in skiing. Skiing is the thing that is interesting to him.*
• Note the abbreviations "math" (for "mathematics") and "rep" (for "representative"). These are quite common in spoken American English. A "sales rep" is the same as a salesperson although normally a sales rep works for a manufacturer or distributor rather than a store.
• Remind the students to listen to their partners so that their choices for slot 6 correspond (e.g. A: Would you like to be a tour guide? B: A tour guide? Yes, I think I'd like that.).

Conversation Tapescript

Employment Officer: Please have a seat, Ms. Green.
Woman: Thank you.
EO: Now, what kind of job are you interested in?
W: Well, I enjoy helping people and I'm good at languages.
EO: Can you use a computer?
W: Yes, I can.
EO: How about a job as a secretary?
W: Well, that doesn't sound very challenging. Is there anything else?
EO: Would you like to be a tour guide?
W: A tour guide? Yes, I think I'd like that.
EO: OK. Let's think about that.

DUET-A

Who does what?

Can	Hiromi you	type? use a computer?		Yes, she can. No, I can't.
Does	Peter she	have	a college education?	Yes, he does. No, she doesn't.
Do	you	like to	work outside? work with people?	Yes, I do. No, I don't.

Fill in the chart. Ask *B* for the information.

Name		Can type	Can drive	Can use a computer	Likes to work outside	Likes to work with people	Has a college education
Hiromi		Y	N		N		N
Peter		N	Y	N	Y	N	N
Gerri		N		N	Y		
John				Y		Y	Y
Chen		Y	Y		N	Y	
Ron		N	Y		Y	Y	N
You							
Your Partner							

Y = yes N = no

Choose someone for each job.

1. secretary for an import company ____________
2. hotel clerk for a large hotel ____________
3. gardener for the city parks department ____________

What does ______ mean?

Bonus!

Find three things you and **B** can both do.
Find three things **B** can do that you can't.

Objective: The students will talk about abilities and preferences.
Function: ask / tell about abilities, preferences, and qualifications
Structures: *yes/no* questions with *do* modal auxiliary verb: *can*
Vocabulary Area: occupations, skills
Classroom language:
What does ____ mean?

Procedure

1. Divide the class into pairs. One student in each pair is **A**. The other is **B.** T: *Row one, you are **A's*** (Point to row one). *Row two, you are **B's*** (Point to row two). *Row three, you are **A's*** (etc.).
2. T: ***A's**, look at page 61. **B's**, look at page 62.*
3. Point out the language box at the top of the page. T: *Look at the box.* (Optional) *Listen and say.* Say the sentences in the box. Have students practice by repeating after you.
4. T: *Look at the page. Are there any words you don't know?*
5. Introduce the task. T: *You will find out things these people can do and things they prefer. You know some of the information. You partner knows the rest of the information.*
6. While the other students watch, direct one pair through the first step of the exercise. T: (to any student **A**): *Ask **B**, "Can Hiromi can use a computer?"* Prompt **B** to answer. (Yes, she can.) Gesture for **A** to write "yes" in the space.
7. T: *Find out about the rest of the people. You will also talk about yourself and ask about your partner. Then choose one person for each job at the bottom.* When the students understand the task, have them do it in pairs.
8. As the students work, circulate, answer questions and note areas for later work.
9. As students finish the main task, have them continue by doing the *Bonus!* task. Have them find three things they both can do and three things their partners can do that they can't.
12. Do consolidation, correction and expansion as desired.

Grammar and Usage

• You may wish to point out that the use of "can" and "do/does" eliminates the need for a final "-s" on the third person form of the main verb. (e.g., "Can Hiromi type?" "Does Peter like to work outside?")

General Notes

• Students should take turns. The best person for each job is not necessarily clear. Students should indicate their preference. You may want to ask them to explain their decisions.
• Of course, most jobs include working with people to some degree. The question on the chart refers to jobs where the worker deals with people most of the time (hotel clerk, teacher, sales clerk, etc.)
• See the introduction (•Corrections) for suggestions on ways to correct during pair work.

Additional Activity

(This activity can be used anytime during this unit).
Ability/preference find someone who... Work as an entire class. See the Unit 3 expansion for instructions. Make one copy of the "find someone who..." (next page) for each student. See the Unit one, Ensemble for more complete instructions for "Find someone who..." Students may want to refer to the language boxes on pages 61-62 for support.

Who does what?

DUET-B

Can	Hiromi you	type? use a computer?		Yes, she can. No, I can't.
Does	Peter she	have	a college education?	Yes, he does. No, she doesn't.
Do	you	like to	work outside? work with people?	Yes, I do. No, I don't.

Fill in the chart. Ask *A* for the information.

Name	Can type	Can drive	Can use a computer	Likes to work outside	Likes to work with people	Has a college education
 Hiromi	Y		Y	N	Y	N
 Peter	N		N		N	N
 Gerri	N	Y		Y	N	
 John	Y			N	Y	
 Chen			N	N		Y
 Ron	N		Y	Y	Y	N
Your Partner						
You						

Y = yes N = no

Choose someone for each job.

1. secretary for an import company ____________
2. hotel clerk for a large hotel ____________
3. gardener for the city parks department ____________

What does ______ mean?

Bonus!

Find three things you and **A** can both do.
Find three things **A** can do that you can't.

Find someone who...

1. can drive a truck.

____

2. can type.

____

3. likes winter more than summer.

____

4. can fix machines.

____

5. likes his or her job.

____

6. can sew.

____

7. can not swim.

____

8. usually works alone.

____

9. has a professional license.

____

10. has two jobs.

____

Answer Key

Answers will vary.

Checking answers as a whole class should not be necessary. You may wish to have the pair look at both books to make sure they have correctly filled in all blanks. Answers for A's page are on page 62 and answers for B's page are on page 61 .

Expansion Activities

Grouping jobs.
As a whole class, students list as many jobs as they can think of on the chalkboard.

In pairs, they pick 10 jobs and divide them into two more more categories (e.g., works indoors/outdoors, well-paid/ poorly paid, dangerous/ safe, etc.).
Each pair then circulates. They show their lists to other pairs. The new pair must guess how the jobs were grouped.

Fluency Frames:
Three "fluency frames" are introduced in the "extra activities" sections of Units 1, 2 and 3. Use any one of the "frames" with this topic for Unit 7:

• *The job I want someday.*

SOLO Presenting yourself

Read about Sue Chang.
Fill out the form for her.

My name is Sue Chang. I'm an 18-year-old university student. I'm fairly outgoing. I like sports, especially tennis. I also like to read and go to the movies. I can play the piano and speak English. I enjoy jobs where I can meet a lot of people.

SUMMER ABROAD INCORPORATED

(Name)

(Age) (Sex)

Rate yourself (circle one)
very outgoing — somewhat outgoing
somewhat reserved — very reserved

Abilities and Interests

■ Do you like sports? yes☐ no☐
Which ones? ______

■ Can you speak any foreign languages? yes☐ no☐
Which ones? ______

■ Can you play any musical instruments? yes☐ no☐
Which ones? ______

What are you interested in?

What type of work do you enjoy?

You want to stay with a family in another country.
Fill out the form for yourself.
Then write about yourself.
Use some of these words:

____ I am... ____ I can...
____ I like... ____ I enjoy...
____ I'm interested in...

SUMMER ABROAD INCORPORATED

(Name)

(Age) (Sex)

Rate yourself (circle one)
very outgoing — somewhat outgoing
somewhat reserved — very reserved

Abilities and Interests

■ Do you like sports? yes☐ no☐
Which ones? ______

■ Can you speak any foreign languages? yes☐ no☐
Which ones? ______

■ Can you play any musical instruments? yes☐ no☐
Which ones? ______

What are you interested in?

What type of work do you enjoy?

Objective: The students will read about someone's abilities and interests and fill out a form. They will fill out a form and write about their own abilities and interests.
Function: describe abilities and interests
Structures: WH- questions, modal auxiliary verb: *can*
Vocabulary Area: abilities and interests

Procedure

1. T: *Open your books to page 63. This is Sue Chang. She is going on a homestay. You will read about her. As you read, fill in the homestay form for Sue.*
2. T: *Now, fill out the form for yourself. Then write about yourself. Use some of these words: I am, I like, I can, I enjoy, I'm interested in.*

You may wish to assign this activity as homework.

In-class Follow-up

Students copy the form and role play a homestay interview in pairs. One student plays the part of the interviewer. The other plays the applicant. They can include questions not on the form -- other personal preferences and habits, country or area preferred, etc. You may wish to remind them that such an interview is likely to be more formal than some of the personal information activities they have done previously.

General Notes

- This form is an application for a homestay program. Students stay with a family in a foreign country for a month or two in order to have the experience of living in another culture and to improve their foreign language skills.
- An "outgoing" person is a friendly person.
- A "reserved" person is someone who is usually rather quiet, but not necessarily shy.
- Remind the students that "enjoy" is followed by "---ing." (I enjoy swimming.) "Can" is followed by the plain form of the verb. (I can ski.) "Like" can be followed by either "---ing" or the infinitive. (e.g., I like skiing. I like to ski.)
- Sue Chang is Chinese -- that is, her name and ethnic background are Chinese. Chinese family names normally come before personal names (e.g., Chang Su). However in some Chinese speaking areas such as Taiwan and Hong Kong, it is common for people to adopt Western names (like "Sue") for use when dealing with foreigners. When this is done, Western name order is used (like "Sue Chang").

Optional Skill-building Activity

Skill: Scanning for specific information

Have the students write their paragraph on separate pieces of paper. Collect the paragraphs and post them on the walls. Tell each student whose paragraph he or she will read. Give each student a copy of the "Summer Abroad" form. Students must leave the forms at their desks. They go to the posted paragraph, read it and try to remember as much as they can. They return to their desks and begin to fill out the form for the person. They write as much as they can remember and return to wall to read for more information as many times as necessary.

Answer Key

Task one:
Name: Sue Chang
Age: 18 Sex: Female
Rate yourself: somewhat outgoing
Do you like sports? Yes, tennis
Can you speak any foreign languages?
Yes, English
Can you play any musical instruments?
Yes, the piano
What are you interested in?
reading and movies
What type of work do you enjoy?
jobs where I can meet a lot of people.

Task two:
Answers will vary.
Example:
See Sue's paragraph.

Occupations

Work in groups of five.

If you want to find out about people's jobs, what questions can you ask?
Think of five yes/no questions. Write your questions below.

Do you usually work indoors? ____________

Do ____________ *?*

____

____

____

____

Now, each person chooses one occupation.
Ask your questions:
Try to guess their occupations.

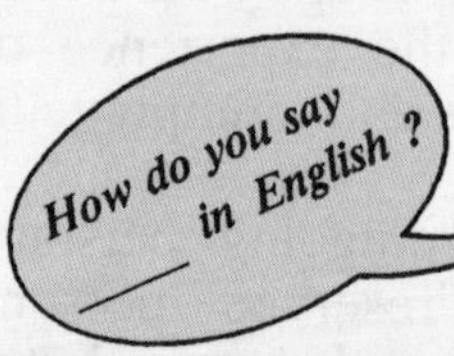

Try This!

Work with your partners.
What are the five best jobs in the world? Why?
What are the five worst jobs? Why?

Objective: The students will learn to ask and answer questions about occupations.
Function: ask / tell about job qualifications and characteristics
Structures: "yes/no" questions with *be* and *do*.
Vocabulary Area: occupations
Classroom language:
How do you say _____ in English?

Procedure

1. T: *Look at page 64. This is a guessing game about jobs.*
2. T: *Look at the pictures. Do you know the names of these jobs? Look at the "Idea box." Are there any words you don't know?* Answer questions about vocabulary.
3. *T: Think of five "yes-no" questions you could ask to find about which job a person has. For example, Do you usually work indoors? Use the "Idea box" to help you.*
4. Divide the class into groups of 5.
5. Introduce the task. T: *You will think of one of the jobs. Your partners will try to guess. You can only answer, "yes" or "no."*
6. Give an example. Think of one of the jobs. T: *I'm thinking of a job. What is it? Ask some of your questions.* Encourage them to ask. When they think they know, they can say, "Are you a ______?"
7. When the students understand the task, have them begin.
8. As the students work, circulate, answer questions and note areas for later work.
10. As groups finish the main task, have them continue by doing the *Try this!* task. Have them list the five best and worst jobs in the world and give reasons.
11. Do consolidation, correction and expansion as desired.

Grammar and Usage Notes

• Point out the idea box so that students may more easily form correct questions.
• "License" in the idea box can refer either to a specific occupational permit (e.g., a teaching certificate) or a more general permit (e.g., a driver's license.).

General Notes

• The students must ask one of the questions they have written before they ask about a specific job. Encourage them to ask questions that narrow choices (e.g., Do you work with other people? Do you need a lot of education?) rather than questions only about a certain job (Do you work at a gas station? Do you use a camera?)
• See the introduction (• **corrections**) for suggestions on ways to correct student errors.

Answer Key

Answers will vary.

Examples:
Do you wear a uniform?
Do you work outside?
Do you work with people?
Is your job dangerous?
Are you well-paid?

Occupations illustrated are as follows (clockwise from top right):
(grocery) store clerk, photographer, computer operator (or programmer), football player (or athlete), musician, paramedic (or ambulance driver), fire fighter , (clothing) store clerk (or salesperson), cook (or chef), mechanic, police officer, doctor, pilot, gas station attendant, teacher

Notes

CHECK YOURSELF

Who are they talking to? Write the job. (5 points)

dentist	doctor	engineer	teacher
store clerk	waiter	police officer	mechanic

1. 
I'm sorry.
I forgot my homework.
teacher

2. 
I'll have the steak.
____

3. 
I feel tired all the time
and I have a fever.
____

4. 
Do you have this
in a smaller size?
____

5. 
I'd like to report a robbery.
Someone stole my car.
____

6. 
I have a bad toothache.
____

Put the letters in the right order (5 points)

	gglinncahie	She has a very challenging job.
1.	ccaiemhn	The ________ fixed my car.
2.	tggnooui	He likes to meet people. He's very ________.
3.	eeaystrrc	A ________ works in an office.
4.	tdcneioua	You need a college ________ to be a teacher.
5.	eiogfnr	She can speak several ________ languages.

Match the questions with the answers. (10 points)

j	1. Can you speak any foreign languages?	a. Yes, he majored in business.
____	2. Can you type?	b. Yes, it's very interesting.
____	3. What kind of work do you enjoy?	c. Yes, I do.
____	4. Do you have a driver's license?	d. He's somewhat reserved.
____	5. How about a job as a clerk?	e. Yes, I like to play the guitar.
____	6. Does he have a college education?	f. She's a doctor.
____	7. What's she good at?	g. I like working with people.
____	8. What does she do?	h. Yes, 65 words a minute.
____	9. Do you enjoy your work?	i. She writes very well.
____	10. Can you play any musical instruments?	j. Yes, French and Spanish.
____	11. What's he like?	k. Well, that doesn't sound very interesting.

Your score

Procedure

Exercise one.
1. T: *Look at page 65.* Point to the first exercise. T: *Who are these people talking to? Write the jobs.*
2. (Optional:) Point to item one. T: *Number one. I'm sorry. I forgot my homework. Who is she talking to?* Encourage the students to answer (A: A teacher). Gesture for them to write the job in the space provided.
3. T: *Do 2-6 the same way.*

Exercise two.
1. Point to the second exercise. T: *These letters are not in the right order. Read the sentences. Put the letters in the right order.*
2. (Optional). T: *Look at the example: She has a (blank) job. What word goes in the blank?* Encourage the students to answer (A: challenging). Gesture for students to write the word in the blank.
3. T: *Do 1-5 the same way.*

Exercise three.
1. Point to the third exercise. T: *Look at the sentences. Match the questions on the left with the answers on the right..*
2. (Optional). T: *Number one: Can you speak any foreign languages? What's the answer?* Encourage students to answer (A: [j.] Yes, French and Spanish.). Gesture for them to write "j" in the space.
3. T: *Do 2-11 the same way.*

You may wish to assign the page as homework.

In-class Follow-up

• T: *Work in pairs. Did you both get the same answers?* As students compare their answers, circulate to make sure that all students have completed the homework. You may wish to have some students write their answers on the board.

General Notes

• The "Check yourself" pages are each worth 20 points. Each item is worth one point.

Answer Key

Exercise one:
1. teacher
2. waiter
3. doctor
4. store clerk
5. police officer
6. dentist

Exercise two:
1. The mechanic fixed my car.
2. He likes to meet people. He's very outgoing.
3. A secretary works in an office.
4. You need a college education to be a teacher.
5. She can speak speak several foreign languages.

Exercise three:
1. j. Yes, French and Spanish.
2. h. Yes, 65 words a minute.
3. g. I like working with people.
4. c. Yes, I do.
5. k. Well, that doesn't sound very interesting.
6. a. Yes, he majored in business.
7. i. She writes very well.
8. f. She's a doctor.
9. b. Yes, it's very interesting.
10. e. Yes, I like to play the guitar.
11. d. He's somewhat reserved.

Unit 8 What's playing?

LISTENING Getting information

Getting ready

Here are some ways to talk about time.

It's five o'clock.
He goes to work at seven-thirty.
The movie starts at a quarter to seven.
It finishes at half past eight.
School starts at twenty past eight.
We'll leave at ten till four.

Write other ways to say these times.

a quarter to one

____

____

eight-thirty

____

____

fifteen after one

____

____

Objective: The students will identify times, prices, dates, days and seat numbers related to entertainment events.
Function: ask for/ receive information, request
Structures: WH- questions
Vocabulary Area: entertainment

Procedure

1. Do the optional warm-up activity listed below.
2. T: *Open your books to pages 66-67. Look at the pictures.*
3. T: *You will hear some people talking about times and entertainment events.*
4. T: *Look at "Getting Ready" on page 66. There are many different ways to talk about time in English.* Play the first part of the tape.
5. T: *Look at the clocks. Write other ways to say the times.* You may want students to do this in pairs.
6. Check what they wrote. T: *What's another way to say a quarter to one?*
(See the answer key on the next page.)
OR have the students check their answers in pairs.
7. (Optional) If your students find listening very difficult, do the "additional preparation" exercise below.
8. T: *Look at the "First Listening"on page 67. Listen to part A. Write the times.* Play the "First Listening, part A" segment of the tape. You may want students to do this in pairs so they can help each other. You may wish to stop after each item to check.
9. (Optional) T: *Work in pairs. Did you both get the same answers?*
10. Play the tape again if necessary.
11. Check by asking the students the questions (e.g., T: *What time does "Mystery Train" start?* A: 7:00 and 9:15.) and eliciting their answers OR by having students work in groups of 2-4. They should compare answers and ask you about any they couldn't catch.
(See the answer key on the next page.)
12. T: *Look at the "First Listening, Part B." Listen and write the missing information.* Play the "First Listening, Part B."
13. Check the answers as in step 11.
(See the answer key on the next page.)

Additional Preparation

Students work in pairs. They identify the types of entertainment in items 1-7 on page 67 (movies, a play, a rock concert, a classical concert). Then they decide typical showtimes and prices for similar events in their city.

General Notes

- Part A contains the names of movies.
- *Les Miserables* is a Broadway play. (The speaker on the tape gives a French-like pronunciation, though most native speakers of English would give a more "Anglicized" pronunciation.)
- Universities in the U.S. generally do not charge for admission to graduation ceremonies, but they often do issue tickets to control seating. This ensures that there will be enough seats for the graduates who invite guests.

Optional Warm-up Activity

Body clocks. Draw a large clock on the chalkboard and elicit different ways to read times (such as those listed on the answer key below). Students then work in pairs. They pantomime times, using their bodies as clocks. One arm is extended farther than the other to represent the minute hand. Partners guess the times. The first team to pantomime and guess 20 different times is the winner.

Tapescript

First listening. Part A. Listen to each conversation. Write down the times of the shows.

Number 1.
Theater information: Hello, Cinema Studio 1.
Customer: Hi. What's playing now?
T: Mystery Train is playing, sir.
C: Mystery Train? What time are the shows?
T: Seven o'clock and nine-fifteen.
C: Seven and a quarter after nine. OK. Thanks a lot.
T: You're welcome.
C: Bye.

Number 2.
Theater information: Thank you for calling the Regency Theater, located at Fifty-fifth Street and Broadway. Presently playing is the ever popular Hitchcock thriller, Rear Window. Show times are six

First Listening

PART A. **Listen to each conversation. Write down the times of the shows.**

1.

2.

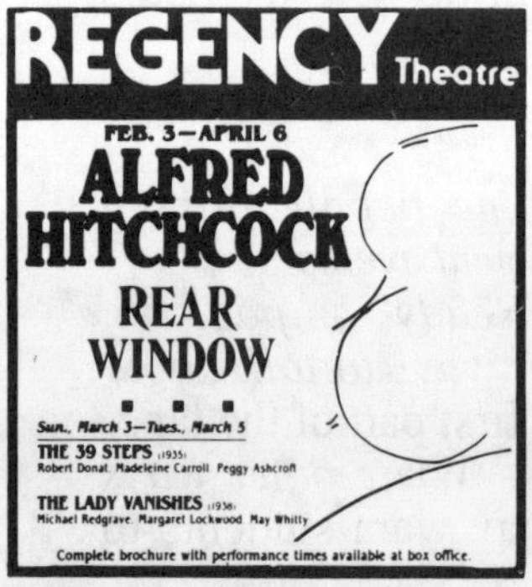

3.

4.

PART B. **Listen and fill in the information.**

5. Tickets for *Les Misérables*

6. Tickets for a Bruce Springsteen concert

7. Tickets for the Boston Symphony

8. Tickets for a graduation ceremony

forty-five and nine ten. Once again, show times are six forty-five and nine ten. The ticket price is $6.50 for adults and $5.25 for children under 12.

Number 3.
Theater information: Hello, Guild Theater.
Customer: Hi. I'm calling about Beyond the Walls. That's playing now, right?
T: Yes, that's right.
C: What times?
T: Well, the next show is at seven-thirty and after that, nine forty-five.
C: Seven-thirty and a quarter to ten. OK, thanks.
T: Uh-huh.

Number 4.
Theater information: This is Lowe's Theater. Today through the end of this month we are featuring Michael J. Fox's smash hit Back to the Future 3. Daily there's a matinee showing at two o'clock and evening showings at six forty-five and eight fifty-five. Ticket prices for the matinee are four fifty. Evening show time tickets are seven dollars.

Part B. Listen and fill in the information.
Number 5.
Ticket information: Ticketron.
Customer: Hello. I'd like some tickets for Les Miserables.
T: Um, for what day? There's uh, there's nothing available for this weekend.
C: Hum? When is the next available show?
T: Friday. That's November fourth...but there are only two orchestra seats left.
C: Only orchestra seats?
T: Yes.
C: How much are those?
T: They're thirty-five dollars each.
C: OK. Could I have those two tickets?
T: OK. The two orchestra seats for Friday, November fourth. Ah, will you be paying by credit card?
C: Yeah, could I?
T: Yeah. What's your name please?

Number 6.
Ticket information: Ticket Hotline. Can I help you?
Customer: Yeah. Bruce Springsteen concert. Is it sold out yet?
T: No, we have some "B" seats for twenty dollars.
C: "B" seats? Are they decent seats?
T: Ah. Well, they're "B" seats...up in the second balcony. You can hear the concert, but I'm not sure how much you'll be able to see.
C: And they're twenty dollars?
T: That's right.
C: No thanks. Forget it.
T: OK. Thanks for calling.

Number 7.
Ticket information: Hello. Gidrich Hall.
Customer: Hello. I'd like to inquire about tickets for the Boston Symphony Orchestra.
T: Yes?
C: How many shows will they be giving here?
T: Three. One on Friday. One on Saturday. One on Sunday. They're all evening shows starting at seven-thirty.
C: All at 7:30? Could I reserve three of the best seats you have for the Saturday evening show ?
T: OK.
C: My name is Finley.
T: Finley? F-I-N-L-E-Y?
C: Yes, that's right.
T: OK, Ms. Finley. I'll reserve three twenty-five dollar seats for the Saturday performance.

Number 8.
Ticket clerk: Yes?
Student: Hi. Can I have some tickets for the graduation ceremony on Sunday?
T: Sure. Are you going to be graduating?
S: Yes. I need three tickets. My little brother and my parents.
T: OK, sure. But can I see your student ID?
S: Here.
T: OK. Here are the three tickets. These are in the "P" row. That's P-22, P-23, and P-24.

Answer Key

Getting Ready:

12:45 •a quarter to one
•twelve forty-five
•fifteen to one

8:30 •eight-thirty
•half past eight

1:15 •fifteen after one
•one fifteen
•a quarter past (after) one

First Listening:

Part A

1. Mystery Train: 7:00, 9:15
2. Rear Window: 6:45, 9:10
3. Beyond the Walls: 7:30, 9:45
4. Back to the Future III, 2:00, 6:45, 8:55

Part B

5. Les Miserables: $35 each/ November 4
6. Bruce Springsteen Concert: $20
7. Boston Symphony: Saturday/ 7:30
8. Graduation: P-22, P-23, P-24

CONVERSATION What's playing?

★ Would you like to go to a ___1___ ?

◆ I don't feel like a ___1___ .
How about a ___1___ ?

★ Sounds good. What's on?

◆ How about ___2___ ?
It's a ___3___ .

★ Hmm. I don't really like ___3___ (s).
How about ___2___ ?
It's a ___3___ .

◆ That sounds good.
Where is it?

★ It's at the ___4___ .

◆ OK. What time shall we go?

★ Well, it starts at ___5___ .

1	2	3	4	5
Movie	Casablanca	classic	State Theatre	5:30
	Touching	love story	Cinema 7	7:00
	The Eye	science fiction film	Pinemall Cinema	9:10
Play	Annie	musical	Broadway Theatre	7:00
	Just Neighbors	comedy	"Off Stage" Theatre	7:30
	Sweet Revenge	mystery	Civic Auditorium	8:00
Concert	Outside	rock band	Sports Center	7:30
	The Silver Five	jazz group	Backdoor	9:00
	The Vienna Chamber Orchestra	classical orchestra	Merwin Auditorium	8:00

Objective: The students will suggest and agree/disagree with suggestions.
Functions: invite, make a suggestion, agree/disagree with a suggestion, decide on details of a plan
Structures: *WH* -questions,
modal auxiliary verb: *shall*
Would you like + infinitive

Procedure

1. T: *Open your books to page 68. Look at the picture. Where are these people?* (A: someone's home.) *What do you think they are talking about?*
2. Play the tape. Have the students listen and read silently.
3. Answer questions about vocabulary and expressions.
4. (Optional) T: *Listen again. Repeat each line.* Play the conversation again. Pause after each sentence. Gesture for the students to repeat the sentences.
5. T: *Work in pairs.* (Gesture to show how you want the students paired.)
6. T: *Stand up. Practice the conversation.* (After a few minutes) T: *Change parts* (Point to your book to show that students who were playing the part on the left now do the part on the right.).
7. Encourage the students to substitute the words and phrases in the box at the bottom.
8. Encourage the students to make eye contact while they are practicing.
9. As the students work, circulate, answer questions and note areas for later work.
10. When students can do the conversation smoothly, encourage them to make changes other than those listed. This can be done by having them cover the substitution box with a piece of paper, a pencil case, etc. OR have them close their books and try to have similar conversations. They can use current or upcoming events in their city or the items in the listening activity of this unit.

Conversation Variation

Bring enough old newspapers for each pair to have one. Have the students imagine they are really looking at the entertainment section of a newspaper as they practice this conversation. They pass the newspaper to their partner each time they speak. Because passing the paper requires that they look away from the text, this helps build short-term memory.

General Notes

• To establish meaning on the category vocabulary in slot 3, you may wish to ask the students for examples of each that they like.
• Remind the students that it is essential to listen to their partners so that their choices for slots 1, 2 and 3 correspond. The second slot 1 (How about a ___?) is a counter-suggestion and should be different from the original.
• "What's on?" is a way of asking "What movies, etc. are playing? What options do we have?"
• For making offers and soliciting suggestions in American English, "shall" is used instead of "will." (e.g., "What time shall we go?" not "What time will we go?")

Conversation Tapescript

First Woman: Would you like to go to a concert?
Second Woman: I don't feel like a concert. How about a movie?
FW: Sounds good. What's on?
SW: How about *The Eye* ? It's a science fiction film.
FW: I don't really like science fiction films. How about *Touching* ?. It's a love story.
SW: That sounds good. Where is it?
FW: It's at the Cinema Seven.
SW: OK. What time shall we go?
FW: Well, it starts at five-thirty.

DUET-A

That sounds interesting, but...

What	shall we do do you feel like doing would you like to do	tonight?
I don't really feel like I'm not really interested in		rock music. art shows.

Let's	go to a concert.
I feel like	going to an art show.
How about	Mexican food?
Why don't we	go to a play?

How do you say ___ in English

You and **B** must decide what to do tonight. **Choose from the newspaper entertainment section.**

Choose Situation 1 or 2. Read the role card. Decide what to do tonight.

Situation 1

You are a rich business person. You and ***B*** went to college together. You haven't seen ***B*** for a long time. You want to do something exciting. You like concerts and foreign food.

Situation 2

You live in New York City. You enjoy it but don't like crowds and noise. Your friend is visiting from a small town. You enjoy artistic events like ballet and classical music.

What did you and ***B*** decide to do?

Bonus!

Find three things you both like to do.
Find three things ***B*** likes that you don't.

Objective: The students will offer and accept / reject suggestions
Function: make and ask for suggestions, accept / reject, state a preference
Structures: *feel like / How about* + gerund
Let's / Why don't we + verb
Would you like + infinitive
modal auxiliary verb: *shall*
Vocabulary Area: entertainment
Classroom language:
How do you say _____ in English?

Procedure

1. Divide the class into pairs. One student in each pair is **A**. The other is **B**. T: *Row one, you are **A's*** (Point to row one). *Row two, you are **B's*** (Point to row two). *Row three, you are **A's*** (etc.).
2. T: ***A's**, look at page 69. **B's**, look at page 70.*
3. Point out the language box at the top of the page. T: *Look at the box.* (Optional) *Listen and say.* Say the sentences in the box. Have students practice by repeating after you.
4. T: *Look at the page. Are there any words you don't know?*
5. Introduce the task. T: *You and your partner are going to go out tonight. Read the role cards. Decide which situation.*
6. While the other students watch, direct one pair through the first step of the exercise. T: *Which situation?* When they decide, remind them of their roles:
Situation one: *You went to college together. You haven't seen each other in a long time. **A**, you are a business person. **B**, you are an English teacher.*
*You need to decide what to do. **A**, make a suggestion.* Prompt **A** by pointing to the language box.
Situation two: *You are in New York City. **A**, you live in New York. **B**, you are visiting. You need to decide what to do. **A**, make a suggestion.* Prompt **A** by pointing to the language box.
7. T: *Decide what to do.* When the students understand the task, have them do it in pairs.
8. As the students work, circulate, answer questions and note areas for later work.
11. As students finish the main task, have them continue by doing the other situation or the *Bonus!* task. Have them find three things they both like to do and three things their partners like that they don't.
12. Do consolidation, correction and expansion as desired.

Grammar and Usage

• You may wish to point out that "shall" is used in American English almost exclusively to give offers or ask questions about arrangements.
(e.g., "Shall we dance?" "When shall we leave for the concert?")

General Notes

• You may need to remind the students that there is certain information that they should not tell their partners. For example, if they cannot afford something, they are not likely to say that directly. Rather, they should suggest a place that is less expensive.
• Note that prices are listed on the ads.
• Two of the clubs list "cover charges." This means the admission price. Birdland also has a two drink minimum. Customers must buy at least two drinks in addition to paying the cover charge.
• See the introduction (•Corrections) for suggestions on ways to correct during pair work.
• Since this activity is designed to encourage fluency, corrections are not recommended at this time.

Additional Activity

(This activity can be used anytime during this unit).
Coin flip invitations. Work as an entire group. Have students think of places and events that they invite their friends to. List the suggestions on the board. Have each student take out a coin. Show them how to flip the coin. Tell them that one side means "yes" and the other side means "no." Tell them which is which. Each student must invite 10 other students to different places or events. The invited student flips the coin to decide if he will accept or reject the invitations. Students should count the number of times their invitations are accepted. They may want to refer to the language box on page 72 for support.

DUET-B

That sounds interesting, but...

What	shall we do do you feel like doing would you like to do	tonight?	Let's	go to a concert.
			I feel like	going to an art show.
			How about	Mexican food?
			Why don't we	go to a play?
I don't really feel like I'm not really interested in		rock music. art shows.		

How do you say ____ in English ?

You and ***A*** must decide what to do tonight. **Choose from the newspaper entertainment section.**

Choose Situation 1 or 2. Read the role card. Decide what to do tonight.

Situation 1

You are an English teacher. You and ***A*** went to college together. You haven't seen ***A*** for a long time. You want to have a quiet evening together so you and ***A*** can talk. You can't afford to spend very much money (but don't tell ***A***).

Situation 2

You live in a small town. You are visiting a friend who lives in New York City. It is your first visit to New York. You want to go to a place (or even two or three) that is wild and exciting. You like jazz and rock music.

What did you and ***A*** decide to do? ______________________

Bonus!

Find three things you both like to do.
Find three things ***A*** likes that you don't.

Expansion Activity

Notes

What's the word?
Each student looks quickly through Unit 8 (or anywhere from Units 1-8) and writes down eight words that are a little difficult.

Students then work in pairs. They give hints about the words. Partners must guess the words. Students take turns. The pair that guesses all 16 words the most quickly is the winner.

Note: You may wish to have them write their words as homework before the class in which would will do the activity.

This vocabulary review activity can be used at any time, not just during unit 8.

Fluency Frames:
Three "fluency frames" are introduced in the "extra activities" sections of Units 1, 2 and 3. Use any one of the "frames" with this topic for Unit 8:

• *My favorite kind of entertainment.*

Answer Key

Since the students are role-playing, **answers will vary**. The students should write down their answers -- what they decided to do -- on the line at the bottom of pages 69-70.

SOLO Invitation

Lori is inviting a friend to a concert.
Read her note.

Renee,

I'm going to the Bon Jovi concert this Friday. Would you like to come?

They play great hard rock. The concert starts at 8:00 at the Meadowlands Arena.

Let's go out to eat after the concert.

Please call me tonight.

Lori

Write a note to a friend. Invite your friend to a rock concert.
Include these things:

- who is playing
- where it is
- the kind of music they play
- when it starts

Objective: The students will read and write invitations.
Function: invite, make a suggestion
Structures: present continuous as future:
I'm going to the Bon Jovi concert.

Procedure

1. T: *Open your books to page 71. Look at the Bon Jovi advertisement. Lori is going to a concert. She is inviting her friend Renee to go with her. Read her note.*
2. T: *Look at the other advertisement. What is the name of the band?* (A: The Lazers.) *Where is the concert?* (A: The Ritz, 54th street, west of Broadway.) *When is it?* (A: Friday, 9 p.m.)
3. T: *You want to invite a friend to a concert. Use the Lazers advertisement or think of a real concert. Write a note. Include these things: who is playing, where it is, the kind of music they play, when it starts.*

You may wish to assign this activity as homework.

In-class Follow-up

Students work in pairs. They read their notes to each other. The partner quickly writes/draws an advertisement for the concert. The advertisement should include the musician(s), the place, the kind of music and the time.

General Notes

• You may want to ask the students to find and bring in an advertisement for a concert .
• If your students do not like rock music, they may invite a friend to any kind of concert they like, using the same format.
• "The Meadowlands Arena" is near New York City. "The Ritz" is a rock concert theater in New York.

Optional Skill-building Activity

Skills: increasing reading speed, scanning for specific information

Have the students open their books to page 71 and turn the books face down on their desks. Tell them that you will ask a question. When you say "go" they should look at page 71 and try to find the answer as quickly as possible. When they know the answer, they should call it out. Do the two example questions in this way.

Question 1. Where is the Bon Jovi concert?
(Answer: the Meadowlands Arena)
Question 2. When is Renee supposed to call Lori? (Answer: tonight)

Now divide the class into groups of four. In each group, one person is the "quizmaster." That student asks the questions. Give each quizmaster a copy of the question and answers below. Then continue with the activity.

Questions and Answers:

1. Where is the Ritz Theater?
(Answer: 54th Street, West of Broadway)
2. What does Lori want to do after the concert?
(Answer: Go out to eat)
3. Which concert begins earlier?
(Answer: The Bon Jovi concert)
4. What kind of music does Lori like?
(Answer: hard rock)
5. How much would it cost of Lori goes to both concerts?
($46.50 or $40.50)

Answer Key

Answers will vary.
Example:
See Lori's note.

Would you like to...

Would you like to go to How about going to	a disco? a movie? a restaurant?	When?	
Monday night at 7:30. Friday at 3:30.		Sure. It sounds like fun.	
		I'm sorry, but	I have to work. I'm going to a concert. I have other plans.
Great. Let's plan on it.			
That's too bad. Maybe another time.			

Work in a large group.

First, write *YOUR* schedule for next week.
Include: - classes
- work
- any plans you have.

Next, decide on *THREE THINGS* you want to do in your free time.
(For example, PLAY TENNIS - SATURDAY, 9:00 A.M.)
Write them on your schedule.

***THEN* invite other people to these events. Find three people who say *YES*.**

ACCEPT THREE INVITATIONS.
Write them on your schedule.

Monday

Tuesday

Wednesday

Thursday

Friday

Saturday

Sunday

Try This! Work in groups of six. Each person lists a food, a sport, an entertainer, and a place they like. Then list one of each you don't like. Take a poll. Ask your partners, "Do you like _____ ? Why?" How many people agree with you?

Objective: The students will learn to invite and to accept / reject invitations and give reasons.
Function: invite, accept / reject an invitation, give reasons
Structures: *Would you like* + infinitive conjunction: *but*
Vocabulary Area: entertainment and leisure activities.

Procedure

1. (Optional) T: *What kinds of things do you invite your friends to do?* Write their ideas on the chalkboard.
2. T: *Look at page 72. This is an activity for inviting people to do something.*
3. T: *Look at the language box at the top of the page. Are there any words you don't know?* Answer questions about vocabulary.
3. (Optional) T: *Look at the box. Listen and say.* Say the sentences in the box. Have students practice by repeating after you.
4. T: *Look at the schedule. Write your schedule for the next week. Include classes, work and any plans you have.*
5. T: *Decide three things you want to do in your free time. When do you want to do them? Write them on the schedule.*
6. Introduce the task. T: *You must invite people to do those things.*
7. While the other students watch, invite one student to do something. T: *Would you like to go to a movie Saturday night?* If the student says, "yes" write the name on your schedule. If the student says, "no" prompt a reason by pointing the that section of the language box.
8. T: *When you say "no," always give a reason. When someone says "yes," write that person's name next to the event. When you say "yes," write it on your schedule.*
9. When the students understand the task, have them begin.
10. As the students work, circulate, answer questions and note areas for later work.
11. As students finish the main task, have them continue by doing the *Try this!* task. Have them list foods, sports, entertainers and places they like and dislike. They then poll other students.
12. Do consolidation, correction and expansion as desired.

General Notes

• This activity can be done either in large groups or as a whole class.
• Normally, reasons are given when refusing an invitation. Not to do so is considered by many people to be rude.
• See the introduction (• **corrections**) for suggestions on ways to correct student errors.

Answer Key

Answers will vary.

See box at the top of the page for sample conversations.

Notes

CHECK YOURSELF

Find a sentence with a similar meaning. Put the words in order. There is one extra word in each group. (2 points each = 12 points)

1. Let's go to a movie.
   How about a movie? ____________ [movie, when, about, a, how]
2. That sounds like fun.
   ____________ [idea, want, that's, good, a]
3. I don't feel like staying home.
   ____________ [want, somewhere, to, going I, go]
4. I don't like that.
   ____________ [interesting, not, in, I'm, interested, that]
5. I saw it last week.
   ____________ [already, I've, seen, been, it]
6. When shall we go?
   ____________ [time, want, left, you, go, what, to, do]
7. Sorry, but I can't.
   ____________ [I, afraid, I'm, plans, other, busy, have]

Circle the correct words. (8 points)

- [Do / Would / Will] you like to go to a movie tomorrow night?
- ■ What's [on / movie / that] ?
- *Summer Romance* is on [in / at / to] the Regency.
- ■ I [won't / doesn't / don't] really like love stories.
- Well, [how about / let's / why don't] *Batman Two?*
- ■ That [looks / is / sounds] good. What time [do / shall / will] we go?
- The last show is at 8:55. [How about / Let's / We will] meet at 7:00 and have dinner first.
- ■ Fine. See you tomorrow.

Your score

Procedure

Exercise one.

1. T: *Look at page 73.* Point to the first exercise. T: *Find a sentence with a meaning similar to the sentence by the number. Put the words in the right order. There is one extra word in each group.*

2. (Optional) T: *Number one: Let's go to a movie. What sentence has the same meaning?* Encourage students to answers (A: How about a movie?). Gesture for them to write the sentence on the line. T: *The extra word is "when."*

3. T: *Do 2-7 the same way.*

Exercise two.

1. Point to the second exercise. T: *Find the conversation. Circle the correct words.*

2. (Optional:) Point to the first line. T: *(Blank)____ you like to go to a movie tomorrow night? Which word goes in the blank?* Encourage the students to answer. (A: Would). Gesture for them to circle the word.

3. T: *Find the rest of the conversation.*

You may wish to assign the page as homework.

In-class Follow-up

• T: *Work in pairs. Did you both get the same answers?* As students compare their answers, circulate to make sure that all students have completed the homework. You may wish to have some students write their answers on the board.

• T: *Work in pairs. Practice the conversations in part two.*

General Notes

• The "Check yourself" pages are each worth 20 points. The sentences in the first activity are worth two points each. Each item in the second activity is worth one point. If you are giving grades, you may wish to keep track of student scores.

Answer Key

Exercise one:

1. How about a movie?
2. That's a good idea.
3. I want to go somewhere.
4. I'm not interested in that.
5. I've already seen it.
6. What time do you want to go?
7. I'm afraid I have other plans.

Exercise two:

•Would you like to go to a movie tomorrow night?

•What's on?

•*Summer Romance* is on at the Regency.

•I don't really like love stories.

•Well, how about *Batman Two?*

•That sounds good. What time shall we go?

•The last show is at 8:55. Let's meet at 7:00 and have dinner first.

•Fine. See you tomorrow.

Notes

Unit 9 What are you going to do?

LISTENING Talking about plans

Getting ready

Here are some ways of talking about what you plan to do.

I'll probably go to the beach.
I might go to a movie.
I think I'll go to the museum.
I don't know what I'll do—maybe go to a baseball game.
If the weather is good, I'll go to the park.

What are you going to do this weekend? Write four things.

I'm going to ______________________.

I'll probably ______________________.

I might ______________________.

I think I'll ______________________.

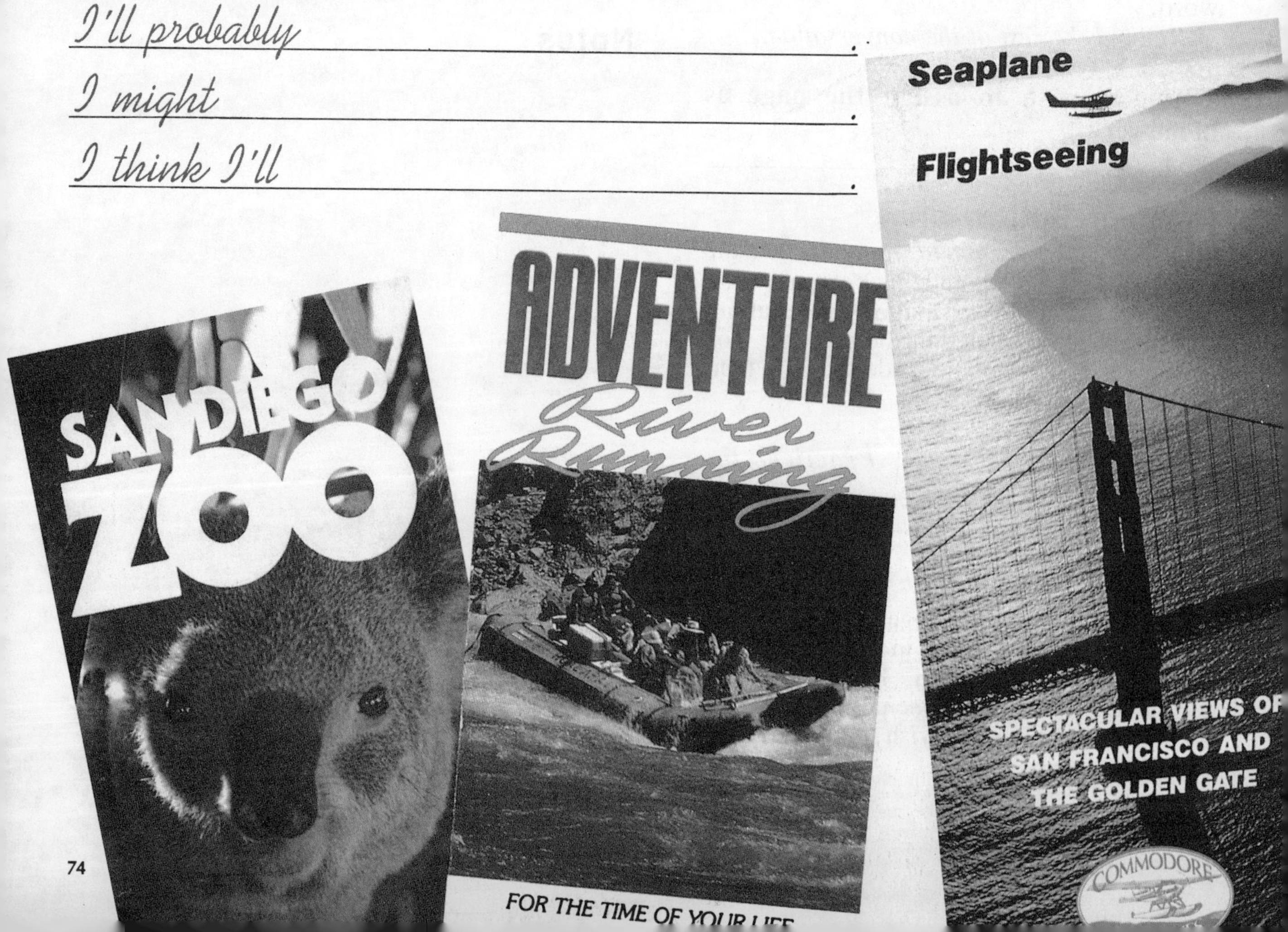

Objective: The students will identify where people are going, staying and what they are planning to do during upcoming vacations.
Function: talk about plans
Structures: *will* and *going to* future, present continuous as future
Vocabulary Area: vacation plans, accommodation

Procedure

1. Do the optional warm-up activity listed below.
2. T: *Open your books to page 74. Look at the travel brochures.*
3. T: *You will hear some people talking about vacation plans.*
4. (Optional). If your students find listening very difficult, do the "additional preparation" exercise below.
5. T: *Look at "Getting Ready" on page 74. These are some ways of talking about what you plan to do.* Play the first part of the tape.
6. T: *What are you going to do this weekend? Write four things.*
7. (Optional) Have several students tell you what they wrote and have other students who wrote the same thing raise their hands.
8. T: *Look at the "First Listening"on page 75. Listen. Where will these people go? Where will they stay? What will they do?* Play the "First Listening" segment of the tape. You may want students to do this in pairs so they can help each other. You may wish to stop after each item to check.
9. (Optional) T: *Work in pairs. Did you both get the same answers?*
10. Play the tape again if necessary.
11. Check by asking the students the questions (e.g., T: *Where will Brenda go?* A: Los Angeles.) and eliciting their answers OR by having students work in groups of 2-4. They should compare answers and ask you about any they couldn't catch. (See the answer key on the next page.)

Additional Preparation

Write "Places to stay" and "Ways to travel" on the chalkboard. Students work in pairs to make a list of as many options for each as they can.

Possible answers:
Places to stay: hotel, motel, campground, friend's house, with relatives, bed and breakfast, youth hostel.
Ways to travel: car, plane, train, bus, bicycle, boat, on foot.

General Notes

• When you ask the students to think of places people stay when they travel, they may stop after they think of "hotels" and "motels." You may want to give them one or two less common examples (a bed and breakfast home, youth hostels, camping) and make the second step (above) a contest to see who can think of the most places.

Optional Warm-up Activity

...and after that? Work in pairs. One student begins a story (real or fictitious) about her weekend plans. After the first sentence, that student's partner asks "and after that?" The student continues the story. Each time she finishes a statement, the partner asks the same question. The speaking student's goal is to make as many statements as possible. The listening student counts the number of statements that the partner makes. When the first student is unable to continue, they change roles. The student who makes the most statements is the winner.

Unit 9

First Listening

Some people are talking about their holiday plans.
Listen and fill in the table.

Brenda 	Los Angeles / hotel	
Sandra 	/	
Michael 	/	
Larry 	/	
Jack 	/	
Kim 	/	
Alan 	/	
Carol 	/	

Tapescript

Number 1: This is Brenda.
Brenda: I'm going to spend the weekend in Los Angeles. I really want to see Disneyland. In fact, I'm planning to stay at the new Disneyland Hotel. I've...I've been to Los Angeles before but I've never been to Disneyland, so I'm really excited.

Number 2: This is Sandra.
Sandra: I'm going to New York. I enjoy seeing Broadway plays and films and art museums and all that kind of thing. And a friend of mine from college lives in New York. She said that I can stay at her place while I'm there.

Number 3: This is Michael.
Michael: I'll be going to San Diego for a couple of weeks. I have some relatives there so I'll stay with them, save the money. I hope to visit the San Diego zoo, too. People say it's one of the best in the world. I also hope I'll be able to do some swimming in the ocean.

Number 4: This is Larry.
Larry: Well, I'm going to go camping with my brother. We're going to the Grand Canyon and we have a tent, so we'll use that. We're going out to Arizona by bus. We figure we'll go hiking and camping around the area. Both of us really love the outdoors and we can't wait.

Number 5: This is Jack.
Jack: My wife and I are planning to take a trip to Europe this year. Actually just to France. We're going to stay in an old hotel in France. We want to see a lot of historical places and small towns and villages and maybe take a bicycle trip around the south of France. We can't wait to get there. It'll be great.

Number 6: This is Kim.
Kim: I'm leaving for Taiwan next Friday. I have reservations at The Grand Hotel in Taipei. The Grand is a really famous hotel there. I'm going to do some business first and then do some sightseeing. I've never been to Taiwan but my friend says it's beautiful and just full of energy.

Number 7: This is Alan.
Alan: I'm going to visit my mom and dad. Ah, my parents live in Florida. And, so I want to do some swimming but mostly I just want to spend time with mom and dad. I haven't seen them for a while.

Number 8: This is Carol.
Carol: We're going to Mexico, to Acapulco. We've rented a beach house. I've been working too hard so I'm not going to do anything but sit on the beach and get a suntan. They have great seafood in Mexico, so I'm going to eat as much as I want and just relax.

Answer Key

First Listening:

1. Brenda: •Los Angeles/ hotel (the Disneyland Hotel) > go to Disneyland

2. Sandra: •New York / stay with a friend > go to Broadway plays, to films and to museums

3. Michael: •San Diego / stay with relatives > go to the zoo and go swimming in the ocean

4. Larry: •Grand Canyon / camping in a tent > go hiking and camping

5. Jack: •France / hotel > see historical places, small towns; take a bicycle trip

6. Kim: •Taiwan / hotel (the Grand Hotel) > business and sightseeing

7. Alan: •Florida / stay with his mother and father > go swimming and visit his parents

8. Carol: •Mexico (Acapulco) / beach house > sit on the beach, get a suntan , eat (seafood) and relax

CONVERSATION I'll probably visit my parents.

★ What are you planning to do during the ___1___ ?

◆ I'm not sure.
I'll probably visit ___2___
and do some ___3___ .
How about you?

★ I'm going to spend ___4___ in ___5___ .

◆ ___5___ ? Oh, really?
What are you going to do there?

★ I plan to ___6___ and
maybe ___7___ .

◆ ___8___ .

1. vacation summer holidays	2. my parents California my boyfriend/girlfriend	3. swimming sightseeing studying	4. two weeks some time a weekend
5. China Hawaii New York City	6. see some famous places relax go to the museums	7. watch TV try hang gliding go to a disco	8. What? Huh? You must be kidding!

Objective: The students will discuss future plans.
Functions: talk about future plans, express surprise
Structures: *will* and *going to* future
I'll visit my parents.
I'm going to China.

Procedure

1. T: *Open your books to page 76. Look at the picture. Where are these people?* (A: At a coffee shop). *This lesson is called, "I'll probably visit my parents." What do you think they are talking about?*
2. Play the tape. Have the students listen and read silently.
3. Answer questions about vocabulary and expressions.
4. (Optional) T: *Listen again. Repeat each line.* Play the conversation again. Pause after each sentence. Gesture for the students to repeat the sentences.
5. T: *Work in pairs.* (Gesture to show how you want the students paired.)
6. T: *Stand up. Practice the conversation.* (After a few minutes) T: *Change parts* (Point to your book to show that students who were playing the part on the left now do the part on the right.).
7. Encourage the students to substitute the words and phrases in the box at the bottom.
8. Encourage the students to make eye contact while they are practicing.
9. As the students work, circulate, answer questions and note areas for later work.
10. When students can do the conversation smoothly, encourage them to make changes other than those listed. This can be done by having them cover the substitution box with a piece of paper, a pencil case, etc. OR have them close their books and try to have similar conversations.

Conversation Variation

Have the students experiment with their voices as they practice. First, students playing the part on the right speak with very low voices while students playing the part on the left speak in high voices. After a few minutes, have them change so students playing the part on the right speak in high voices.

General Notes

• In general, "going to" is used when future events have already been decided or can be clearly seen to be coming. (e.g., "She's going to have a baby." "He's going to fall!")
• "Will" is used to talk about future events if the speaker is less certain (e.g., "I will visit my parents." is less definite than "I'm going to visit my parents." "Will" is also used at the moment of making a decision to do something (e.g., "I guess I will go.").
• The second speaker is surprised by the first speaker's plans. They either involve doing ordinary things in unusual places (watching TV in China) or doing things considered daring or unusual for the first speaker (going hang gliding). All the expressions in slot 8 are used for expressing surprise. "I don't believe you." would be too strong or rude in this situation.

Conversation Tapescript

Man: What are you planning to do during the vacation?
Woman: I'm not sure. I'll probably visit my parents and do some swimming. How about you?
M: I'm going to spend two weeks in China.
W: Oh, really? What are you going to do there?
M: I plan to see some famous places and maybe watch TV.
W: What?

DUET-A

Palm reading

What is this line called? What is the first line called? What does this line mean?			
You	will will probably won't are going to aren't going to	be become	very smart. rich.
		live a long time. get married when you are young.	

Some people believe that you can learn about your future from palm reading.
Look at the sentences below. Ask *B* for the missing information.

LINE 1 **LIFE LINE**

If this line is long, you will have a long life.

LINE 2 ____________ **LINE**

If this line is ____________ ,

you will ____________ .

LINE 3 **HEART LINE**

If you have a long, curved line, you are very kind.
If you have many small lines, you will have many romances.

LINE 4 ____________ **LINE**

If this line starts ____________ ,

you are going to be ____________ .

If it starts ________ from the bottom, you'll be

____________ .

LINE 5 **MARRIAGE LINES**

If your marriage lines are close together, you will probably get married when you are very young.

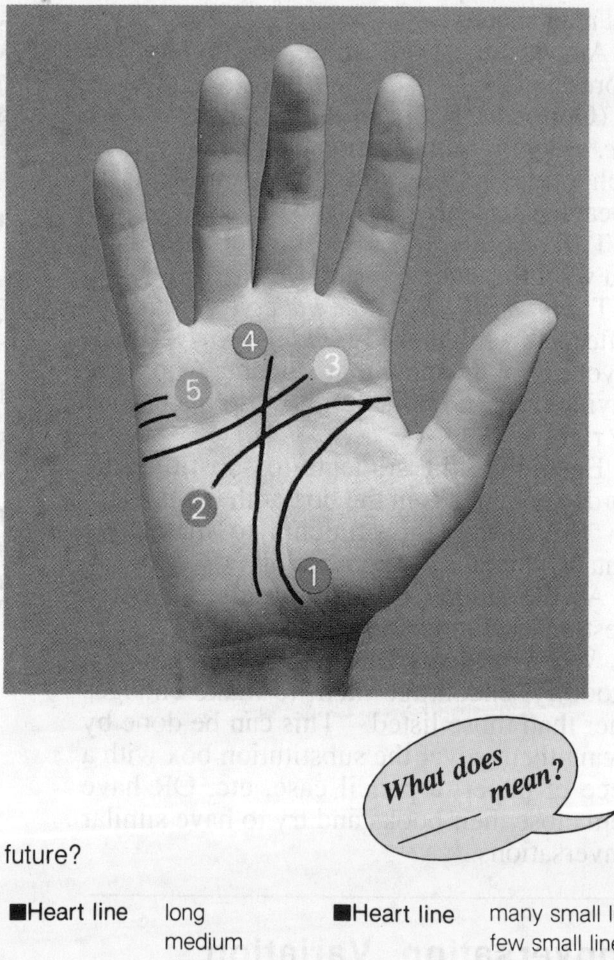

Look at *B*'s right hand. Circle the words. What is ***B***'s future?

■Life line	long medium short	■Head line	long medium short	■Heart line	long medium short	■Heart line	many small lines few small lines
■Sun line	starts at the bottom of ***B***'s hand starts far from the bottom			■Marriage lines	far apart close together		

Bonus! Make five more predictions about ***B***'s future. Does ***B*** agree?

Objective: The students will talk about the future with varying degrees of certainty.
Function: talk about / predict the future.
Structures: *going to* and *will* future
Classroom language: *What does ____ mean?*

Procedure

1. (Optional). T: *How do people try to find out about the future? How many ways do you know?* List their answers on the chalkboard. Possible answers: palm reading, horoscopes (astrology), crystal balls, reading tea leaves, etc. T: *Do you believe in any of these? Have you ever been to a fortune teller? What were you told?*
2. Divide the class into pairs. One student in each pair is **A**. The other is **B**. T: *Row one, you are* ***A's*** (Point to row one). *Row two, you are* ***B's*** (Point to row two). *Row three, you are* ***A's*** (etc.).
3. T: ***A's****, look at page 77.* ***B's****, look at page 78.*
4. Point out the language box at the top of the page. T: *Look at the box.* (Optional) *Listen and say.* Say the sentences in the box. Have students practice by repeating after you.
5. T: *Look at the page. Are there any words you don't know?*
6. Introduce the task. T: *You will learn how to read your partner's palm.*
7. While the other students watch, direct one pair through the first step of the exercise. T: (to any student **B**): *Look at line 1 in the picture. It is the "life line." Ask* ***A****, "What does this line mean?"* Prompt **A** to answer ("If this line is long, you will have a long life." Gesture for **B** to write it.
8. T: *Find out what the lines mean. Then read your partner's palm.* When the students understand the task, have them do it in pairs.
9. As the students work, circulate, answer questions and note areas for later work.
10. As students finish the main task, have them continue by doing the *Bonus!* task. Have them make five more predictions about their partners.
11. Do consolidation, correction and expansion as desired.

Grammar and Usage

• Though individual speakers may vary, *Will* plus the dictionary form of the verb (e.g., "You will probably be very smart.") is generally used for predictions or talking about decisions made at the moment (Thanks for the flowers. I'll put them in a vase.)
• *Be* plus *going to* is used to talk about a decision that has already been made (e.g., "I'm going to the United States next year."), especially when the speaker wants to stress his or her certainty of the thing happening. In the example of fortunetelling, the fortuneteller might use "going to" when he or she is very certain of the prediction.

General Notes

• Not all people have all the lines. Students should not worry if they are missing one or more.
• If some of your students are married, have them compare their own marriage lines to the facts. How many of those who got married when they were older have marriage lines that are far apart?
• While palm reading exists in many different cultures, specific ways to do it differ. In some cultures, the right hand indicates the future and the left hand indicates what has already happened. In other cultures, men read their right hands while women read their left.
• While most people are skeptical about attempts to forecast the future, many people enjoy speculating about the future and hearing about different methods like palm-reading and astrology.
• See the introduction (•Corrections) for suggestions on ways to correct during pair work.

Additional Activity

(This activity can be used anytime during this unit).

In five years... This is a dictation activity. Dictate the following sentences. Have the students complete them in whatever way they like. Then have them compare their answers in groups of three or four. Students should ask one follow-up question about each partner's response. (see next page)

Palm reading

DUET-B

What is this line called? What is the first line called? What does this line mean?			
You	will will probably won't are going to aren't going to	be become	very smart. rich.
		live a long time. get married when you are young.	

Some people believe that you can learn about your future from palm reading.
Look at the sentences below. Ask *A* for the missing information.

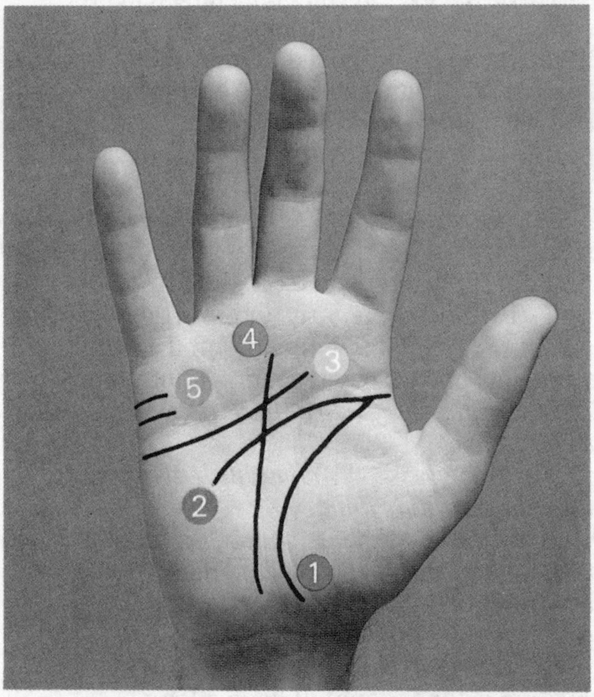

LINE 1 — LIFE LINE

If this line is ______________ ,
______________________________ .

LINE 2 — HEAD LINE

If this line is long, you will be very intelligent.

LINE 3 — ______________ LINE

If you have a long, curved line, you are ________ .

If you have many small lines, you ______________
______________________________ .

LINE 4 — SUN LINE

If this line starts at the bottom of your hand, you are going to be rich and successful.
If it starts far from the bottom, you'll be successful when you are old.

LINE 5 — ______________ LINES

If these lines are ______________ , you will probably get married when you are young.

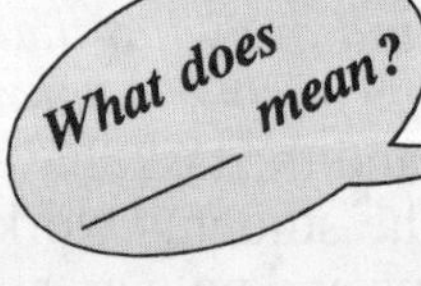

Look at *A*'s right hand. Circle the words. What is ***A***'s future?

■Life line	long medium short	■Head line	long medium short	■Heart line	long medium short	■Heart line	many small lines few small lines
■Sun line	starts at the bottom of ***A***'s hand starts far from the bottom			■Marriage lines	far apart close together		

Bonus! Make five more predictions about ***A***'s future.
Does ***A*** agree?

1. In five years I will blank.

2. This weekend, I'm going to blank.

3. Someday, this school will probably blank.

4. I'm going to blank after class today.

5. In a few years, my teacher will blank.

Expansion Activity

What are they going to do?

Collect magazine pictures of people interacting, being in unusual places or doing unusual things. There should be one picture for each person in the class.

Give one picture to each student. Students work in groups of three. They look at the pictures and make up a story about the people in the pictures. The story should tell what is happening now and what will happen next.

Each group joins another group and tells their story. The new members listen. After the story has been told, the new members retell the story, changing at least five facts.

Note: Collecting enough magazine pictures can be time consuming. To save time, have each student bring two or three magazine pictures to use with the activity.

Fluency Frames:

Three "fluency frames" are introduced in the "extra activities" sections of Units 1, 2 and 3. Use any one of the "frames" with this topic for Unit 9:

• *My plans for the weekend* or
My plans for the next holiday.

Answer Key

Checking answers as a whole class should not be necessary. You may wish to have the pair look at both books to make sure they have correctly filled in all blanks. Answers for A's page are on page 78 and answers for B's page are on page 77.

Notes

SOLO Announcement

Some students are going to have a beach party.
They wrote an announcement and placed it on the bulletin board.
There are *FIVE MISTAKES* in the announcement.
Circle the mistakes.

Attention English Students

S.C. approved 6 - 7

Beach Party!

We are going to hold a party at Kincade Beach on Sunday afternoon, June 15.

We are going to bicycle from the Student Center. Let's meet there at 10p.m. It will probably be hot so be sure to wear warm clothing.

We plan to have a cookout on the beach. All the food is going to be provided by the Student Association. There will be swimming and sailing. Don't forget to bring your swimsuit and hiking shoes. You'll need to bring your own hot dogs, soda, etc.

If you are coming, please sign up before Wednesday, June 18.

Write an announcement for a different event.
(For example, a picnic, a camping trip, a volleyball game)
Include these things:

- *What* the event is
- *When* and *where* it will be held
- *Who* should come
- *What* people should bring

Objective: The students will read an announcement and identify errors. They will write an announcement for a different event.
Function: describe future plans, give instructions, remind someone to do something
Structures: *will* and *going to* future, present continuous as future, prepositions of place and time: *at, on*

Procedure

1. T: *Open your books to page 79. Look at the picture. This is an announcement for a beach party. There are five mistakes in the ad. Read it. Circle the mistakes.*
2. T: *Now, write an announcement for a different event like a picnic, a camping trip or a volleyball game. Include the following things: what the event is, who should come, when and where it will be held, what (if anything) people should bring.*

You may wish to assign this activity as homework.

In-class Follow-up

Students work in pairs. Students change their own announcements to include about five mistakes. They then read their announcements to their partners. Partners try to identify the mistakes.

General Notes

• The "S.C. approved" stamp in the corner means that the students had permission from the University Student Center or Student Council to put the announcement on the bulletin board.
• "Dorm" in the sample paragraph below means "dormitory", a university residence hall.

Optional Skill-building Activity

Skill: scanning for specific information

Have the students write five comprehension (test) questions about their own paragraphs. They then exchange paragraphs and questions with a partner. The partners read the questions first and then quickly read the paragraphs and find the answers.

Answer Key

Task one:
Mistakes:
1. meet at 10 p.m. (afternoon picnic)
2. wear warm clothing (it will be hot)
3. hiking shoes (not needed at the beach)
4. You'll need to bring your own hot dogs, soda, etc. (All the food is going to be provided by the Student Association.)
5. sign up before Wednesday, June 18 (party is June 15).

Task two:
Answers will vary.
Example:
We going to have a picnic on Sunday, June 12 at 1 p.m. All residents of the dorm are invited. Meet in front of Bayside Park at 1 p.m. Bring your own hot dogs and hamburgers. The dorm will provide drinks and salads.

Predictions

- There might be…
- There will probably be…
- People will probably…
- I think that…..will happen.
- In ten years, perhaps…
- I predict that…
- I bet that people will…
- I think the world will…

What will life be like 10 years from now? 20 years from now? 100 years from now?

Work in groups of four.

Make predictions for your city, your country, and the world.

Change groups. Tell your predictions to the members of your new group.

How many people agree with your predictions?

Try This!

Your group is going to be given $100,000.
You must spend it in one month. You can not put it in the bank.
What are you going to buy? What will you do? Make a list.

Objective: The students will learn to discuss and predict future events.
Function: talk about / predict the future, give an opinion.
Structures: *will* and *going to* future, time clauses
Classroom language:
Could you repeat that?

Procedure

1. (Optional) T: *What are the most important changes that have taken place in the past 50 years?* (After several students have given ideas, ask the next question.) *What changes do you think will take place in the next 50 years?* (Don't specify "this city" or "this country" yet. You just want them thinking about the topic generally.)
2. T: *Look at page 80. You will predict the future.*
3. T: *Look at the language box at the top of the page. Are there any words you don't know?* Answer questions about vocabulary.
4. (Optional) T: *Look at the box. Listen and say.* Say the sentences in the box. Have students practice by repeating after you.
5. Divide the class into groups of 4.
6. Introduce the task. T: *You will make predictions about this city, this country and the world.*
7. While the other students watch, direct one group through the first step of the exercise. T: *What do you think will happen in this city in 10 years?* Encourage answers. When they agree, gesture for them to write it. T: *Do the rest the same way.*
8. When the students understand the task, have them begin.
9. As the students work, circulate, answer questions and note areas for later work.
10. As students finish, introduce the next step. T: *Change groups. Read your predictions. Do your partners agree?*
11. As students finish the main task, have them continue by doing the *Try this!* task. Have them image that they will be given $100,000 (or the equivalent in local currency). What will they buy?
12. Do consolidation, correction and expansion as desired.

Grammar and Usage Notes

- See Pairwork 9 for notes on "will" and "going to."

General Notes

- Encourage the students to give reasons for their predictions and to make them as specific as possible.
- When students are doing the *Try this!* be sure to word the statement "Your group is going to be given $100,000. What are you going to buy?" rather than "If you got $100,000, what would you do?" so they use the future tenses rather than the conditional.
- If certain students tend to monopolize discussions, make them "discussion monitors." The job of "discussion monitor" is to make sure that every member of the group gives an opinion about each place at every time.
- Since this activity is designed to encourage fluency, corrections are not recommended at this time.

Answer Key

Answers will vary.

Examples:
In ten years, this city is going to be much bigger.
I think that this country will be much richer.
I predict the world will be much safer in ten years.

CHECK YOURSELF

Match the phrases with similar meanings. (10 points)

__c__ 1. She's going tomorrow.	a. I'd like to...
_____ 2. Don't forget to...	b. in 10 years...
_____ 3. She may...	~~c.~~ She's going to go.
_____ 4. I'm planning to...	d. I must...
_____ 5. Maybe I will...	e. I don't really know.
_____ 6. 10 years from now...	f. Remember to...
_____ 7. I bet that...	g. I'm going to...
_____ 8. I'll probably...	h. I might...
_____ 9. I want to...	i. I think that...
_____ 10. I have to...	j. I'm almost sure I'll...
_____ 11. I'm not sure.	k. Perhaps she'll...

Write will or be (is, am, are) going to in the blanks. (10 points)

1. She is pregnant. She __________ have a baby in June.
2. After I graduate I __________ probably work for a bank.
3. I __________ watch TV tonight.
4. If you don't drive more slowly you __________ have an accident.
5. Watch out! You __________ hit that truck.
6. If your life line is long, your life __________ be long too.
7. Those clouds are really black. I think it __________ rain.
8. This city __________ probably have a population of 1,000,000 in ten years.
9. If I don't feel better by tomorrow, maybe I __________ stay home.
10. He bought the present yesterday. He __________ give it to her tonight.

Remember

- Use **going to** when you are sure something will happen.
- Use **will** if you are less certain or at the time you decide something.

Your score

Procedure

Exercise one.

1. T: *Look at page 81.* Point to the first exercise. T: *Match the phrases with similar meanings.*

2. (Optional) T: *Number one: She's going tomorrow. Which sentence on the right has the same meaning?* Encourage the students to answer (A: [c.] She's going to go.). Gesture for them to write "c" on the line.

3. T: *Do 2-11 the same way.*

Exercise two.

1. Point to the second exercise. T: *Finish the sentences. Write "will" or "be (is, am, are) going to" in the blanks.*

2. T: *Look at the "remember" box. Remember that you use "going to" when you are sure something will happen. You use "will" if you are less certain or at the time you decide.*

3. (Optional:) Point to item one. T: *Number one. She is pregnant. She (blank) have a baby in June. What goes in the blank?* Encourage the students to answer. (A: is going to). Gesture for them to write "is going to" in the space provided.

4. T: *Do 2-10 the same way.*

You may wish to assign the page as homework.

In-class Follow-up

• T: *Work in pairs. Did you both get the same answers?* As students compare their answers, circulate to make sure that all students have completed the homework. You may wish to have some students write their answers on the board.

General Notes

• The "Check yourself" pages are each worth 20 points. Each item is worth one point. If you are giving grades, you may wish to keep track of student scores.

Answer Key

Exercise one:

1. c. She's going to go.
2. f. Remember to…
3. k. Perhaps she'll…
4. g. I'm going to…
5. h. I might…
6. b. in 10 years…
7. i. I think that...
8. j. I'm almost sure I'll...
9. a. I'd like to...
10. d. I must...
11. e. I don't really know.

Exercise two:

1. She's pregnant. She is going to have a baby in June.
2. After I graduate I will probably work for a bank.
3. I am going to watch TV tonight.
4. If you don't drive more slowly you will have an accident.
5. Watch out! You are going to hit that truck.
6. If your life line is long, your life will be long too.
7. Those clouds are really black. I think it is going to rain.
8. This city will probably have a population of 1,000,000 in ten years.
9. If I don't feel better by tomorrow, maybe I will stay home.
10. He bought the present yesterday. He is going to give it to her tonight.

Unit 10 How much is this?

LISTENING Getting the price

Getting ready

There are different ways to say prices.
For example, you can say $57.25 as:

—Fifty-seven twenty-five
—Fifty-seven dollars and twenty-five cents
—Fifty-seven and a quarter

Say these prices: $1.95 $3.75 $17.50 $85.00

How much do you *THINK* these items might cost?

a magazine	between	$1.50	and	$2.50
a jacket	between	______	and	______
an English phrase book	between	______	and	______
a hotel bill for one night	between	______	and	______
dry cleaning for one dress	between	______	and	______
a roll of film	between	______	and	______
a bus tour of a city	between	______	and	______
a service charge for traveler's checks	between	______ %	and	______ %

Objective: The students will identify prices of items and services.
Function: ask for/give information, shopping routines
Structures: WH-questions, numbers, comparatives.
Vocabulary Area: shopping

Procedure

1. Do the optional warm-up activity listed below.
2. T: *Open your books to page 82. Look at the pictures.*
3. T: *You will hear some people shopping.*
4. (Optional) If your students find listening very difficult, do the "additional preparation" exercise below.
5. T: *Look at "Getting Ready" on page 82. There are different ways to say prices.* Play the first part of the tape.
6. T: *Say the prices. How much do you think these items might cost?* You may want to have them do this step in pairs.
7. (Optional) Have the students tell you how much they thought the items would cost. You may want to write the price range (the highest and lowest price for each item) on the chalkboard.
8. T: *Look at the "First Listening" on page 83. Listen. Circle the prices.* Play the "First Listening" segment of the tape. You may want students to do this in pairs so they can help each other. You may wish to stop after each item to check.
9. (Optional) T: *Work in pairs. Did you both get the same answers?*
10. Play the tape again if necessary.
11. Check by asking the students the questions (e.g., T: *How much was Newsweek magazine?* A: $2.75.) and eliciting their answers OR by having students work in groups of 2-4. They should compare answers and ask you about any they couldn't catch. (See the answer key on the next page.)

Additional Preparation

Tell the students they will hear people buying things. Before they open their books, play the "First Listening." For each item, students should try to identify the following:

Is the shopper a man or a woman?
What do they think the person is buying?

General Notes

• Price range varies greatly so some students may resist trying to guess. It may be helpful to give them examples from both ends of the range (e.g., How much would a jacket cost at a discount store? How much would one cost at a very expensive boutique or department store?).
• If your students are not familiar with the value of U.S. money, you may want to tell the students the value of U.S.$1 compared to their national currency. The students may want to figure the price ranges in their national currency and convert those prices to U.S. $.
• In segment 2, the bank charges a "service charge" for traveler's checks, one percent of the total. This is standard.
• "Exposures" (segment 5) refers to the number of photos that can be taken, the "size" of the roll of film.

Optional Warm-up Activity

Shopping - comparative blackboard race. Work in groups. Make 3-6 (depending on your class size and the size of your chalkboard) sets of index cards with the following words written on them (one per card): colorful, big, small, interesting, beautiful, expensive, cheap, new, old, popular, easy, good, quality, variety, selection, fashionable. Mix up the cards so each set is in a different order. If necessary, teach the meanings of the words on the cards.

Divide the class into teams. You should have the same number of teams as sets of cards. Set the cards face down on chairs that are an equal distance from the blackboard (at least 10 feet/ 3 meters is ideal). Students line up behind the chairs. When you say "go", the first student from each team looks at the first card, runs to the blackboard and writes a sentence using the word to compare two stores or items of clothing (e.g., Leather coats are more expensive than cloth coats. [Store A] has better quality than [Store B].) That student then runs back to the group and gives the chalk to the next student, who picks up the next card and continues the process. The items compared can be used only one time by each team. The team with the most correct sentences is the winner.

First Listening

Listen. Circle the prices.

1.

2.

3.

4.

5.
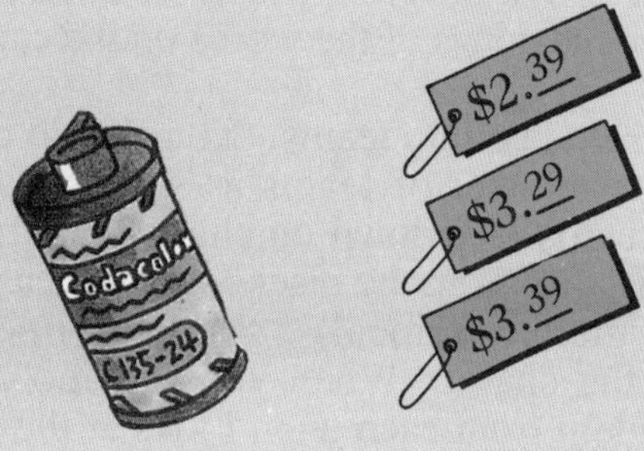

6.

7.

8.
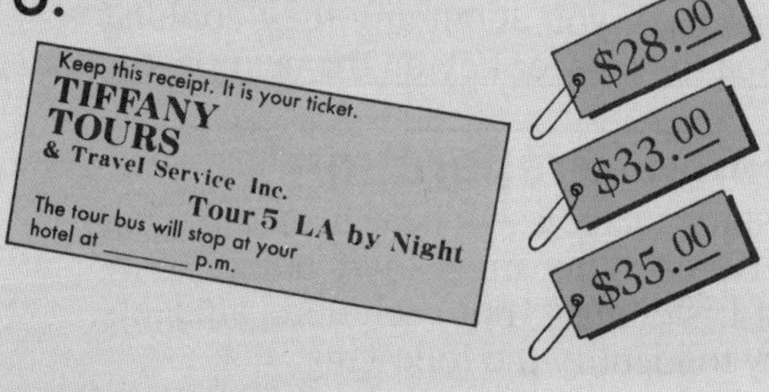

Tapescript

Number 1.
Man: Excuse me...uh...you got Newsweek magazine?
Clerk: Yeah, it's a two dollars and seventy-five cents.
M: Two seventy-five? OK.
C: OK. And a quarter's your change.
M: Thanks.

Number 2.
Teller: Good afternoon, may I help you?
Customer: Yes, I'd like travelers checks please. American Express traveler's checks.
T: OK, and in what denomination?
C: Uh, two hundred fifty dollars...uh, in fifties.
T: In fifties? OK, two hundred fifty dollars in fifties.
C: Right.
T: There's a two dollar fifty cent service charge -- that's 1 percent -- so it comes to two hundred fifty two fifty.
C: Two fifty two fifty.
T: Thank you. Now could you please sign them on this line before you leave the bank?
C: All right. Do you have a pen?
T: Here you are.
C: Thank you.

Number 3.
Man: Excuse me. Could you help me a minute?
Clerk: Yes, Sir. What can I do for you?
M: How much is this jacket?
C: Usually that's eighty-five fifty, but we have it on sale now for just seventy-two ninety-five. It's a very good buy.
M: Seventy-two ninety-five? That is a good buy.

Number 4.
Clerk: Front desk.
Guest: Hello. This is Mrs. Schumacher in 317 (Uh-huh). I have a dress that I need to have pressed by tomorrow morning. Can you get it to me buy eight?
C: Yes, overnight service. That's nine dollars fifty cents. It'll be ready by seven a.m.
G: Nine-fifty? OK. Could you send someone up for it?
C: Yes. I'll send somebody up right away.
G: Thank you.

Number 5.
Clerk: Can I help you?
Woman: I want 200 ASA film.
C: How many exposures will that be?
W: Um... twenty-four.
C: That's three thirty-nine a roll. How many would you like?
W: Just one roll.
C: OK. Here you are. That's three thirty-nine.

Number 6.
Man: Excuse me. How much is this phrasebook?
Clerk: Ah, let's see. That's six twenty-five.
M: Six dollars twenty-five cents? Do you have any that are cheaper?
C: I'm sorry, that's the only one we have.
M: OK, I'll take it.

Number 7.
Guest: Yes, I have a reservation for tonight and tomorrow night.
Clerk: Ah, your name please?
G: Smith. William B. Smith.
C: Um, just a minute. Yes, Smith. That was for a single?
G: Yes, yes. What was the rate on that?
C: It's one hundred and fifteen dollars.
G: I'm sorry. Did you say one fifteen or one fifty?
C: One fifteen.
G: Yes, that's fine.
C: OK, fine, we'll check you in.

Number 8.
Clerk: Yes, sir?
Man: Yes. I'd like some information about night bus tours of Los Angeles.
C: Uh-huh. Yeah. We've got two tours. There's a $28.00 tour and a $33.00 tour. The 33 is with dinner.
M: The 33 dollar one is with dinner? How about the 28 dollar tour?
C: Same tour. Just the food is not included, the meal is not included.
M: Oh. Well, I'd like the 33 dollar tour, the one with dinner, please.
C: OK.

Answer Key

Getting Ready
Answers will vary.

First Listening:

1. magazine: $2.75
2. traveler's checks: $252.50
3. a jacket: $72.95
4. pressing (ironing) a dress: $9.50
5. film: $3.39
6. a phrase book: $6.25
7. a hotel room: $115
8. a tour: $33.00

CONVERSATION May I help you?

★ May I help you?

◆ I'm looking for a ___1___ .

★ What ___2___ ?

◆ I'm not sure. ___3___ , I guess.

★ Here's a nice one.

◆ Hmm... This is ___4___ .
Do you have any that are ___5___ ?

★ This one is much ___6___ .

◆ How much is it?

★ It's ___7___ dollars.

◆ Did you say ___8___ ?

★ ___7___ .

◆ Oh.

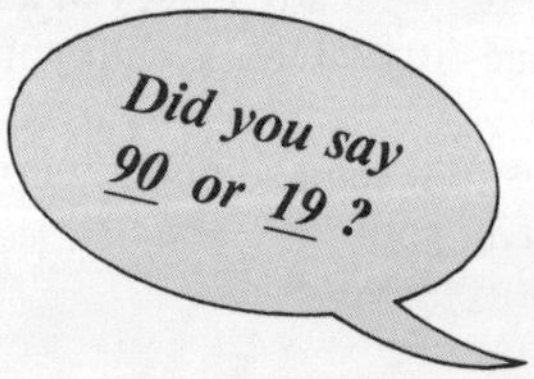

1. sweater
   jacket
   shirt
2. size
   kind
   color
3. Medium
   Leather
   Blue
4. gray
   150 dollars
   silk
5. more colorful
   less expensive
   less difficult to take care of
6. brighter
   cheaper
   easier
7. $90.00
   62.50
   30.00
8. ninety or nineteen
   sixty-two fifty or sixty-two fifteen
   thirteen or thirty

Objective: The students will practice shopping for things.
Functions: shopping routines: offering assistance, asking/telling about size/price/color/kind, ask for clarification
Structures: comparative adjectives: *This is cheaper. This is more colorful.*
present continuous: *I'm looking for...*
Classroom language:
Did you say ___ or ___?

Procedure

1. T: *Open your books to page 84. Look at the picture. Where are these people?* (A: At a store.) *What do you think she is shopping for?*
2. Play the tape. Have the students listen and read silently.
3. Answer questions about vocabulary and expressions.
4. (Optional) T: *Listen again. Repeat each line.* Play the conversation again. Pause after each sentence. Gesture for the students to repeat the sentences.
5. T: *Work in pairs.* (Gesture to show how you want the students paired.)
6. T: *Stand up. Practice the conversation.* (After a few minutes) T: *Change parts* (Point to your book to show that students who were playing the part on the left now do the part on the right.).
7. Encourage the students to substitute the words and phrases in the box at the bottom.
8. Encourage the students to make eye contact while they are practicing.
9. As the students work, circulate, answer questions and note areas for later work.
10. When students can do the conversation smoothly, encourage them to make changes other than those listed. This can be done by having them cover the substitution box with a piece of paper, a pencil case, etc. OR have them close their books and try to have similar conversations.

Conversation Variation

Have the students playing the part on the left imagine that they are "high-pressure salespeople." They speak quickly with strong voices. Students playing the customer are very relaxed. They speak slowly.

General Notes

• Slots 5 and 6 contain comparative forms. You may wish to remind students that generally one-syllable adjectives and adjectives ending in "y" take "er" to become comparative (bright-brighter, pretty-prettier). For two- or three-syllable adjectives, add "more" before the word (more colorful).
• Remind the students to listen to their partners so that their choices for slots 7 and 8 correspond.

Conversation Tapescript

Clerk: May I help you?
Customer: I'm looking for a sweater.
Clerk: What size?
Customer: I'm not sure. Medium, I guess.
Clerk: Here's a nice one.
Customer: Hmm. This is gray. Do you have any that are more colorful?
Clerk: This one is much brighter.
Customer: How much is it?
Clerk: It's ninety dollars.
Customer: Did you say ninety or nineteen?
Clerk: Ninety.
Customer: Oh.

DUET-AB

Shopping spree!

You are going to play a shopping game.

You must buy these things:

A's shopping list	*B*'s shopping list
___ some film (24 or 36 exposures)	___ a sweater (red or blue?)
___ a CD player (What brand?)	___ a dictionary (What kind?)
___ a drill. (What kind?)	___ U-2's new album (CD or tape?)
___ a notebook (How many pages?)	___ 1 dozen (12) roses (What color?)
___ a pair of shoes (What kind?)	___ some aspirin (How many?)
___ a pair of jeans (What brand?)	___ a pair of boots (What kind?)

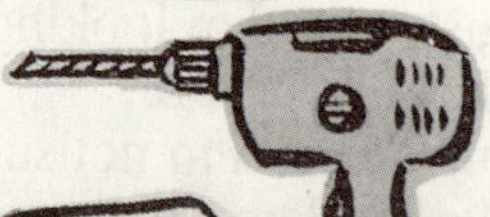

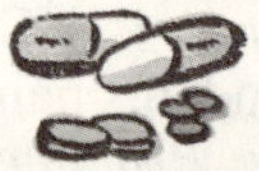

Who bought all 6 things first? ______

How to play:

Use ***A***'s book (this page) for your shopping lists.
Use ***B***'s book (page 86) for the game board.

space

spaces

1. Roll dice or flip a coin to see how many spaces to move. Use a marker (eraser, coin, etc.) to show where you are.
2. When you land on a store, you are the **shopper.** Your partner is the **clerk.**
3. Follow the "shopping conversation" on page 86.
   - Decide the kind you want to buy.
   - If you don't want to buy anything at that store, say, "No, thank you. I'm just looking."
4. When you buy something, check (✓) it on your shopping list.
5. The first player to buy everything on the list wins.

Objective: The students will shop for things.
Function: shopping routines, ask for / state color, size, brand and type
Structures: present continuous
Vocabulary Area: shopping items

Procedure

Note: Unlike the other Duet activities, in this unit students both look at the same pages. The shopping lists and game rules are on page 85. The game board is on page 86.

1. Divide the class into pairs. One student in each pair is **A**. The other is **B.** T: *Row one, you are **A's*** (Point to row one). *Row two, you are **B's*** (Point to row two). *Row three, you are **A's*** (etc.).

2. T: *Look at page 85. This is Shopping Spree! It is a shopping game. Look at your shopping lists.* ***A****, your list is on the left.* ***B****, your list is on the right. You must buy everything on the list. You will decide what kind of each thing you want. For example,* ***A****, you want do buy film. Do you want 24 or 36 exposures?* ***B****, you want to buy a sweater. Do you want a red one or a blue one ?*

3. T: *Look at page 86. This is the Shopping Spree! game board. Are there any words you don't know?*

4. T: *Look at the language box at the top of page 86.* (Optional) *Listen and say.* Say the sentences in the box. Have students practice by repeating after you.

5. Introduce the game. T: *Use **A's** book for the shopping lists. Use **B's** book for the game board. You need a marker to show where you are on the board. Use an eraser or a coin.* Put your marker on "start." You will also need dice or a coin.*

6. While the other students watch, direct one pair through the first part of the game. T: (to any student **A**): *Roll the dice (or flip the coin). Move that many spaces. You are at the* _*(store name)*_ *. Look at your list. Do you want to buy anything here?*

(If yes, point to the language box to prompt the pair to go through the shopping routine at the top. T: *You bought* _*(item)*_ *so check it on your shopping list.*

(If no, prompt them to say the last line of the language box: **B:** May I help you? **A:** No, thank you. I'm just looking.)

7. T: *Take turns. The first player to buy all six things is the winner.* When the students understand the task, have them do it in pairs.

8. As the students work, circulate, answer questions and note areas for later work.

9. As students finish the main task, have them continue by doing the *Bonus!* task. Have them list the five stores they like the best and write the reasons.

10. Do consolidation, correction and expansion as desired.

General Notes

• If dice are not available, students can flip coins. The "head" side means go one space. The "tail" side means go two spaces. If your coins do not have a head on one side, decide which side the students will use as a head.

• If neither dice nor coins are available, have students move five spaces each time. Eventually they will land on all the squares.

• The students will need to go around the game board several times to buy everything on their lists.

• If you want students to practice asking prices while the play, have students decide the prices for their partner's items (i.e., **A** sets the prices for the items on **B**'s list.). Add the lines, "How much is it? It's _(price)_." to the language box. Students write the price paid on the shopping list.

• Much shopping language is formulaic. "I'm looking for a sweater " is a very common way to ask a clerk's help in finding a sweater. "I'm just looking" announces that the speaker wishes no help, but prefers to browse.

• "Shopping spree" is an idiom which means to buy many things without thinking much about price.

• See the introduction (•Corrections) for suggestions on ways to correct during pair work.

Additional Activity

(This activity can be used anytime during this unit).

My numbers. Understanding spoken numbers is often difficult for students long after they know the numbers in lists or in isolation. Ask the students what numbers are important to them. On the chalkboard, list

DUET-AB

The Shopping spree! game board

Read the instructions on page 85.

Shopping conversation:

Store clerk	Shopper	
May I help you?	I'm looking for I'd like	a sweater. some film.
What I color? How many exposures?	Blue, please. 24, please.	
Here you are.	Thank you.	
You're welcome.		

OR

May I help you?	No, thank you. I'm just looking.

Bonus! What five stores do you both like the best? List them. Why do you like them? Write your reasons.

types of numbers they suggest (telephone number, student identification number, birth date, video club membership number, postal code, etc.). Tell the students to write down five numbers that are important to them. Write the following on the board:

I think _____ is your _____ number.
number

What does _____ mean?
number

Have students dictate their number to partners. The partner write the numbers and guesses what each number means. If the partner is unable to guess, "What does _____ mean?" can be used.
After the numbers have been dictated, students change partners and continue.

Answer Key

Since students are generating original language, **answers will vary**. They should follow the basic dialogue in the language box on the top of page 86.

Expansion Activity

Word chains
Make two or three copies of the "Word chains" worksheet for each student. Students look through unit 10 (or Units 1-10) and write a new word in the first box of each chain. In pairs, students work with one sheet at a time. They look at their partner's sheet and write a word connected with the word their partner wrote. Then the first partner write a word connected with the second word. It does not need to be connected with the first word (e.g., hardware > drill > English class > study > college > graduate, etc.). They do this with each sheet.
Variation 1: Have students say a sentence for each new word.
Variation 2: Instead of using the worksheets, have them do the activity orally, counting how many new words they add to each chain.

Word chains

This is a vocabulary review game.

Write a word in the top box. Use words that you know but that are a little difficult.

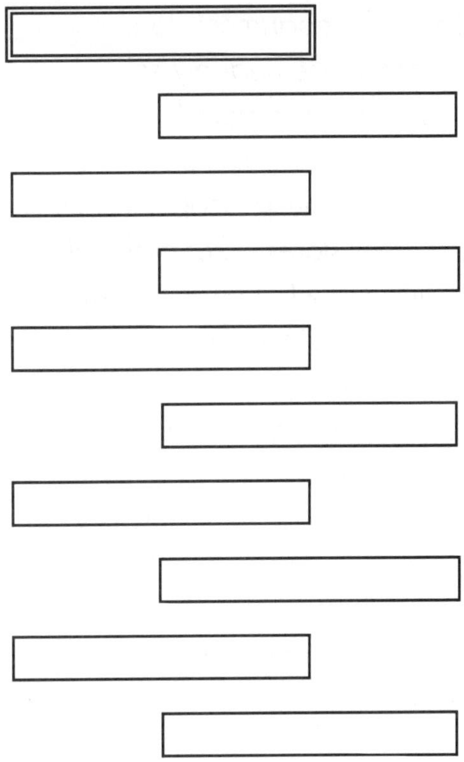

Work with a partner.
Look at one of your partner's words.
What word does it make you think of?
Write it. Use the word in a sentence.

Now you partner looks at your word and thinks of another word.

SOLO My favorite department store

Read what Ken wrote.

My favorite department store is Marui. There is one near my school. It is very popular with people my age. They have a bigger selection and a wider variety of young people's clothes than most other stores. That makes it easier to find just what I want. They have a wide selection of designer fashions. I especially like Issey Miyake's designs. Of course, they're more expensive than other clothes but the quality is better. Besides, I think they are more fashionable than a lot of cheaper clothes.

I love shopping at Marui.

Write about your favorite department store. Use some of these words:

___ cheap	___ expensive	___ easy	___ good (better, best)
___ quality	___ variety	___ selection	___ fashionable

Objective: The students will read and write about favorite department stores.
Function: describe a place, give reasons
Structures: comparatives, clauses of reason, qualitative adjectives

Procedure

1. (Optional) T: *What is your favorite department store? Why?*
2. *Open your books to page 87. Look at the picture. This is a Marui Department Store in Tokyo. Read about it.*
3. T: *Now, think about your favorite department store. Why do you like it? Write about it. Use some of these words: cheap, expensive, easy, good, quality, variety, selection, fashionable.*

You may wish to assign this activity as homework.

In-class Follow-up

Group students according to the department stores they chose. The read their paragraphs and, based on what they wrote, make a list of all the reasons they like given stores. If too many students choose the same store, divide them into smaller groups. If some students were the only ones to pick a particular store, have them form a group and find reasons they prefer their choices to the more popular stores.

General Notes

- Ken's paragraph is about an actual Japanese department store popular with young people. One reason for Marui's popularity is that it offers credit cards to young people. They are easier to get than most other credit cards.
- "Selection" as used here refers to the range and number of clothing items available.

Optional Skill-building Activity

Skill: reading for details

Tell the students that you are going to read the paragraph that Ken wrote. You will intentionally make some "mistakes". The students should read along silently and, when they hear a mistake, circle it in their books. After you read the script (below), have them tell you the mistakes they found.

(Note: the "mistakes" are underline in the following script. As you read, do not stress the mistakes.)

Script:
My favorite appliance store is Marui. There is one near my house. It is very popular with people my age. They have a better selection and a wider variety of young people's goods than most other stores. They makes it easier to find just what I want. They have a wide selection of designer fashions. I especially like Pierre Cardin's designs. Of course, they're more expensive than other clothes but the style is better. Besides, I think they are just as good as a lot of cheaper clothes.
I love shopping at Macy's.

Variation: Have the students make their own changes and do the activity in pairs. Students read their "mistake" paragraphs aloud while partners listen for the changes.

Answer Key

Answers to the task will vary.
Example: See Ken's paragraph.

Shop talk

Store clerk			Shopper	
May I help you?			I'm looking for a	jacket. shirt.
			Do you have any	skirts? suits?
What	kind color size	do you want?	Checked, Yellow, Size 8,	please.
Here you are.			How much	is it? are they?
It's They're		$27.50.	I'll take	it. them.
			I think I'll look some more.	

OR

Sorry, we don't have any	checked ones. yellow ones. size 8's.	Thanks anyway.

Work as a large group.

You are in a clothing store. Some of you are shoppers. Some of you are clerks.

Read your "role card" (for SHOPPER or STORE CLERK). Then begin.

SHOPPERS

- You want to buy these things.
- Circle the *STYLE* or *PATTERN* you want.
- When you buy something, WRITE THE PRICE.
- You can spend $400.
- Buy as many things as you can.

coat **checked/solid**

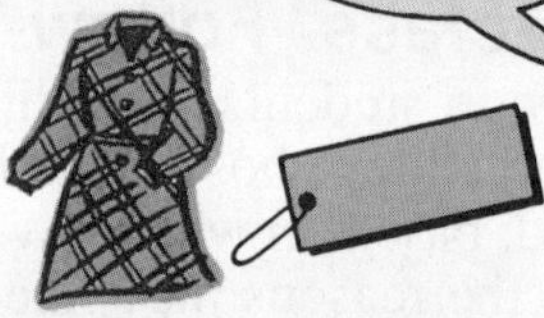
dress **striped/plaid**

jacket **leather/down**

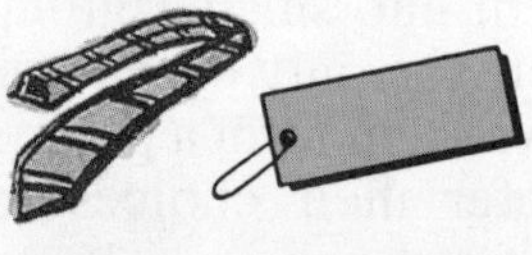
necktie **solid/striped**

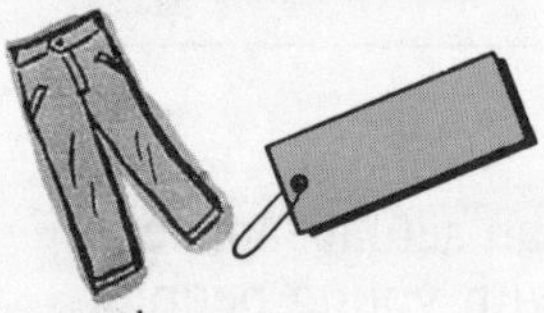
pants (trousers) **checked/solid**

shirt **short-sleeved/long-sleeved**

skirt **solid/flowered**

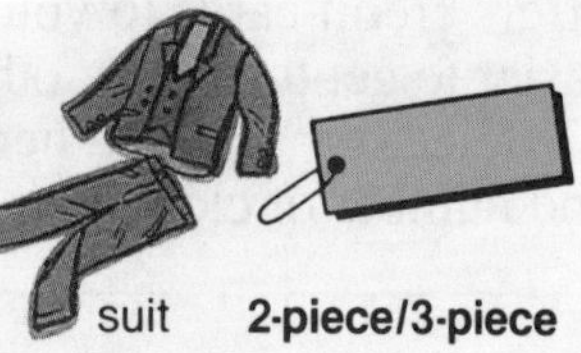
suit **2-piece/3-piece**

How many things did you buy? ______

How much money did you spend? ______

STORE CLERKS

- Half of you are STORE CLERK A.
- Half are STORE CLERK B.

Your store has the following things:

Clerk A:		Clerk B:	
checked coats	$ ___ . ___	solid coats	$ ___ . ___
striped dresses	___ . ___	plaid dresses	___ . ___
down jackets	___ . ___	leather jackets	___ . ___
solid ties	___ . ___	striped ties	___ . ___
solid pants	___ . ___	checked pants	___ . ___
long-sleeved shirts	___ . ___	short-sleeved shirts	___ . ___
flowered skirts	___ . ___	solid skirts	___ . ___
2-piece suits	___ . ___	3-piece suits	___ . ___

Write the prices.

Try This!

You have $200 more. Continue with the activity.
Try to buy all eight things.

Objective: The students will learn to shop for clothing.
Function: shopping routines: ask for / state clothing availability, size, price, material
Structures: present continuous, *any* in interrogative / negative sentences
Vocabulary Area: clothing
Classroom language:
Did you say ___ or ___?

Procedure

Note: Before you begin, decide if the students will do the activity using dollars (as listed on the page) or in other currency.

1. T: *Look at page 88. You will do a shopping activity.*

2. T: *Look at the language box at the top of the page and the clothing and styles. Are there any words you don't know?* Answer questions about vocabulary.

3. (Optional) T: *Look at the box. Listen and say.* Say the sentences in the box. Have students practice by repeating after you.

4. Divide the class into two groups, shoppers and store clerks.

5. Divide the store clerks group in half. T: *Half of you are **A's**. The other half are **B's**. Your stores have these things.* Point to the items in the "store clerks" box. *T: How much do these things cost at your store? Decide and write your prices.* Note: Store clerks do this individually.

6. While the clerks are deciding prices, work with the shoppers. T: *Shoppers, read the "shoppers' box." You want to buy all these things.* Point to the clothing. *Decide which style or pattern you want.*

7. (Optional) T: *Store clerks , stand along the edge of the room so shoppers will know who you are.*

8. T: *Shoppers, you want to buy all the pieces of clothing. Go to the stores. When you buy something, write the price you paid. You can only spend $400.*

9. While the other students watch, go to one store clerk and give an example. Prompt the clerk to say, "May I help you.?" T: *Do you have any jackets?* Continue through the conversation. If the clerk has the item, buy it and write the price. If the clerk does not have the item, ask for something else.

10. When the students understand the task, have them begin.

11. As the students work, circulate, answer questions and note areas for later work.

12. As students finish the main task, have them continue with the *Try this!* task. They have $200 more. They should try to buy everything.

13. Do consolidation, correction and expansion as desired.

General Notes

- In EFL situations, you may wish to have the students use local prices and measurements.
- You may want to require students to go to a different store after each purchase.
- Clerks have many of each item so they can sell the same product several times. Shoppers and Clerks can not change the styles they want/have once the activity has started.
- "Down" jackets are winter jackets filled with goose feathers.
- "Plaid" is similar to checked but usually includes more colors and has squares of different sizes. Scottish "tartans" are among the most famous plaid designs.
- "Pants," "trousers" and "slacks" all have similar meanings in American English.
- Since this activity is designed to encourage fluency, corrections are not recommended at this time.

Answer Key

Answers will vary. Students will have conversations similar to those in the language box.

Notes

CHECK YOURSELF

Finish the questions. Use these words. (16 points)

coats	does	what	where	that	may	do	one
these	many	ones	much	cost	any	take	are

Match the answers to the questions.

f 1. What color would you like?
_____ 2. How _____ is this sweater?
_____ 3. _____ I help you?
_____ 4. How much do _____ shoes cost?
_____ 5. What size do you _____ ?
_____ 6. Do you have any less expensive _____ ?
_____ 7. _____ you have a bigger one?
_____ 8. Do you have any leather _____ ?
_____ 9. May I see a yellow _____ , please?

a. Medium.
b. Yes, sir. What size?
c. They're $75.00.
d. It's $25.00.
e. Yellow? Of course. Here you are.
~~f.~~ Blue, please.
g. Yes. I'm looking for a present for my wife.
h. This should be big enough. It's a 42.
i. I'm afraid this is the cheapest one we have.

Read the ad. Compare the CD players. (4 points)

1. The Teac is bigger than the Sony.
2. The Sony is _____ (expensive)
3. _____ (heavy)
4. _____ (new)
5. _____ (small)

Remember

- Use **-er** with short (one-syllable) adjectives and **-ier** with two-syllable adjectives that end with **y.**)
- Use **more** with long adjectives.

Sale!

CD Players

Teac Compact Disc Player

- 16-selection memory
- 3 kg
- 35 cm × 30 cm × 10 cm
- Special discount on last year's model:

$159.95

Sony D-17 Discman

- 22-track memory
- 1 kg
- 14 cm × 14 cm × 3 cm
- new model only:

$239.95

Your score

Procedure

Exercise one.

1. T: *Look at page 89.* Point to the first exercise. T: *Finish the sentences. Use words from the box. Then match the answer to the questions.*

2. (Optional) Point to item one. T: *Number one. (blank) color would you like? What word goes in the blank?* Encourage the students to answer (A: What). Gesture for them to write "What" in the space provided. T: *What is the answer?* (A: [f.] Blue please). T: *Write that.*

3. T: *Do 2-9 the same way.*

Exercise two.

1. Point to the second exercise. T: *Read the ad. Compare the CD players.*

2. T: *Look at the "remember" box. Remember than you use "-er" with short adjectives and "-ier" with two-syllable adjectives that end with "y." You use "more" with long adjectives.*

3. (Optional:) Point to item one. T: *Look at the ad. How big is the Teac?* Encourage the students to answer (35 by 30 by 10 centimeters). T: *How big is the Sony?* (A: 14 by 14 by 3 centimeters.) Point to sentence one. T: *The Teac is bigger than the Sony.*

4. T: *Do 2-5 the same way.*

You may wish to assign the page as homework.

In-class Follow-up

• T: *Work in pairs. Did you both get the same answers?* As students compare their answers, circulate to make sure that all students have completed the homework. You may wish to have some students write their answers on the board.

General Notes

• The "x" that indicates size in the advertisement (14 cm x 14 cm x by 10 cm.) is read "by" (14 by 14 by 10 centimeters).

• The "Check yourself" pages are each worth 20 points. Each question is worth one point.

If you are giving grades, you may wish to keep track of student scores. Alternatively, if you have assigned the pages as homework and class size makes keeping track of individual points impractical, you may want to note which students have completed the assignment, those who did only part of it, and those who didn't do it.

Answer Key

Exercise one:

1.	What	f. Blue, please.
2.	much	d. It's $25.00.
3.	May	g. Yes. I'm looking...
4.	these	c. They're $75.00.
5.	take	a. Medium.
6.	ones	i. I'm afraid this is ...
7.	Do	h. This should be ...
8.	coats	b. Yes, sir. What size?
9.	one	e. Yellow? Of course..

Exercise two:

1. The Teac is bigger than the Sony.
2. The Sony is more expensive than the Teac.
3. The Teac is heavier than the Sony.
4. The Sony is newer than the Teac.
5. The Sony is smaller than the Teac.

The students could also compare the two products negatively :

1. The Sony isn't as big as the Teac.
2. The Teac isn't as expensive as the Sony.
3. The Sony isn't as heavy as the Teac.
4. The Teac isn't as new as the Sony.
5. The Teac isn't as small as the Sony.

Unit 11 How was it?

LISTENING Talking about emotions

Getting ready

Here are some words for emotions:

happy
grateful
scared
worried
bored
confident
angry
disappointed
embarrassed
surprised
uncomfortable

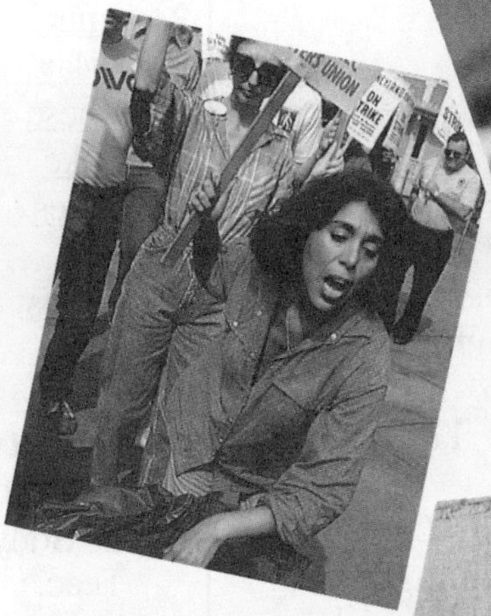

Think of something that makes you

happy ______________________________

sad ______________________________

scared ______________________________

bored ______________________________

Objective: The students will identify emotions of speakers and the causes of the reactions.
Function: express feelings, give reasons
Structures: simple past, interjections
Vocabulary Area: emotions

Procedure

1. Do the optional warm-up activity listed below.
2. T: *Open your books to page 90. Look at the pictures.*
3. T: *You will hear some people talking about how they feel*
4. T: *Look at "Getting Ready" on page 90. These are some words for emotions.* Play the first part of the tape.
5. T: *Think of things that make you feel these emotions.* Point to the four blanks at the bottom of page 90.
6. (Optional) Have some students tell you what they wrote and see how many others wrote the same thing OR have students compare their lists in groups of 4-6.
7. (Optional) If your students find listening very difficult, do the "additional preparation" exercise below.
8. T: *Look at the "First Listening"on page 91. How do they feel? Write the words.* Play the "First Listening" segment of the tape. You may want students to do this in pairs so they can help each other. You may wish to stop after each item to check.
9. (Optional) T: *Work in pairs. Did you both get the same answers?*
10. Play the tape again if necessary.
11. Check by asking the students the questions (e.g., T: *How does Michael feel?* A: Disappointed.) and eliciting their answers OR by having students work in groups of 2-4. They should compare answers and ask you about any they couldn't catch. (See the answer key on the next page.)
12. T: *Look at the "Second Listening." Listen again. Why do they feel that way? Finish the sentences.* Play the "Second Listening."
13. Check the answers as in step 11.
(See the answer key on the next page.)

Additional Preparation

Students work in pairs. They write things that make them feel each of the emotions listed at the top of page 90.

General Notes

• Language related to emotions is not often taught at an elementary level. We have included it because learning a language and adapting to or learning about a new culture can be a very emotional experience for students and they need to be able to express their feelings clearly. However, we caution teachers to use care in making sure students are not embarrassed or judged by other students during any discussion or exercise that deals with emotional experiences.
• When students are doing the "Second Listening" activity, you can adjust the level of precision according to the individual students' abilities. For example, in question 1, a student with above average ability might be required to respond, "He feels disappointed because he fell down during the race and couldn't finish." A student with less ability may respond, "He feels disappointed he lost (didn't win)."
• A "marathon" is a footrace lasting 26 miles, 385 yards. (segment 1) Other races are usually referred to by length (e.g., a "10 K" is a 10 kilometer race).
•"Surprise birthday parties" are not uncommon in North America. The person's friends hide and then jump out and yell, "Happy Birthday!" or "Surprise!" when the person comes into the room. Then the party begins.
• In segment 5, the men feel angry at the referees or officials in a soccer game.

Optional Warm-up Activity

Match the emotion. On the chalkboard, write:

A: I'm <u>(situation)</u> .

B: Oh. You must be <u>(emotion)</u>.
(or)
Oh, really? That's <u>nice</u> .
too bad

Unit 11

First Listening

How do they feel?
Write the words.

1. Michael
   the marathon race ______
2. Judith
   the party ______
3. Alice
   the sweaters ______
4. Pat and Daniel
   the hotel room ______
5. Mark, Bill, Andy
   the soccer match ______

Second Listening

Listen again. Complete each sentence.

1. He feels *disappointed* because he didn't ______
   ______
2. She feels ______ because her friends ______
   ______
3. She feels ______ because her mother ______
   ______
4. He feels ______ because he ______
   ______
5. They feel ______ because their team ______
   ______

Each student folds a piece of paper into 6 squares. In three of the squares they write an emotion or feeling (e.g., bored). On the other three squares, they write something that makes them feel that way (e.g., watching golf on TV). They then tear all the squares apart, separate the feelings and situations and give them to the teacher. The teachers shuffles the feeling squares and the situations (separately) and gives each student one of each. Each student must circulate and try to find an emotion square that matches the situation square. They do this by approaching other students and going through the phrases on the board (e.g., I'm watching golf on TV.). If the partner has an emotion that makes sense in that situation, she answers (e.g., Oh. You must be bored.) and gives the person the emotion square. If that person's emotion square doesn't match (e.g., scared) she says, "Oh, really? That's nice/too bad."

Students collect as many matches as possible. When they give away a square or match their own, they get new squares from the teacher. The student who collect the most squares wins.

Tapescript

Number 1: This is Michael.
Friend: Well, Michael, how did it go?
Michael: Well, it was a bit of a disappointment, I'd say. I had trained for a long time for that marathon, real hard. I was going really well in the race. About half way through, I tripped over something. I fell. I hurt my knee. I couldn't even finish. I was really upset about that.

Number 2: This is Judith.
Crowd: (whispering)...Surprise!
Judith: I don't believe it. I don't believe it.
C: Happy birthday to you...

Number 3: This is Alice.
Alice: Hi, mom. Hi. This is Alice. Good...I wanted to tell you I got the sweaters. They're beautiful. I love them...thanks so much...yeah, yeah, they all fit fine...

Number 4: This is Pat and Daniel.
Daniel: Hi, Mary. I'm back...(Oh!)...Oh, I'm sorry. Isn't this room 205?
Pat: 205? Uh, 205? No, this is 204.
D: I'm really sorry. Excuse me. I thought I...I'm staying in 205 and...
P: That's OK.

Number 5: This is Mark, Bill, and Andy.
Group speaking: I don't believe that...Yeah, we shouldn't have lost that game...Yeah, man...What was a terrible call!....Could you believe that call in front of the goal... Could you believe they took the goal away from us? I can't believe it...

Answer Key

First Listening:
1. disappointed
2. surprised or happy
3. happy or grateful
4. embarrassed
5. angry

Second Listening:
(wording will vary)
1. disappointed
(he didn't finish the race)
2. surprised or happy
(her friends gave her a surprise party)
3. happy or grateful
(her mother sent her some sweaters)
4. embarrassed
(he walked into the wrong hotel room)
5. angry
(they lost the soccer game)

CONVERSATION What did you think of it?

★ Have you ___1___ ___2___ new ___3___ yet?

◆ ___2___ new ___3___? Yeah, I ___4___ it last weekend.

★ What did you think of it?

◆ I really liked it. The ___5___ [was / were] ___6___. How did you like it?

★ I thought it was ___7___.

1. seen heard read	2. The Fabulous Stain's Prince's *The Rolling Stone*'s	3. video album rock review	4. saw heard read
5. special effects music stories	6. fantastic exciting terrific	7. boring just so-so great	

Objective: The students will ask for and give opinions.
Functions: ask/tell about experiences, ask for/give opinions
Structures: present perfect:
Have you seen it?
irregular past tense: *saw, read, heard*
descriptive adjectives (including participles: *exciting, boring)*

Procedure

1. T: *Open your books to page 92. Look at the picture. Where are these people?* (A: At school.)*What do you think they are talking about?*

2. Play the tape. Have the students listen and read silently.

3. Answer questions about vocabulary and expressions.

4. (Optional) T: *Listen again. Repeat each line.* Play the conversation again. Pause after each sentence. Gesture for the students to repeat the sentences.

5. T: *Work in pairs.* (Gesture to show how you want the students paired.)

6. T: *Stand up. Practice the conversation.* (After a few minutes) T: *Change parts* (Point to your book to show that students who were playing the part on the left now do the part on the right.).

7. Encourage the students to substitute the words and phrases in the box at the bottom.

8. Encourage the students to make eye contact while they are practicing.

9. As the students work, circulate, answer questions and note areas for later work.

10. When students can do the conversation smoothly, encourage them to make changes other than those listed. This can be done by having them cover the substitution box with a piece of paper, a pencil case, etc. OR have them close their books and try to have similar conversations.

Conversation Variation

Have the students gesture or touch their partners during each line. For example, they can point to their partners for the first line ("Have you seen...?") or put their hands over their hearts for the fourth line ("I really liked it.").

General Notes

- In slot 2, "The Fabulous Stains" are a (fictitious) rock group. "Prince" is a rock star. "Rolling Stone" is a magazine specializing in rock music and the lifestyles of the young.
- Slot 5 refers to the "special effects"on the video. This is special lighting, sound, or animation.
- Remind the students to listen to their partners so that their choices for slots 2 and 3 correspond.

Conversation Tapescript

First Boy: Have you seen the Fabulous Stain's new video yet?
Friend: The Fabulous Stain's new video? Yeah, I saw it last weekend.
First Boy: What did you think of it?
Friend: I really liked it. The special effects were terrific. How did you like it?
First Boy: I thought it was just so-so.

DUET-A

What do you think?

Answer the questions.
Ask *B*.

I think......is......
I think so too.
I like......the best.
Oh, really? I prefer.....
The one I like the most is......

What is the best movie you have ever seen?

you ______________________

your partner ______________________

What is the most exciting sport to play?

you ______________________

your partner ______________________

How do you spell it?

What is the most boring sport to watch?

you ______________________

your partner ______________________

What is your favorite thing to do on a holiday?

you ______________________

your partner ______________________

What is the worst movie you have seen?

you ______________________

your partner ______________________

Write one more.

you ______________________

your partner ______________________

Did you and ***B*** give the same answer for any questions? How many? ______

Bonus! Think of five more questions.
Ask ***B***.

Objective: The students will ask for and give opinions.
Function: ask for / give an opinion
Structures: *Wh-* questions, superlative adjectives
Vocabulary Area: entertainment and interests
Classroom language:*How do you spell it?*

Procedure

1. Divide the class into pairs. One student in each pair is **A**. The other is **B.** T: *Row one, you are **A's*** (Point to row one). *Row two, you are **B's*** (Point to row two). *Row three, you are **A's*** (etc.).
2. T: *A's, look at page 93. **B's**, look at page 94.*
3. Point out the language box at the top of the page. T: *Look at the box.* (Optional) *Listen and say.* Say the sentences in the box substituting "this" and "that" for "..." Have students practice by repeating after you.
4. T: *Look at the page. Are there any words you don't know?*
5. Introduce the task. T: *You will find out about your partner's opinions.*
6. While the other students watch, direct one pair through the first step of the exercise. T: (to any student **A**): *Look at the first box. What is the best movie you have ever seen? Write your answer. Now, ask **B**, "What is the best movie you have ever seen ?* Prompt **B** to answer. Gesture for **A** to write **B**'s answer.
7. T: *Do the rest the same way. You will need to think of your own question for the last one.* When the students understand the task, have them do it in pairs.
8. As the students work, circulate, answer questions and note areas for later work.
9. As students finish the main task, have them continue by doing the *Bonus!* task. Have them think of five more questions and ask their partners.
10. Do consolidation, correction and expansion as desired.

Grammar and Usage

• You may wish to point out that generally one-syllable adjectives and adjectives ending in "-y" take "-er" to become comparative. For two or three syllable adjectives, add "more" before the word. The same is true for "-est" and "most" in the superlative(e.g., most boring, most exciting). "Good" is irregular: the comparative form is "better" and the superlative form is "best."

General Notes

• Questions which have answers that may not be in English (e.g., best movie) may be answered in the native language with a short English explanation (e.g., "The best movie I've ever seen was _____. It's a love story.") If the students can make a reasonable translation, they may do so.
• "Athlete" rather than "sportsman" or "sportswoman" is generally used to refer to people who engage in sports.
• A "politician" is an elected public official such as a president, prime minister, senator or member of parliament..

Additional Activity

(This activity can be used anytime during this unit).
Match game. Work in groups of three. Have them answers these questions individually:

1. What is your favorite color?
2. Who is your favorite musician?
3. What is the most beautiful place in this country?
4. Which TV star do you like the most?
5. What is your favorite magazine?
6. What is the most important subject at school?
7. What is the most boring subject at school?
8. What is your least favorite holiday?
9. If you could live anywhere in the world, where would it be?
10. What is your favorite food?

After the students have written their answers, have them compare in groups. They get one point every time two people's ideas match.

DUET-B

What do you think?

I think......is......
I think so too.
I like......the best.
Oh, really? I prefer.....
The one I like the most is......

Answer the questions.
Ask *A*.

Who is the best professional athlete in the world?

you ____________________

your partner ____________________

Who do you think is the best politician?

you ____________________

your partner ____________________

How do you spell it?

What is the best book you have ever read?

you ____________________

your partner ____________________

Who is your favorite movie star?

you ____________________

your partner ____________________

What is your favorite type of ethnic food?

you ____________________

your partner ____________________

Write one more.

you ____________________

your partner ____________________

Did you and ***A*** give the same answer for any questions? How many? ______

Bonus! Think of five more questions. Ask ***A***.

They get two points whenever all three students wrote the same answer.

Expansion Activity

Emotional match.

Write the following sentences on the board:

You must feel ____.
That's nice.
That's too bad.

Students each take out a piece of paper and fold it into six squares like this:

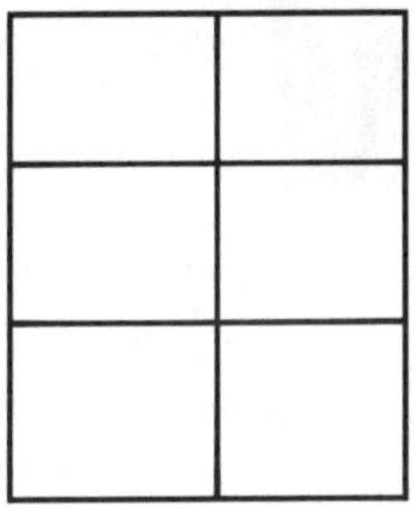

In three of the squares, they write an emotion from the list on page 90. In the other three squares, they write something that would make them feel those emotions (e.g., frustrated > studied but didn't pass the test). They then teach all six squares apart, separate the emotions and reasons and give all the squares to you. Keep the emotions and reasons separate. Give one new emotion and reason to each student. Students stand and circulate. They tell other students what happened (the reason). If the partner has an emotion that fits that reason, he or she says, "You must feel ______." The first student collects the emotion slip. That is a match. Those students get new emotion or reason slips from you. If the student's emotion slip does not match the reason, that student says "That's nice." or "That's too bad." (whichever is appropriate) and moves on to a new partner. The activity continues until all slips are used. The winner is the person with the most matches.

Fluency Frames:

Three "fluency frames" are introduced in the "extra activities" sections of Units 1, 2 and 3. Use any one of the "frames" with this topic for Unit 11:

• *Things that make me very happy.*

Answer Key

Because the students are sharing personal ideas and opinions, **answers will vary**.

Notes

SOLO Advice

Dr. Wells writes a newspaper advice column. People write about their problems and Dr. Wells gives them advice.
Read this letter.

Dear Dr. Wells,

I'm having a terrible time and don't know what to do. Eight years ago I decided to interrupt my career as a successful businesswoman to marry and have children. Our children are now both in school, and I have returned to work. I love my job but am having trouble being a businesswoman as well as a wife and mother. My husband and children agreed to my returning to work but now seem upset with the situation. They help a little, but I still have to do most of the housework and cooking. I'm tired and resentful. What should I do?

Ms. X

What happened to Ms. X?
Put the sentences in order:

_______ She went back to work.

_______ Ms. X's children were born.

_______ Her children entered school.

_______ Ms. X quit her job and got married.

Think of four suggestions for Ms. X:

Why don't you ______________________________?

I think you should ______________________________.

Maybe you could ______________________________.

How about ______________ -ing ______________________________?

Think of a problem. Write to Dr. Wells for advice.
Include these things: ■ the problem ■ why it happened ■ who is involved

Objective: The students will read about a problem and write suggestions
Function: ask for/ give advice
Structures: modal auxiliary verbs: *should, could*
How about + gerund

Procedure

1. (Optional) T: *When people have problems, who do they talk to?* (Possible answers: friends, family, counselor, teacher, etc.)
2. T: *Open your books to page 95. Dr. Wells writes an advice column for a newspaper. When people have problems, they write to her. She answers the letters in the newspaper. Her answers give advice.*
3. T: *Read the letter. What happened to Ms. X ? As you read, put the sentences in order.*
4. T: *What should Ms. X do? Write your suggestions.*
5. T: *Now, think of a problem. Write to Dr. Wells for advice. Include these things: the problem, why it happened and who is involved.*

You may wish to assign this activity as homework.

In-class Follow-up

In groups of 3-4, students compare advice. How many gave nearly the same advice? Were there any different ideas? Did the students think of Ms. X, her husband and/or her children as being "to blame" for the problem?

You may ask students to exchange their "problem" letters and write advice. However, if your students wrote about actual personal matters, it may be better not to ask them to reveal the problems.

General Notes

• Students sometimes use "you had better..." when giving advice. While this phrase can be used, it is very strong. It implies authority (a doctor might say, "You had better get some rest.") or a relationship close enough that one person can give another an order (a good friend saying, "You had better study more."). "You had better..." implies that there is no other reasonable choice.
• Advice columns are common in newspapers in North American. The most famous columnists are Ann Landers and Abigail Van Buren ("Dear Abby").

Optional Skill-building Activity

Skill: scanning for relationships in written texts

Collect a large number of letters from newspaper advice columns such as Ann Landers or Dear Abby. Separate the questions and the advice. Put four or five problem and advice letters in envelopes. Divide the class into groups of three or four. Give one envelope to each group. Have the students read the letters and match the problems and advice as quickly as possible.

Answer Key

Task one:
4. She went back to work.
2. Ms. X's children were born.
3. Her children entered school.
1. Ms. X quit her job and got married.

Task two:
Answers will vary.
Examples:
•Why don't you <u>talk to your family and tell them your feelings?</u>
•I think you should <u>ask everyone to help out a little with the housework and cooking.</u>
•Maybe you could <u>ask your husband and children for more help.</u>
•How about <u>work</u>ing <u>part-time</u>?

Task three:
Answers will vary.
Example:
See Ms. X's letter.

Class poll

Do you think Would you say	that crab tastes better than steak? that soccer is more exciting than golf?	Yes, I really do. Yes, I think so. No, I don't think so. I really don't know.

Step one:

Work alone. Finish the sentences.

__________ is more exciting than __________ .
(sport) (sport)

__________ taste(s) better than __________
(food) (food)

__________ is more interesting than __________ .
(kind of music) (kind of music)

__________ is a wonderful movie star.
(actor/actress)

__________ is funnier than __________ .
(comedian/comedienne) (comedian/comedienne)

__________ is easier than __________ .
(subject/class) (subject/class)

__________ is more important than __________
(subject/class) (subject/class)

The most important world problem is __________ .
(problem)

Write one more.

____

AGREE	DISAGREE	NO OPINION

Step two:

Ask at least five other people for their ideas.
Mark (////) their answers.

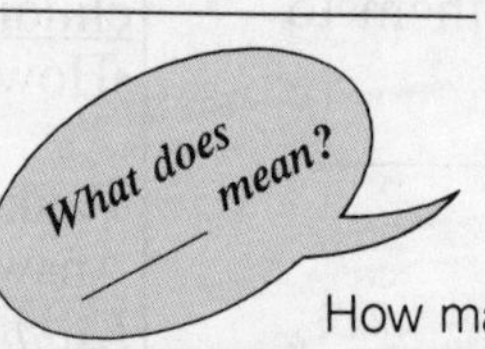

How many times did people agree? ____

Try This!

Pick a category (education, the world, etc.)
What are the five most important problems?
List them. Decide the order of importance (1-5). Why?

Objective: The students will ask for and give opinions.
Function: ask or / give opinions, state preferences
Structures: "yes/no" questions with *do* and *would,* comparative/ superlative adjectives
Classroom language: *What does _____ mean?*

Procedure

1. T: *Look at page 96. You will find out about other people's opinions.*
2. T: *Look at the language box at the top of the page. Are there any words you don't know?* Answer questions about vocabulary.
3. (Optional) T: *Look at the box.* Listen *and say.* Say the sentences in the box. Have students practice by repeating after you.
4. Introduce the task. T: *You will do a "class poll." Look at the sentences. Write one word in each blank. For example, number one is about sports. __Blank__ is more exciting than __blank__. What sports could you write?* Elicit examples and gesture for the students to write their ideas.
5. When they have finished, show them how to conduct the poll. Go to one student and read your first question (e.g., T: *Do you think that soccer is more exciting than golf?*). Mark the student's answer under "agree," "disagree" or "no opinion." T*: Ask your questions to at least five other people. Mark their answers.*
6. When the students understand the task, have them begin.
7. As the students work, circulate, answer questions and note areas for later work.
8. As students finish the main task, have them continue by doing the *Try this!* task. In pairs or small groups, they pick a category and identify the five most important problems. They decide the order of importance along with reasons.
9. Do consolidation, correction and expansion as desired.

Grammar and Usage Notes

- See the manual notes for the Duet in this unit. It has a note on forming comparative/ superlative adjectives.

General Notes

- To save class time, you may want to have students prepare their answers to the poll questions as homework prior to the class.
- Remind the students that they are practicing language. They should spend more time speaking to their partners than agonizing over their choices.
- Since this activity is designed to encourage fluency, corrections are not recommended at this time.

Answer Key

Answers will vary.

Examples:

Do you think tennis is more exciting than wrestling?
No, I don't think so.

Would you say English is easier than math?
Yes, I think so.

Notes

CHECK YOURSELF

How would you feel? Write one word on each line. Use these words. (10 points)

nervous	excited	disappointed	angry	sad
scared	tired	embarrassed	happy	bored

1. Someone gives you a nice present. ____________
2. You are alone in an old house. You hear noises and then a scream. ____________
3. You apartment is very dirty and your aunt comes to visit. ____________
4. Someone breaks your new CD player. ____________
5. You worked very, very hard today. ____________
6. A friend dies. ____________
7. You are waiting in someone's office. You have an interview for a job you really want. ____________
8. A friend who lives in a different city was going to visit you. She telephones to say she can't come. ____________
9. You are home with nothing to do. ____________
10. The score in the baseball game is 8 to 8. It is the last inning. ____________

Put the words in order. Make sentences. There is one extra word in each group. (2 points each = 10 points)

1. was I be surprised very ____________
2. enjoyed really could we party the ____________
3. about did like how it you ____________?
4. you read yet heard album their have new

____________?

5. you will best is movie the ever what seen have

____________?

Your score

Procedure

Exercise one.

1. T: *Look at page 97.* Point to the first exercise. T: *How would you feel? Write one word on each line. Use the words from the box..*

2. (Optional:) Point to item one. T: *Number one. Someone gives you a nice present. How would you feel?* Encourage the students to answer. (A: Happy). Gesture for them to write the feeling in the space provided.

3. T: *Do 2-10 the same way.*

Exercise two.

1. Point to the second exercise. T: *These words are in the wrong order. Put the words in the right order. Make sentences. There is one extra word in each group.*

2. (Optional) T: *Look at number one. What is the sentence?* Encourage the students to answer (A: I was very surprised.). Gesture for them to write the sentence on the line. T: *The extra word is "be."*

3. T: *Do 2-5 the same way.*

You may wish to assign the page as homework.

In-class Follow-up

• T: *Work in pairs. Did you both get the same answers?* As students compare their answers, circulate to make sure that all students have completed the homework. You may wish to have some students write their answers on the board.

General Notes

•"inning" (item 10): a period of a baseball game during which each team has three outs.

• The "Check yourself" pages are each worth 20 points. The items in the first activity are worth one point each. Each sentence in the second activity is worth two points.

Answer Key

Exercise one:

1. happy
2. scared
3. embarrassed
4. angry
5. tired
6. sad
7. nervous
8. disappointed
9. bored
10. excited

Exercise two:

1. I was very surprised.
2. We really enjoyed the party.
3. How did you like it?
4. Have you heard their new album yet?
5. What is the best movie you have ever seen?

Notes

Unit 12 How do you make it?

LISTENING Following instructions

Getting ready

Do you know these cooking words?

stir	add	put	peel	brown
boil	chop	bake	take out	

Work with a partner.
How many other cooking words do you know?
Write them.

First Listening

You are watching a TV cooking show. This week, they are making lasagne.
The pictures are NOT in order. **Listen. Number the pictures(1-8).**

Objective: The students will identify steps in a process.
Function: give instructions, sequence
Structures: imperatives, sequence markers: *first, then, next*
Vocabulary Area: cooking

Procedure

1. Do the optional warm-up activity.
2. T: *Open your books to page 98. Look at the pictures.*
3. T: *You will hear a TV cooking show.*
4. T: *Look at "Getting Ready" on page 98. Do you know these cooking words?* Play the first part of the tape.
5. T: *Work with a partner. How many other cooking words do you know? Write them.*
6. (Optional) Have the students tell you the words they wrote. Write them on the board.
7. T: *Look at the "First Listening"on page 98. This is a TV cooking show.*
8. (Optional) If your students find listening very difficult, do the "additional preparation" exercise below.
9. T: *The pictures are not in order. Listen. Number the pictures.* Play the "First Listening" segment of the tape.
10. (Optional) T: *Work in pairs. Did you both get the same answers?*
11. Play the tape again if necessary.
12. Check by asking the students the questions (e.g., T: *Which picture is first?*) and and have them point to the correct picture. To confirm, point to the picture in your book or draw eight squares on the chalkboard and point to the one in the same position. (See the answer key on the next page.)
13. T: *Look at the "Second Listening." Listen again. Write the verbs.* Play the "Second Listening."
14. Check the answers as in step 12. (See the answer key on the next page.)

Additional Preparation

Before they listen, have students work in pairs. They should look at the pictures and identify each as likely to come near the beginning (B), in the middle (M) or near the end (E) of the process. They write B, M or E next to each.

General Notes

• In cooking, "brown" may be used as a verb referring to cooking something (usually meat) just long enough for it to become light brown.
• Lasagne (also spelled "lasagna") was chosen for this activity because it is a dish many people have heard of but do not know how to make. If any of your students happen to know how to make lasagne, ask them to notice any differences between their recipe and Mario's.

Optional Warm-up Activity

A recipe. Find a recipe for some food the students do not know how to prepare. Write each step of the recipe on a slip of paper. Include a lot of sequence markers (e.g., first...; after you ___, ...; finally..., etc.). Students work in groups. Give one slip to each student . The student say their sentences and try to find the sequence.

Tapescript

First listening.
Number 1.
Announcer: Welcome to "What's Cooking." Today, my guest is the internationally famous chef, Mario DiPietro. And Mario, what are you going to teach us to make today?
Mario: Well, today we're going to learn to make everybody's Italian favorite, lasagne.
A: Mario, how do we begin?
M: Well, what we do first is boil some water. And now, into that boiling, salted water, we're going to put the dry lasagne pasta. Can you do that?
A: Just put it right in there?
Number 2.
M: We need some onions, mushrooms, and tomatoes. (OK). We're going to chop the onions and the mushrooms... And, uh, while I'm chopping these, would you like to peel the boiled tomatoes, please?
Number 3.
M: That's the next step, browning the meat . (Oh) And you simply brown it, by heating it over a low to medium fire.
Number 4.
M: We're going to add the vegetables to the meat. And at the same time we need to add some water (OK.)
Number 5.
A: And the next step is to add the cheese?
M: That's right. We recommend using ricotta cheese, but you can substitute cottage cheese or something like that.

Second Listening

Listen again. Write the verbs:

put, add, take out, brown, chop, bake, boil, stir, peel, put, add

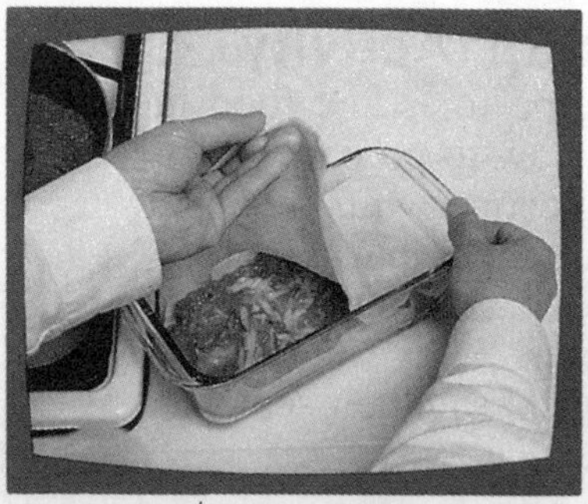

(____)

________ layers of pasta and the meat sauce into a pan.

(____)

________ the vegetables and water while you ________

(1)

Put the pasta into ________ing water.

(____)

________ the cheese.

(____)

________ it ________ of the oven.

(____)

________ the meat.

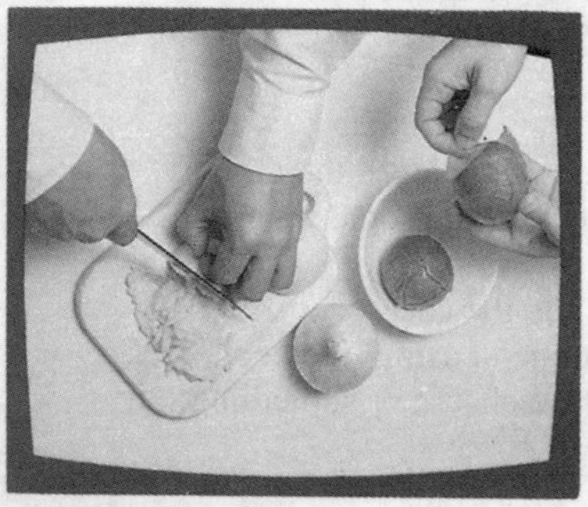

(____)

________ the vegetables and ________ the tomatoes.

(____)

________ at 190 degrees for 30 minutes.

Number 6.
M: So I'm going to put a layer of pasta and then I'm going to take the meat sauce -- that's the meat, the vegetables and the cheese mixed together. All right, I'm going to lay a layer on top of the pasta, then another layer of pasta.
Number 7.
M: And now we're ready to bake it. (I see) We need to put it into the oven for about thirty minutes and bake it at a low to medium heat.
Number 8.
A: And we've waited for just about 30 minutes, and Mario, it looks like it's about time to take it out.
M: All right, Let's have a look at it. And it looks, um, just right. I'll take it out carefully.

Second listening.
Announcer: Welcome to "What's Cooking," the show that introduces you to ethnic dishes from around the world. Today, my guest is the internationally famous chef, Mario DiPietro. And Mario, what are you going to teach us to make today?
Mario: Well, today we're going to learn to make everybody's Italian favorite, lasagne.
A: Mario, How do we begin?

M: Well, what we do first is boil some water. You're going to need about two liters of water. Oh, I see you've started boiling the water already. (yes) OK, we need to add a bit of salt to that. And now, into that boiling, salted water, we're going to put the dry lasagne pasta. Can you do that?
A: Just put it right in there?
M: Uh-huh. That's right.

M: Now while that's boiling, we are going to make the meat, vegetable, and cheese mixture.
A: OK. How do we do that?
M: OK. Well, let's start with the vegetables. We need some onions, mushrooms, and tomatoes. (OK). We're going to chop the onions and the mushrooms... And, uh, while I'm chopping these would you like to peel the boiled tomatoes, please?
A: Oh, yes, sure. So we have two peeled tomatoes, some chopped onions and mushrooms...right?
M: Mm.

M: Right. Now let's keep this to the side here until we have browned the meat.So that's the next step, browning the meat. (Oh.) And you simply brown it, by heating it over a low to medium fire. (OK) All right, that's fine. That's good. We'll brown this now over a low fire.

M: We're going to add the vegetables to the meat. Now, it is very important to stir the entire time that the meat and vegetables are simmering. (I see) And at the same time, we need to add some water (Oh, OK)

A: And the next step is to add the cheese?
M: That's right. We recommend using ricotta cheese, but you can substitute cottage cheese or something like that.
A: I see. Here I've got the cheese and...
M: OK, then add that into the mixture.

M: Now by this time, our pasta should be done.
A: Yes, it's been boiling for several minutes and now it's ready.
M: Yes, let me check that a minute. Un-huh, that's fine... Good...all right, so we've drained the pasta. Now, in this casserole dish, I'm going to put a layer of pasta -- I'm going to put a layer of pasta, and then I'm going to take the meat sauce, that is the meat, the vegetables and the cheese mixed together. All right, I'm going to lay a layer on top of the pasta, then another layer of pasta.
A: Another layer of pasta, I see.
M: Um, yeah, we'll have about three or four layers of each...

M: And now we're ready to bake it. (I see) We need to put it into the oven for about thirty minutes and bake it at a low to medium heat.

A: OK, viewers, we've put the lasagne into the oven and we've waited for just about 30 minutes, and Mario, it looks like it's about time to take it out.
M: All right. Let's have a look at it. It looks, um, just right. I'll take it out carefully.
A: Oh, it looks delicious.
M: And I'll, I'll set it up here to cool...
A: Could I try some of this?
M: Of course, go ahead.
A: Oh, it's wonderful. Absolutely delicious. So, viewers, we hope your lasagne turned out just as good as this one. And we'd like to thank you for joining us again this week on "What's Cooking?"
M: Thank you.

Answer Key

Getting Ready
Anwers will vary:
Possible answers:
cook, burn, mix, cut, chop, fry, steam, pour, etc.

First Listening:

6	4
1	5
8	3
2	7

Second Listening:
1. Put the pasta into boiling water. **2.** Chop the vegetables and peel the tomatoes. **3.** Brown the meat. **4.** Add the vegetables and water while you stir. **5.** Add the cheese. **6.** Put layers of pasta and the meat sauce into a pan. **7.** Bake at 190 degrees for 30 minutes. **8.** Take it out of the oven.

CONVERSATION How does this work?

★ Excuse me. I want to ___1___
What do I have to do?

◆ Well, first ___2___ .

★ OK. Then what?

◆ Next ___3___ .

★ I see. What's next?

◆ ___4___ .

★ I ___4___ ? Is that all?

◆ Well, finally you have to ___5___ .

★ Oh, I see. Thanks.

1. get a driver's license
   take out some money
   send a fax
2. fill out this form
   put in your card
   put the paper here
3. take the written test
   press your secret number
   dial the number
4. take the driving test
   press the amount
   push this button
5. pay the fee
   push the "OK" button
   wait for it to finish

Objective: The students will give and confirm instructions.
Functions: attract someone's attention, give/confirm instructions
Structures: imperative mood:
Fill out this form. Push this button.
Sequencing language: *first, then, next, finally*
want + infinitive
phrasal verbs: *take out, put in, fill in.*

Procedure

1. T: *Open your books to page 100. Look at the picture. Where are these people?* (A: At a bank cash machine). *What do you think the problem is?*
2. Play the tape. Have the students listen and read silently.
3. Answer questions about vocabulary and expressions.
4. (Optional) T: *Listen again. Repeat each line.* Play the conversation again. Pause after each sentence. Gesture for the students to repeat the sentences.
5. T: *Work in pairs.* (Gesture to show how you want the students paired.)
6. T: *Stand up. Practice the conversation.* (After a few minutes) T: *Change parts* (Point to your book to show that students who were playing the part on the left now do the part on the right.).
7. Encourage the students to substitute the words and phrases in the box at the bottom.
8. Encourage the students to make eye contact while they are practicing.
9. As the students work, circulate, answer questions and note areas for later work.
10. When students can do the conversation smoothly, encourage them to make changes other than those listed. This can be done by having them cover the substitution box with a piece of paper, a pencil case, etc. OR have them close their books and try to have similar conversations.

Conversation Variation

When receiving instructions, it is very common for the listener to repeat the the instructions to confirm that they were understood. Have students playing the part on the left change each of their partner's line to the first person and repeat it (e.g., B: Well, first you put in you card. A: Oh, first I put in my card? OK. Then what?)

General Notes

• Slot 1 (take out some money) refers to an automatic teller machine (a cash machine) --a device to get money when the banks are closed.
• The first speaker is talking to a stranger next to him/her or behind him/her in line.
• You may want to call attention to the sequence language in this conversation (first, next, finally).

Conversation Tapescript

Man: Excuse me. I want to take out some money. What do I have to do?
Woman: Well, first put in your card.
M: OK. Then what?
W: Next press your secret number.
S: I see. What's next?
M: Press the amount.
S: I press the amount? Is that all?
M: Well, finally you have to push the "OK" button.
S: Oh, I see. Thanks.

DUET-A

Following instructions

Do you understand what I said? Have you got that? OK? Can I continue? Did you do that? Should I say that again?	Did you say….? What does……mean? Can you explain that again? Could you say that a different way? I'm sorry. I'm really confused.

Origami is Japanese paper folding. You are going to teach ***B*** to make an origami wallet. ***B*** will need a 15 cm × 15 cm (about 6″ by 6″) paper.

Teach *B*.

Two ways are given to say each step. Do not let ***B*** see this page.

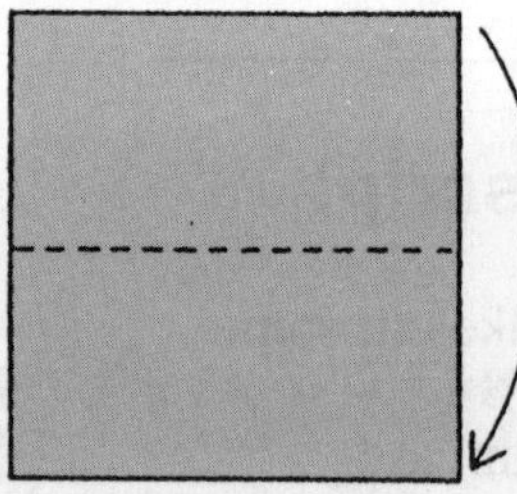

1. First, fold your paper in half horizontally.
∗ First, fold the top edge of the paper down to the bottom edge.

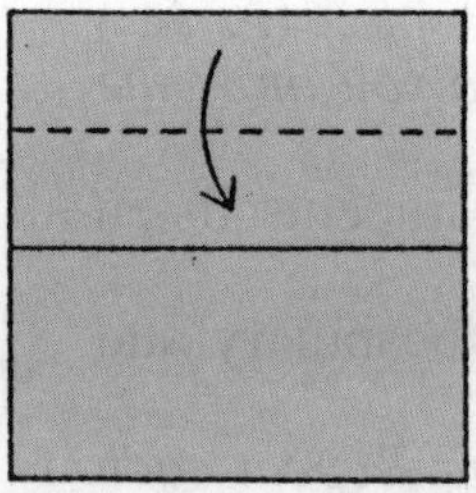

2. Next, unfold it and fold the top to the center line.
∗ Next unfold it. Then make a fold halfway between the top and the center line.

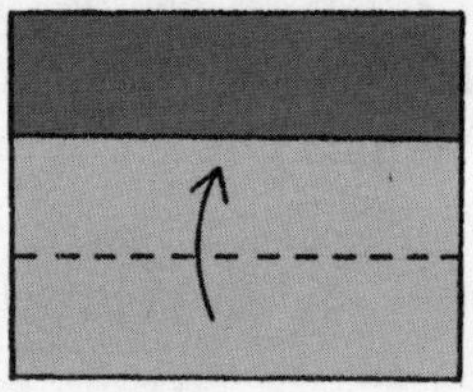

3. Fold the bottom to the center line.
∗ Repeat the last step but make the fold between the bottom and the center.

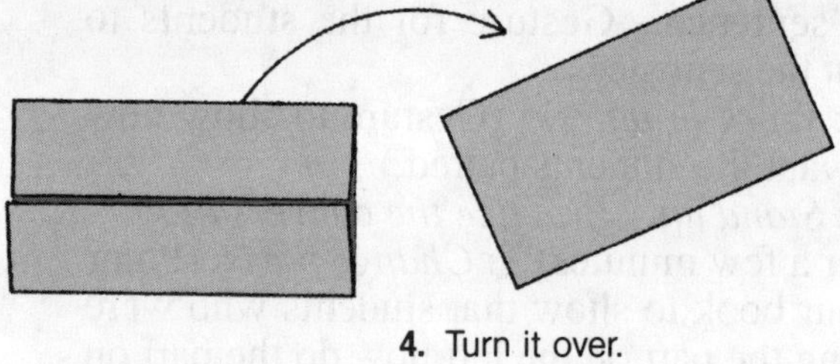

4. Turn it over.
∗ Turn the paper over.

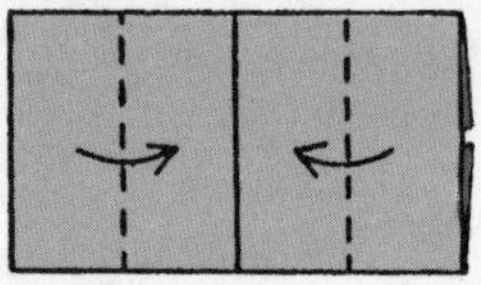

5. Make a square by folding the outside edges to the center.
∗ Fold the left and right edges to the middle.

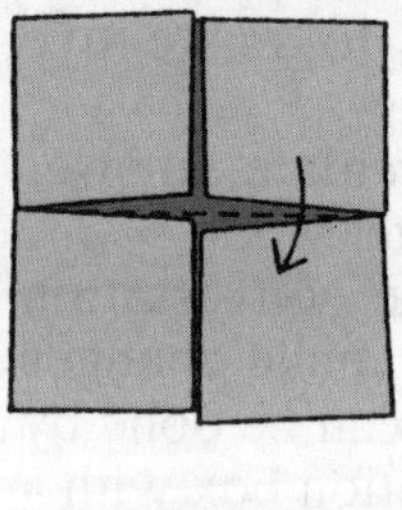

6. Finally, fold the paper in half so that the top edge meets the bottom.
∗ Last, fold it along the center line. The top and bottom edges should meet.

7. Now you have a small Japanese paper wallet.

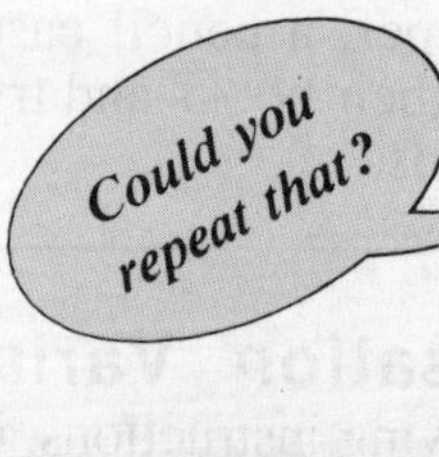

Bonus! Think of something you know how to make or cook.
Tell ***B***. ***B*** will list the steps.

Objective: The students will give sequential instructions. They will also learn to ask for and give clarification.
Function: give instructions
Structures: imperative mood
sequencing language: *first, next, then, finally*
prepositions: *in, to, by, along*
Classroom language:
I don't understand.
Could your repeat that?

Procedure

1. Divide the class into pairs. One student in each pair is **A**. The other is **B.** T: *Row one, you are **A's*** (Point to row one). *Row two, you are **B's*** (Point to row two). *Row three, you are **A's*** (etc.).
2. T: ***A**'s, look at page 101. **B**'s, look at page 102.*
3. Point out the language box at the top of the page. T: *Look at the box.* (Optional) *Listen and say.* Say the sentences in the box. Have students practice by repeating after you.
4. T: *Look at the page. Are there any words you don't know?*
5. Introduce the task. T: *You will teach your partner how to make an origami object. You need a piece of paper about fifteen centimeters by fifteen centimeters.*
6. T: *Two ways are given to say each step. If your partner doesn't understand the first one, say it the other way.* While the other students watch, direct one pair through the first step of the exercise. T: (to any student **A**): *What should **B** do first?* Prompt **A** to say, "First, fold your paper in half horizontally." Encourage **B** to follow the instruction.
7. T: *Teach your partner to make the objects. Do not let your partner see your book. Watch what your partner is doing to make sure all the steps are OK.* When the students understand the task, have them do it in pairs.
8. As the students work, circulate, answer questions and note areas for later work. If students get confused, tell them which step to go back to.
9. As students finish the main task, have them continue by doing the *Bonus!* task. Have them tell how to make something they know how to cook. Partners should list the steps.
10. Do consolidation, correction and expansion as desired.

Grammar and Usage

• You may want to call your students' attention to the use of the imperative mood (Fold your paper..., etc.) in this exercise. Imperatives are used for giving instructions and orders, making suggestions and encouraging people to do things. Often it is the speaker's tone of voice and the situation that indicates if an imperative is an order, a direction, an instruction or a suggestion. Generally, imperatives do not have subjects. The exception is when a subject is necessary to indicate who is to do the action. (e.g., Mike, answer the door.) "You" preceding an imperative often indicates anger (e.g., "You be quiet!")

General Notes

• You may want to teach the words "horizontal," "vertical" and diagonal" before students begin the task.
• The "x" in "15 cm x 15 cm" is pronounced "by": fifteen centimeters by fifteen centimeters.
• Thin paper (regular origami paper or newsprint) is easier to work with than thick paper. If regular origami paper (available in craft shops and some stationery stores) is used, the students should begin with the colored side down.
• Urge the "instructor" (the student explaining the steps) to watch his or her partner carefully to make sure each step is done correctly.
• See the introduction (•Corrections) for suggestions on ways to correct during pair work.

Additional Activity

(This activity can be used anytime during this unit).
Blindfolded TPR ("Total Physical Respons"). Students work in pairs. Make one copy of the following list per 6 students (or write similar tasks) and cut the tasks into separate slips. Prepare any necessary items (books, rods, etc.) One member of each pair is blindfolded. The other member is given

DUET-B

Following instructions

Do you understand what I said? Have you got that? OK? Can I continue? Did you do that? Should I say that again?	Did you say....? What does......mean? Can you explain that again? Could you say that a different way? I'm sorry. I'm really confused.

Origami is Japanese paper folding. You are going to teach ***A*** to make an origami penguin. ***A*** will need a 15 cm × 15 cm (about 6″ by 6″) paper.

Teach *A*.

Two ways are given to say each step. Do not let ***A*** see this page.

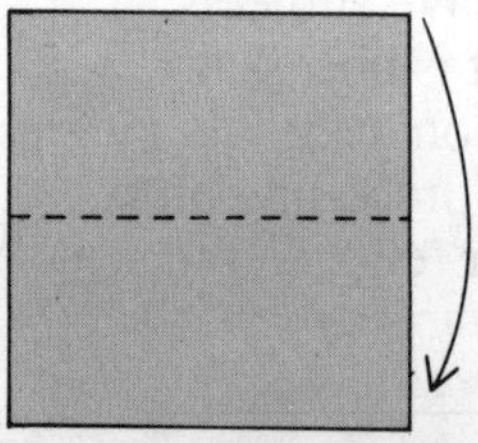

1. First, fold your paper in half horizontally.
∗ Fold the top edge of the paper to the bottom edge.

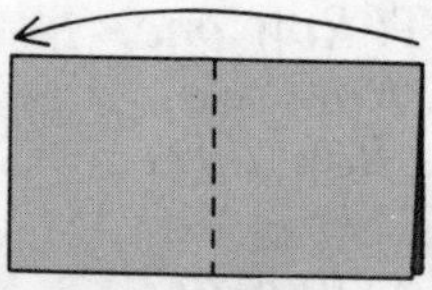

2. Make a square by folding it in half again.
∗ Fold the right edge to the left edge.

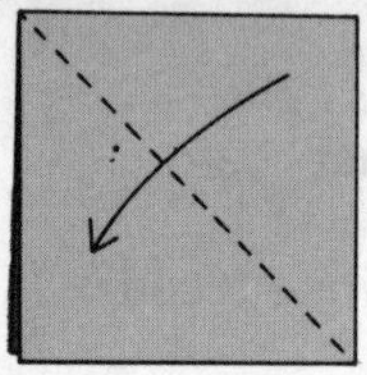

3. Make a triangle by folding the top right corner to the bottom left corner.
∗ Fold the opposite corners together. It should be a triangle.

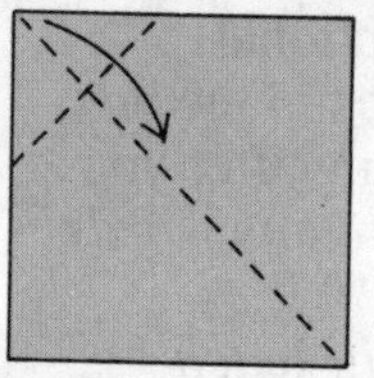

4. Unfold the triangle. Fold the top left point halfway to the middle. This is the penguin's head.
∗ Unfold the triangle. Find the middle of the paper. Fold the top left corner halfway to that point.

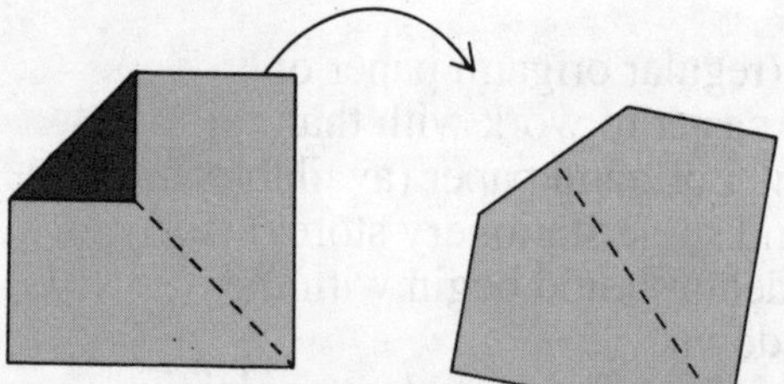

5. Turn it over.
∗ Turn the paper over.

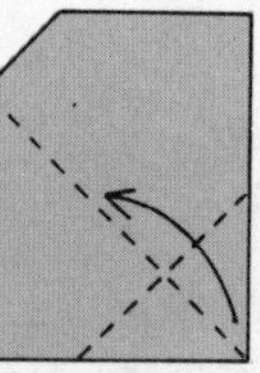

6. Fold the bottom right corner to the middle. This is the bird's tail.
∗ Find the corner opposite the head. Fold it to the center.

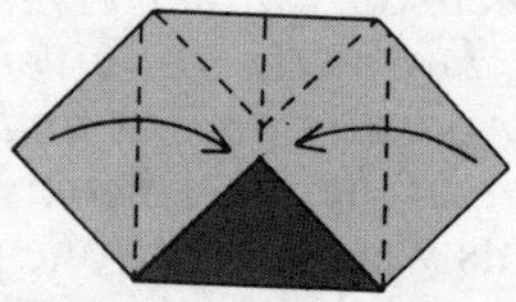

7. Fold the other two corners to the middle. They should touch the tail. These are the wings.
∗ Fold the top right and bottom left corners to the middle.

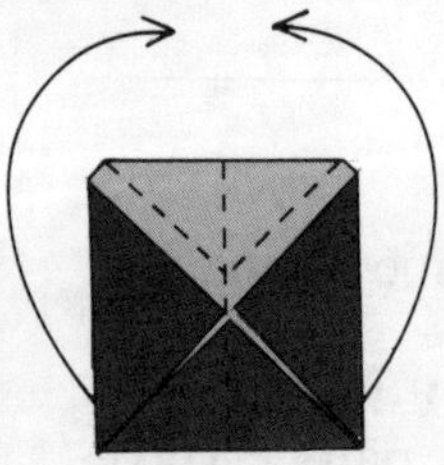

8. Finally, fold along the center line and pull the bird's head halfway out of its body.
∗ Last, fold the sides of the body together. Pull out the bird's head halfway.

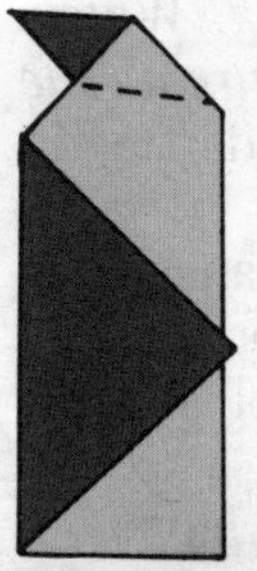

9. Stand the bird on its back legs. Now you have an origami penguin.

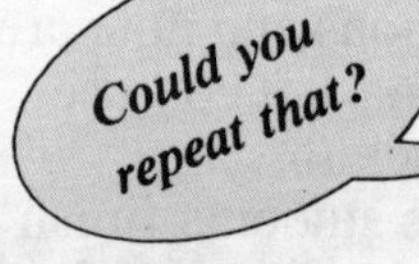

Bonus! Think of something you know how to make or cook. Tell ***A***. ***A*** will list the steps.

one of the tasks. He must guide his partner in doing the task.
The blindfolded partner should not be told what the task is, just how to do it.

Sample TPR tasks:

• Put five books in alphabetical (A-B-C) order.

• Draw a map of your country on the chalkboard.

• Pick up a book and carry it to the other side of the room.

• Open all the windows in this room. Then close them.

• Write the teacher's name backwards on the chalkboard.

• Line up pencils or rods so they spell the name of this city.

Answer Key

There should be no need to check answers as a whole class. The production of the wallet and penguin are proof of successful communication.

Expansion Activity

Modern art

Have each student draw a "modern art" picture. The picture should include at least five of the following:

circles
rectangles
squares
triangles
lines
stars

In pairs, they tell their partners how to draw their pictures. Partners can not see the pictures as they draw. When the finish, they compare their version to the original.

Fluency Frames:

Three "fluency frames" are introduced in the "extra activities" sections of Units 1, 2 and 3. Use any one of the "frames" with this topic for Unit 12:

• *My favorite food and how to make it.*

Notes

SOLO The farmer's problem

Read the problem. Then write a solution to the farmer's problem.

A farmer was taking a fox, a chicken and some wheat to town. He was going to sell them. He came to a river. He had a boat but it was very small. It could carry him and only one other thing (the wheat or an animal). He had to take everything across the river, one thing at a time.

He had two problems.

He couldn't leave the fox and the chicken together. The fox would eat the chicken.	He couldn't leave the chicken and the wheat together or the chicken would eat the wheat.

How did he get all three of them across the river?

Write a puzzle that you know.
Use some of these words:

____ first
____ second
____ next
____ then
____ after that
____ finally

Objective: The students will read a puzzle and try to write a solution. Then they will write a puzzle.
Function: describe a sequence
Structures: past continuous, future in the past, simple past, sequence discourse markers: *first, second, next, after that, finally*

Procedure

1. T: *Open your books to page 103. This story is a puzzle. Read it.*
2. T: *The farmer had two problems: He couldn't leave the fox and the chicken together. The fox would eat the chicken. He couldn't leave the chicken and the wheat together or the chicken would eat the wheat. How did he get all three across the river?*
3. T: *Think of a puzzle you know. Write it. Use some of these words: first, second, next, then, after that, finally.*

You may wish to assign this activity as homework.

In-class Follow-up

In groups of about 4, students compare their solutions. Did they say everything in exactly the same way? Then they share the puzzles they wrote. The groups try to discover the solutions.

General Notes

• This puzzle or riddle comes from American folklore. Many cultures have a stock of such riddles, often told in the form of stories, which are popular among children. Many adults too, of course, enjoy working out the solutions to these puzzles.

Optional Skill-building Activity

Skill: identifying steps in a sequence

Have students draw simple pictures to illustrate the sequence of events in the answer to "The Farmer's Problem." Then, in pairs have them read their partner's story and illustrate the answer.

Answer Key

Task one:
Wording will vary.

Example:
First he took the chicken across the river. He left it and went back. Next, he took the wheat across the river. He left the wheat and then he took the chicken back. After that, he left the chicken and took the fox across. Finally, he went back and got the chicken.

(Note: It would also be possible to take the fox across before the wheat.)

Task two:
Answers will vary.
Any puzzle that involves a series of steps is acceptable.

How does it work?

Work in groups of three.

Step one:

Read the sample instruction card. What is the machine?

What is it? ______________________________

First select what you want. Then put the correct amount of money into the machine. Next, push the button for the thing that you want to buy. It will come out at the bottom of the machine.

Step two:

Think of a machine. Write instructions for how to use it.

Step three:

Read your instructions to the class. Can anyone guess the name of the machine?

Try This!

Invent (think of) an unusual machine.
Draw a picture.
Write the instructions.

Objective: The students will learn to give instructions.
Function: give instructions
Structures: imperative mood, sequence language: *first, then, next*
Vocabulary Area: operating machines

Procedure

1. (Optional) Have the students tell you how to operate a simple machine such as a tape recorder. Follow their instructions exactly (e.g., If they don't tell you to plug it in, don't). T: *I want to play a tape. What do I do first?* etc.

2. *Look at page 104. You will explain how to operate a machine.*

3. T: *Read the instruction card. What machine are they talking about?* (A: a vending machine).

4. T: *Think of a machine you know how to use. How does it work? Write the instructions. Do not write the name of the machine.* (You may want to have them do this activity in pairs).

5. T: *Read the instructions. Guess what people's machines are.*
(This step can be done as a whole class or in groups of 8-10. Groups can exchange paragraphs and continue.)

6. As students finish the main task, have them continue by doing the *Try this!* task. Have them work in pairs or small groups and think of an unusual machine. They should draw a picture and write instructions.

7. Do consolidation, correction and expansion as desired.

Grammar and Usage Notes

• See notes on the imperative mood (Unit 12, Duet).

General Notes

• Instruction language of this type tends to be rather neutral in English. Students from some cultural backgrounds may make the language overly polite (e.g., "Please put in the correct amount...") Point out that this is not appropriate in this situation.

• Encourage the students to think of machines that everyone is familiar with, but which are not too easy to guess.

• If students are likely to write about very similar machines, give them cards with the name of a machine to write about. Possible machines: a coffee maker, a computer, a CD player, a can opener, a car jack, a typewriter, a knife sharpener, a car, an electric saw, a camera, a video player, a sewing machine, a remote control, an electric drill, a hand drill, a washing machine, a vacuum cleaner, a mixer, a toaster oven, a cash machine (automatic teller).

• Since this activity is designed to encourage fluency, corrections are not recommended at this time.

Answer Key

Step one: a vending machine
(also called a "soda machine" or a "Coke machine.")

Student instructions (Step two) will vary.

Notes

CHECK YOURSELF

Which set of instructions goes with each object? (3 points)

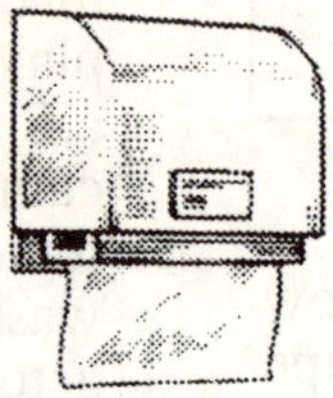

a.
1. Place the paper on the board.
2. Align the paper with the cutting edge.
3. Push the blade down carefully.

b.
1. Insert a sheet of paper between the rollers.
2. Close the protective cover.
3. Press the "print" button.

c.
1. Hold the paper with both hands.
2. Pull down firmly.
3. Tear off by pulling toward you.

Read the sentences. Choose the correct words. (8 points)

ARRIVING IN A NEW COUNTRY

[Next / Before / Then] your airplane lands, the flight attendant will give you a customs declaration card. [Fill / Write / Read] it out. You [might / may / have to] list the items you are bringing into the country. After you land, [come / go / went] to the Immigration counter. The officer will ask about the purpose and length of your visit. [Then / Finally / After] Immigration, pick [up / in / on] your luggage at the baggage claim. [When / Next / Before] you go to customs. They will inspect your luggage. You must give them your declaration card. [Before that / First / Finally] you will be allowed to enter the country.

Read the hints. Unscramble the words. Write them. (9 points)

1. (opposite of "right") = ____________ [nwogr]
2. (has three sides) = ____________ [gtrealin]
3. (opposite of "after") = ____________ [rfbeeo]
4. (opposite of "top") = ____________ [mobtot]
5. (" ——— " this line is) = ____________ [ntrholozia]
6. (center) = ____________ [dldemi]
7. (not separate) = ____________ [eerotthg]
8. (last) = ____________ [lfnia]
9. (opposite of "away from") = ____________ [wdtora]

Your score

Procedure

Exercise one.

1. T: *Look at page 105.* Point to the first exercise. T: *Read the instructions. Which instructions go with each object?*

2. (Optional) T: *Read instructions set A. Which objects do those instructions go with?* Encourage the students to answer (A: The paper cutter).

3. T: *Do the others the same way.*

Exercise two.

1. Point to the second exercise. T: *Read the sentences. Choose the correct words.*

2. (Optional) Point to the first line. T: *(Blank)____ your airplane lands, the flight attendant will give you a customs declaration card. Which word goes in the blank?* Encourage the students to answer. (A: Before.) Gesture for them to circle the word.

2. T: *Do the rest the same way.*

Exercise three.

1. Point to the third exercise. T: *These letters are not in the right order. Read the hints. Put the letters in the right order.*

2. (Optional). T: *Look at the example: opposite of "right." What word is the opposite of right?* Encourage the students to answer (A: Wrong). If students suggest a different word (e.g., left), tell them to check the mixed up letters. When they find the correct word, gesture for them to write the word in the blank.

3. T: *Do 2-9 the same way.*

You may wish to assign the page as homework.

In-class Follow-up

• T: *Work in pairs. Did you both get the same answers?* As students compare their answers, circulate to make sure that all students have completed the homework. You may wish to have some students write their answers on the board.

General Notes

• The "Check yourself" pages are each worth 20 points. Each item is worth one point. If you are giving grades, you may wish to keep track of student scores. Alternatively, if you have assigned the pages as homework and class size makes keeping track of individual points impractical, you may want to note which students have completed the assignment, those who did only part of it and those who didn't do it.

Answer Key

Exercise one:

a. the paper cutter (third illustration)
b. the computer printer (first illustration)
c. the paper towel dispenser (second illustration)

Exercise two:

Before your airplane lands, the flight attendant will give you a customs declaration. Fill it out. You have to list the items you are bringing into the country. After you land, go to the immigration counter. The officer will ask you about the purpose and length of your visit. After Immigration, pick up your luggage at the baggage claim. Next you go to customs. They will inspect your luggage. You must give them your declaration card. Finally you will be allowed to enter the country.

Exercise three:

1. wrong
2. triangle
3. before
4. bottom
5. horizontal
6. middle
7. together
8. final
9. toward

REVIEW ACTIVITIES

The appendix contains four review activities:

THE CLASS NEWSPAPER, is a project which reviews functions, structures, vocabulary, and classroom language from Units 1-6. Guidelines and work space for this project is provided on student book pages ____________ 108-112

SLAP! is a vocabulary game. SLAP! 1 includes words from Units 1-6; SLAP! 2 includes words from Units 7-12. The gameboards are on student book pages ____________ 114-117

Let's Talk reviews functions, structures, vocabulary and classroom language from Units 1-12. The Let's Talk gameboard is on student book pages ____________ 118-119

The PROJECT FAIR reviews a variety of language functions, structures, and vocabulary from throughout the book.

Guidelines for developing and displaying projects are on student book pages ____________ 120-123

Directions and guidelines for the students are provided in the student book with each activity. This manual offers additional suggestions and information about the activities and games.

The Class Newspaper

Objective: The students will create a class newspaper.

General Notes

- Language projects are major tasks which usually take several class periods to complete. Much of the work can be done outside of class. Allow class time, particularly at the beginning of the project, for students to understand the goals and to become excited about the project.
- This project is specifically designed to be practical for students in countries or areas where native English speakers are not readily available for interaction.
- The instructions printed in the student book should provide sufficient information and ideas for the students to get started. It is important that the teacher and students do not get overly frustrated when problems arise in carrying out the project. Part of the advantage of using projects is that they encourage students to solve problems as they arise.
- If necessary, use the instructions printed next to each step of the project to explain what the students should do.

The following are resource notes and suggestions for each step.

Step one: Getting Started

Types of articles:

- travel reports
- movie/concert reviews
- recipes
- advice column
- a horoscope
- advice for travelers
- advice for English students
- a "grammar explained" column
- fashion news or tips
- crossword puzzles
- other word games

Common English newspaper names:

- -Times
- -Sun
- -Star
- -Tribune
- -World

These are usually preceded with the name of a city (e.g. *The New York Times*). Of course, there is no reason for your class newspaper to have a common name! These are provided only as a source of ideas.

• You may want to select two or three people to do the lay out work since it is a big job. Also, if there are at least two, they can speak English while doing the task.

Step two: Getting Information

• Encourage students to be very specific about what information they are looking for and where (or from whom) they will get it.
• Encourage students to help each other identify and contact information sources.
• Most embassies and consulates have English language information about their countries. It is usually free. Have students check the telephone directory or directory assistance for phone numbers.
•If students want to write about The United States or Great Britain, the United States Information Agency or the British Council can be helpful.

Step three: Research

• Remind the students to call to make an appointment with anyone they want to talk to.
• After taking notes, students are asked to underline the most important things. This will help them organize information when they are writing.
• Encourage students to take photographs of (or draw sketches or find a picture of) whatever they are writing about.

Step four: First Draft

• Remind the students that the most important information should go at the beginning of the article.
• Students are asked to write their headlines after they have written the article. This is so the headlines reflect what is really included.
• If students have word processors available, they should use them. It makes the re-writing process much easier.

Step five: Rewriting

• Encourage rewriting in pairs. This allows students to help each other and will allow each writer to see what was and was not clear in the first draft.
• While students are encouraged to help each other with grammar and spelling mistakes, the questions are designed to focus them on the meaning.
• Students should rewrite in the space provided. This is to provide standard size columns to help the layout person. Additional writing space is provided on page 112. Articles can be shorter or longer than a single column.
• Articles do not need to be typed. If students choose to type either on a typewriter or a word processor, tell them the column width. The columns in the book are 5.5 centimeters (about 2.25 inches) wide.
• If students do not want to cut their articles out of their books, they can make photocopies to give to the layout person.
• Make sure the lay out people understand that headlines should not be right next to each other. It makes them hard to read. (Newspaper people call such headlines "tombstoned" because they look like rows of grave stones.)
• If possible, make copies for all students. If this isn't possible, post the newspaper on a bulletin board or wall.

Step six: Reading

• Be sure to allow time for reading the paper. Having students answer the questions on page 111 helps ensure that they think about what they read.

The Class Newspaper

This is an English **PROJECT.**
Your class will make a school newspaper.

Step one: Getting Started

Work with a partner.
What articles could be in your newspaper?
Here are some ideas. **Write at least five more.**

The Class Newspaper

- *interesting places in this city*
- *interviews with new students or teachers*
- *an interview with the head of the school*
- *recent events in this city*
- *news about you or other students*
- *stories*
- *jokes or cartoons*
-
-
-
-
-
-
-

Work as a large group.
Put all of the ideas on the blackboard.

Decide on a name for the newspaper. ______________________
Decide who will write which articles.
Decide who will lay out the newspaper.

Step two: Getting information

Write the topic or title of your article. ______________________
You will need information to write your article.
What do you need to find out?
Write five questions:

____ ?

____ ?

____ ?

____ ?

____ ?

Hints:
Ask **Wh**-questions:
who **where**
what **why**
when **how**

Where can you get the information?
Check (✓) the ones you can use.

- ☐ talking to someone from your country (Who?) ________________
- ☐ talking to someone from another country (Who?) ________________
- ☐ books
- ☐ magazines
- ☐ a library
- ☐ city hall or a tourist information office
- ☐ TV/video
- ☐ other (What or where?) ________________

Step three: Research

Get the information you decided on in *Step two.*
Remember, if you want to talk to someone, you should telephone them first.

Take notes:

The Class Newspaper

who:

what:

when:

where:

why:

how:

Hints:

- Pictures make newspapers more interesting. Draw or take a picture of whatever you are going to write about.

Look at your notes:
Which information is the most important? **Underline it.**

Step four: First draft

Write your article.

The Class Newspaper

by ______________________

(your name)

Hints:

- The most important information should go near the beginning.
- Remember to use the **wh**-question information.

Write a headline (title) for your article.

Step five: Rewriting

Good writers always rewrite their articles to make them better.
Work with a partner.
Exchange articles.
Read your partner's article. Answer these questions:

- Who or what is it about? ______________________
- What is the most interesting thing in the article?

____

- Is the most important information at the beginning? ______________________
- Did you notice any grammar or spelling mistakes? **Circle them.**

Underline anything that is difficult to understand.

Write your article again. Use the space on the right.
Think about things that your partner didn't understand.
How can you make them clear?

Give your article to the layout person.

Hint for the layout person:

- Newspapers are easier to read if headlines are not next to each other. Use pictures.

Like this:

Not like this:

Your teacher will make copies or post the newspaper on a bulletin board.

Step six: Reading

Read the newspaper.
Answer these questions.

- Which article was the most interesting? ______________________
- Which article was the funniest? ______________________
- Which picture did you like the most? ______________________

Write three things you learned from the newspaper:

- ______________________
- ______________________
- ______________________

____

by ______________________

Slap!

(Slap! 1 and Slap! 2)

Objective: The students will play a vocabulary review game.

Procedure

Regular vocabulary review is an important part of language learning. This game (Slap!) is useful for reviewing the key vocabulary items from the book. **Slap 1!** includes words from the first half of the book (Units 1-6); **Slap 2!** includes words from the second half of the book (Units 7-12).

The directions in the student book are sufficient for getting the students started on this vocabulary game.

1. T: (if you are playing Slap 1) *Look at pages 114-115.* [OR (if you are playing Slap 2) *Look at pages 116-117.] This is a vocabulary review game. These words are from the first half of the book.* [OR (if you are playing Slap 2) *These words are from the second half of the book.]*
2. *Work in groups of four or five. Look at the words. Do you remember what they mean?*
3. T: *Put one book in the middle of your group. Look at the words. One person thinks of a word and gives a hint. Try to be the first person in your group to touch the word. Say it.*
4. (Optional) T: *For example, the first hint is. "It's in the kitchen. You wash dishes in it."* (A: sink) Gesture for the students to touch the word "sink" and say it (top, left on page 115).
[OR if you are playing Slap 2, T: *For example, the first hint is. "It doesn't cost very much."* (A: cheap) Gesture for the students to touch the word "cheap" and say it (top, right on page 117).]
5. T: *Continue. Take turns.*

General Notes

• The word *slap* means to hit sharply with the hand.
• Students have to touch the word so they can tell who answered first.
• Discourage students from writing the meanings of any unknown words in their native language next to the word on the page. If they feel it is helpful for them to keep vocabulary lists, they should be kept on a separate paper so students don't see their mother-tongue equivalents while they are playing the game.
• When teaching games such as this one, it is often easier for the students to understand if, instead of giving directions to the entire group at once, you demonstrate with one group while the other students watch. Another way is to teach the game to several students while the others work on something else (for example, checking their homework). The students you teach the game to become group leaders, teaching the game to their groups.

Variations:
• Require the students to use the words in sentences after they guess.
• Have the students give hints in sentences form, changing the target word to "blank" (e.g., I have a BLANK in my kitchen.) The students who guess must repeat the sentences, filling in the target word.

SLAP!

This is a vocabulary review game.

Work in groups of four or five.

Look at all of the words. If there are any words you don't know, ask your partners for the meaning.

Decide who will start That person will think of one word and give a hint.

Example: *It's in the kitchen. You wash dishes in it.*

The first person to touch and say the correct word (*sink*) gets one point. That person gives the next hint.

The one who gets the most points is the winner.

(Note: **SLAP! 1** is for vocabulary items from **UNITS 1-6;**
SLAP! 2 is for vocabulary items from **UNITS 7-12.**)

brother-in-law

breakfast

languages

curly

government

wavy

criminal

famous

hospital

niece

occupation

restaurant

born

study

spicy

bald

nationality

across from

hardly ever

moustache

listen

nephew

weekend

striped

heavy set

sink

block

spill

meter

appliance

supermarket

get up

drive

graduate

post office

signal

activity

rent

finish

stationery

microwave

watch

shelf

museum

newspaper

homemaker

describe

magazine

programmer

plant

pattern

fix

office

cabinet

shape

cushion

beard

instructions

personality

languages

math

clerk

customers

outgoing

ability

mechanic

classical

occupation

schedule

less

favorite

then

classic

next

tools

variety

boring

science fiction

SLAP! 2

license

confident

striped

musical

easy

after that

reserved

smart

cheap

checked

solid

comedy

challenging

secretary

leather

expensive

intelligent

quality

finally

probably

first

representative

mystery

sightseeing

wonderful

worried

concert

embarrassed

outgoing

rock

advice

similar

foreign

disappointed

exciting

phrase book

Let's Talk!

Objective: The students find out about more about each other while playing a conversation game.

Procedure

1. T: *Look at pages 118-119. This is a conversation game. Work in groups of four.*
2. T: *Put one book in the middle of your group. This is your game board. Use a coin, an eraser or a key as a marker. Put your marker on the Let's Talk! mark* (the circle on the game board).
3. (If dice are available, have each group use one. If not, simply have them move from space to space.) T: *Roll the dice. Move that many spaces. You can move in any direction.*
4. T: *When you land on a space, the person to your left asks you that question. Your answer must have three or more sentences.*
5. T: *After you have answered, it is the next person's turn. Continue.*

General Notes

• This is not a competitive game. It is designed to encourage long answers and competition may encourage short responses.
• You may want to encourage the students to ask follow-up questions about what their partners say.
• If dice are not available and you want to add an element of chance to their moves, have each group take out a coin. One side of the coin is good for one space. The other is good for two spaces. Decide which is which and tell the students. To determine how far they can move, students toss the coin into the air. They move the number of spaces determined by the side of the coin that lands face-up.
• Each question is designed to review a grammatical or functional point. Students should have enough time to play to be sure they answer many questions.
• The students should play this game after they finish the book. You may wish to have them play the game periodically before that. It is best if they have new partners each time they play.
• This game can, along with quizzes, "Check yourself" review page scores, attendance and participation, be used to help with students grading and evaluation.

• **Evaluation idea**
Have students work in pairs after they have played the game once or twice. They should make a **tape recording** of themselves playing the game. They continue until they have each had three turns.
While they are allowed to practice before they make their tape, they may not write out their answers. They give the tape to the teacher who listens to it and fills out a form. The form should give points (usually 1-10 or 1-5) for categories such as the following:
1. Fluency (content, naturalness, focus on meaning, etc.)
2. Accuracy (grammar is correct and varied, i.e., students using more complex forms such as perfect tenses and the passive voice should get more points - even if there are a few mistakes - than students staying with very simple forms).
3. Vocabulary (Is the vocabulary appropriate and is there evidence of students using new words?)
4. Pronunciation/intonation (smooth, natural phrasing, etc.)
5. Interaction. (Do students interact with their partners or simply ignore them while they wait for their next turns?)

The categories used and the weight (points) for each depend on what the teacher has emphasized during the course.

Surprisingly, it doesn't take much longer to check this type of test than to correct a traditional "paper and pencil" test. Weaker and less interested students tend to make rather short tapes. It is a useful measure of spoken ability in classes where oral English is the focus.

Let's Talk!

This is a speaking game.

Work in groups of four.

Each player uses a marker.
Put it on the *Let's Talk!* mark.
Follow the lines to any space.

Answer the question.
Your answer must have
three or more sentences.

Take turns.

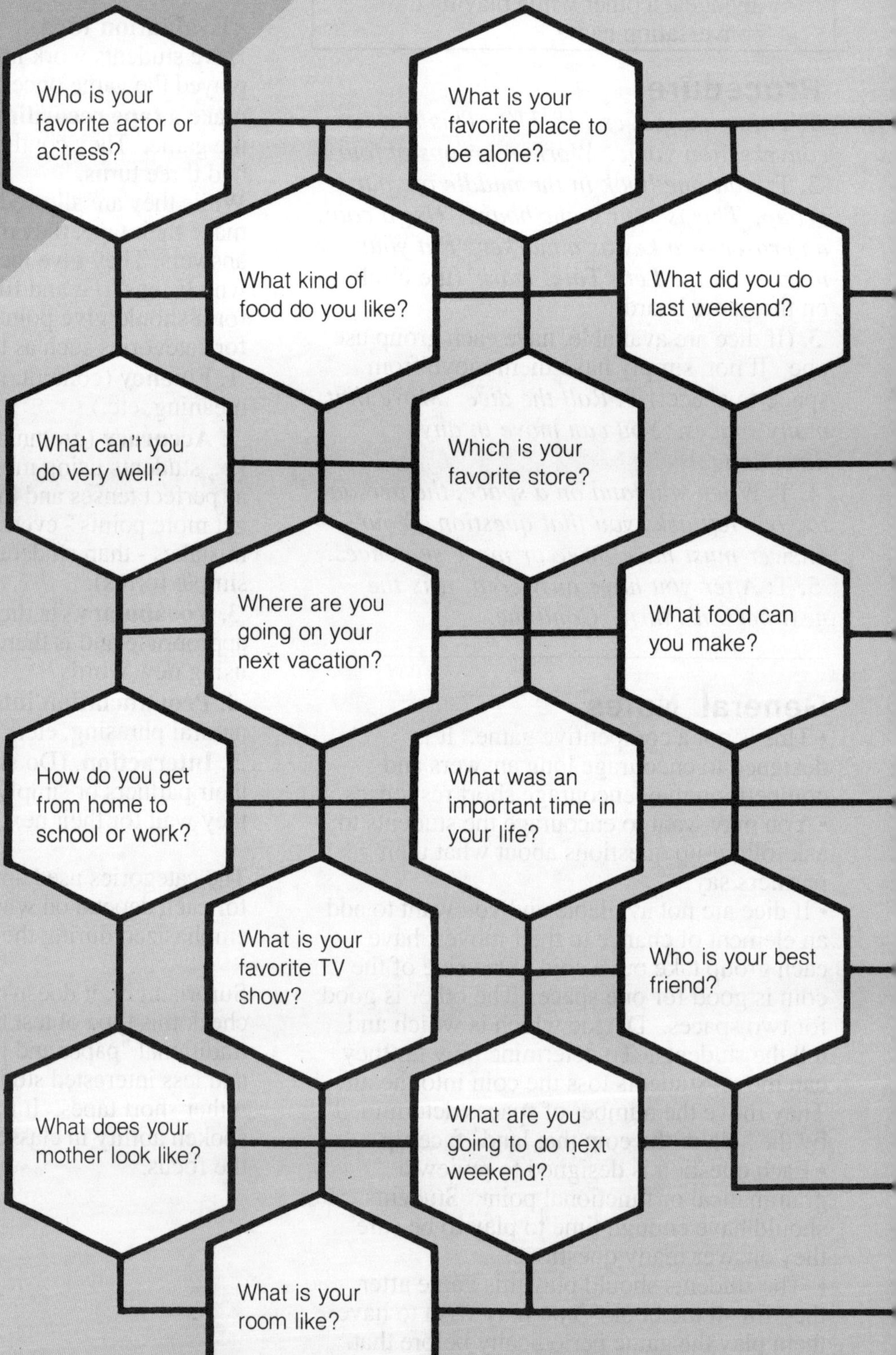

What are you going to do after school today?
What should you do more often?
Who is your most interesting aunt, uncle, or cousin?
What sport do you like?
Can you tell a joke in English?
What is your house or apartment like?
When were you very sad?
What should you do less often?
What will this city be like in 10 years?
What does your father look like?
What kind of clothes do you like?
Where were you born?
When are you bored?
When were you very happy?
What machine can you use?
What can you do very well?
Who is your favorite musician?
What is a good movie you have seen?
Let's Talk!

Project Fair

Objective: The students will create and share projects on topics they are interested in.

General Notes

• Language projects are major tasks which usually take several class periods to complete. Much of the work can be done outside of class. Allow class time, particularly at the beginning, for students to understand and to become excited about the project.

• Because *English Firsthand* incorporates group tasks throughout the syllabus, most students will be familiar with the ideas of using English to achieve a goal rather than simply practicing. In particular, Unit 3 Ensemble (What to they like to do?) and Unit 5 Ensemble (Welcome to my city!) provided miniature projects. In those activities the students were collaborating to produce a clear result. The Class Newspaper (Unit 1-6 review) is an example of a more elaborate project.

• The instructions printed in the student book should provide sufficient information and ideas for the students to get started.

•If necessary, use the instructions printed next to each step of the project to explain what the students should do.

The following are resource notes and suggestions for each step.

Step one: Getting Started

• Most projects will be carried out in pairs. This maximizes the English used.

• You may wish to have students who wish to have more than one partner justify their decision. (Why do they need more than two people?)

• If the project will be used to determine a course grade, you may want to require that projects having more than two people be significantly larger than those done by pairs.

• Teachers interested in more information on project work may want to read *Project Work* by Diana L. Fried-Booth (Oxford University Press.)

Step two: Getting Information

• Virtually any activity that has a clear purpose and a clear result can be a project. Encourage the students to use their imaginations.

• Page 121 provides a list of project ideas and different results. This is to help students realize that a written report -- the only thing approaching a project most students have ever done -- is only one (and perhaps not the most interesting) possibility.

• The first part of the Project idea form (pages 122-123) is a "brainstorming" space. Encourage students to think of a variety of topics before they make their choice.

• Once the students have decided a project topic, encourage them to be very specific about what information they are looking for and where (or from whom) they will get it.

• Encourage students to help each identify and contact information sources.

• Make sure the students are very specific about dividing responsibilities and setting a schedule for coordinating their work.

•If you have access to copying facilities and students are doing a project that requires copying (making a booklet or magazine, for example), let them know your deadline for copying it.

Step three: The Project Fair

• A Project Fair is simply a time when all the students present their projects. Typically, they set up booths around the room to display and talk about what they have done.

• Allow ample time for projects that will be presented to the whole group (e.g., skits, speeches, etc.)

• Since most projects were done in pairs, the partners can take turns being at their booth to answer questions and going around and seeing what other students have done.

• Tell the students well in advance when the Project Fair will be held.

• You may want to invite other teachers or other classes to the Fair. Students may want to invite friends. For most of your students, this will be the biggest accomplishment they have had using English. It can be a source of pride and encouragement if they can them share it with people other than the instructor and their classmates.

• To help keep the students focused onthe purpose of the project fair while it is taking place, you may want to make copies of the following form. As students circulate, they need to learn at least five new things and record them on the form.

Using Projects for Students Evaluation

• Projects, along with the quizzes, "Check yourself" review page scores, attendance and participation, can be used to help with students grading and evaluation. They are especially useful because the amount of effort, as well as student proficiency is very clear.

• Make the criteria clear to the students. Some teachers grade projects entirely on effort and fluency. Others weight such factors as accuracy, presentation (oral or written), etc. If you are using multiple factors, you may want to weight the points (e.g., Effort: 1-10 points, oral presentation 1-5 points, etc.). The categories used and the weight (points) for each depend on what was emphasized during the course.

• You may also want to collect and give points for the form on which students wrote that they learned at the fair. It is often an indication of the degree to which they interacted with other students and listened to what they did.

The Project Fair

Name: ______________________

Visit at least five projects.
Write what you learned.

Project #1
Topic:
____

Who did the project?
What did you learn?

Project #2
Topic:
____

Who did the project?
What did you learn?

Project #3
Topic:
____

Who did the project?
What did you learn?

Project #4
Topic:
____

Who did the project?
What did you learn?

Project #5
Topic:
____

Who did the project?
What did you learn?

The *Project Fair*

Your final task in *English Firsthand* is a project.
Your class will have a project fair.

A RESTAURANT GUIDE FOR YOUR CITY

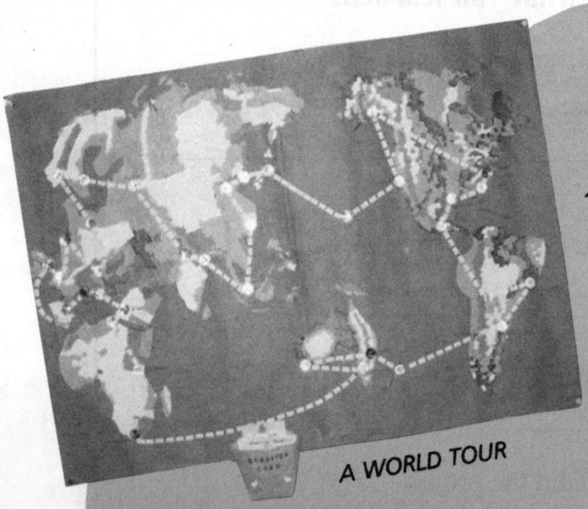

A WORLD TOUR

AN ENTERTAINMENT REVIEW

A RECIPE BOOK

A GUIDE TO YOUR CAMPUS

What is a project?

- A project is a major activity. It has many steps.
  Doing a project will help you use and learn English.
- Projects always have a clear purpose and a clear result.

You have already done some projects:

- *What do they like to do?* (page 32) You created a story.
- *Welcome to my city!* (page 48) You made a map and wrote about your city.
- *The class newspaper* (page 108) was a major project.

Step one: Getting started

Most projects will have two people. **Find a partner.**
If you want to work with more people (for example, to present a play or make a video), talk to your teacher.

Step two: Choosing a project

There are many kinds of projects.

Ideas:

- Make a restaurant, entertainment, or historical guidebook for your city.
- Make a magazine for other students in your school.
- Study a topic you are interested in. Make a report.
  Topics: music, culture, hobbies, business, etc.
- Make a questionnaire. Ask people questions about an important or interesting topic and report the results.
- Interview someone in your first language. Choose a topic (for example, changes in this country). Make an oral or written report in English.
- Interview native English speakers. Choose a topic (for example, things in this culture that are easy/difficult to get used to).
- Make a video about your city or school.
- Prepare and perform a play in English.

With your partner, fill out the project idea form on pages 122-123.

The result

Projects always have a clear result.
You will share what you have done at the **Project Fair.**

These are ideas for the Project Fair.

- An oral report.
- A poster showing what you did and learned.
- A video.
- A play or skit.
- Show people what you made.
- Give a copy of your magazine to everyone. Tell them about it.
- A written report.

Have fun with the project.
Use your imagination.
Challenge yourself!

Project idea form

Names: ______________________________

____

What are some topics you are interested in? Write at least 8.

-
-
-
-
-
-
-
-
-
-

Pick one of the topics. Where can you get the information?

Check (✓) the ones you can use.

☐ talking to someone from your country (Who?) ______________________________

☐ talking to someone from another country (Who?) ______________________________

☐ books

☐ magazines

☐ a library

☐ a government office, embassy, or tourist information center

☐ TV/video

☐ other (What or where?) ______________________________

Your project

What will your project be?
Write a description of your project.

What we will do:

How we will report it:

Do you need any special equipment? (video camera, tape recorder, etc.) ______________________
Where can you get it? ______________________

Schedule

Specific things that need to be done:	When:	Who will do them:
■		
■		
■		
■		
■		
■		

Problems, questions, etc.

QUIZZES

The following quizzes cover main grammar points and vocabulary items presented in ***New English Firsthand.*** They can be used after every second unit (2, 4, 6, 8, 10 and 12). If students are to be given grades, it is recommended that the quizzes be only part of the grading. In addition to the quiz scores, attendance, homework completion and participation should be considered.

Procedure

1. Make a copy of the quiz for each student.
2. Distribute the quizzes. (Have the students write their names at the top, plus any class identification numbers that are necessary.)
3. T: *Look at part one. Write the missing words.*
4. T: *Look at part two. Match the words or expressions.*
5.T: *Look at part three. Find the mistakes. Read each sentence. If the sentence has no mistake, check "OK." If there is a mistake, correct the sentence.*
6. Allow 15 to 20 minutes for the students to take the quiz. As they take the quiz, circulate and make sure that everyone understands what to do. In particular, check that they know they must correct the sentences that are wrong.
7. If you will be checking the quizzes in class, write the "find the mistakes" sentence (in the same form as they appear on the quiz) on the chalkboard.

Checking Procedure

1. (Optional). Redistribute the quizzes. For example, T: *Pass your quiz two people forward. Students in the first two seats, pass yours to the back.*
2. T: *Check the quiz. Use a different color pen or pencil. If there is a mistake, write the correct answer.*
3. Elicit answers from the class. T: *What did you get for number one?* etc. Write the correct answers on the board.
4. Write the "find the mistakes" sentences on the chalkboard (if not done before.)
5. Elicit answers for this section from the class. T: *Is sentence one OK?* (If not,) *What should it be?* Correct it on the board (in a different color chalk if possible).
6. T: *Add up the mistakes. Write it on the "number wrong" line. How many correct? Write it on the "number correct" line.*
7. Return the quiz to the original student. Answer any questions. Collect the quizzes.

Peer-checking Note

While the students may be initially surprised at being asked to correct their own or another student's quiz, the advantages of immediate feedback and the time savings for the teacher make it a useful procedure.

Answer Keys

The following pages provide answer keys to the quizzes. Students may occasionally come up with different answers than the ones presented here that are grammatically correct and meaningful. If they do so, their answers should be accepted.

New English Firsthand
Units 1 & 2 - Quiz

Name: ____________________
Class: ________ No. __________

Part I. Write the missing words.

1. _________ you like some coffee? — Yes, please.
2. What do you _______, Bill? — I'm a student.
3. ______ do you know Mary? — We work in the same office.
4. _______ are you from? — Los Angeles.
5. What does she look ______? — She's tall and has short black hair.
6. What's she _______? — A red coat.
7. What _______ is her hair? — It's brown.
8. ______ do you spell your name? — K-R-I-S.

Part II. Match the words or expressions.

1. _e_ enjoy	a. your aunt's or uncle's child
2. ___ hometown	b. not married
3. ___ slim	c. not outgoing
4. ___ occupation	d. married or single
5. ___ cousin	e. like
6. ___ marital status	f. your brother's or sister's son
7. ___ nephew	g. not fat
8. ___ single	h. your brother's or sister's daughter
	i. job
	k. birthplace

Part III. Find the mistakes. Correct them.
If a sentence has no mistakes, check _√_ OK.

___ OK 1. Where are you live?

___ OK 2. Is he married?

___ OK 3. I live in 5134 Astor in New York.

___ OK 4. He likes skiing.

___ OK 5. She is brown hair.

Number wrong: ______ Number correct: ______ Checked by: ____________________

New English Firsthand

Units 3 & 4 - Quiz

Name: ____________________

Class: __________ No. __________

Part I. Write the missing words.

1. ______ often do you go shopping? Hardly ever.
2. What are you ____________? I'm studying.
3. Where are the pots and pans? _____ are under the sink.
4. ______ you like to go to a movie? That sounds good.
5. What time do you go to work? I usually ______ for work at 8:00.
6. _____ there any pictures? Yes, there are two.

Part II. Match the words or expressions.

1. _b_ won't
2. ___ weekend
3. ___ Could you?
4. ___ The dot (•) is between A and B.
5. ___ The dot is to the left of A.
6. ___ The dot is under B.
7. ___ The dot is next to B.
8. ___ always
9. ___ leaves for

a. Would you....?
b. will not
c. goes to
d. vacation
e. Saturday and Sunday
f. 100 %
g. •A B
h. A • B
i. A B•
j. A B (dot under B)

Part III. Find the mistakes. Correct them.
If a sentence has no mistakes, check _√_ OK.

___ OK 1. I almost get up at 7:00.

___ OK 2. I go to the movies every Saturday. I never go to the movies.

___ OK 3. I go to bed at 9:00 on Monday, Tuesday and Wednesday nights.I never go to bed early.

___ OK 4. How often do you play tennis?

___ OK 5. She usually goes to bed until 11:30.

___ OK 6. She likes to play volleyball.

Number wrong: ______	Number correct: ______	Checked by: ________________

New English Firsthand

Units 5& 6 - Quiz

Name: ______________________

Class: ________ No. __________

Part I. Write the missing words.

1. ________ do I get to the art museum from here?	Go straight ahead about 3 blocks. You'll see it on the left.
2. Is _______ a bookstore near here?	Yes. There's one next to the post office.
3. Where is the Grand Hotel?	_______ on the corner of Main St. and Third St.
4. How long have you lived here?	We moved here when I _____ 10.
5. ______ do you say that in Engish?	It's called "breakfast.".

Part II. Write the missing words.

I ______ a bad day yesterday. I overslept and _____ up at 9:00. I didn't ______ time for breakfast so I ______ an apple in the car. ______ my way to work, I hit another car. I finally ______ to the office at 10:30. During lunch I spilled coffee on my suit. Later, when I _____ fixing dinner, I burned it. I _______ asleep watching TV. I finally ________ to bed at 10:30.

Part III. Find the mistakes. Correct them.
If a sentence has no mistakes, check _√_ OK.

___ OK 1. How do I get to there?
___ OK 2. It's next to the hotel.
___ OK 3. Last year, she go to Los Angeles.
___ OK 4. Turn left the corner.
___ OK 5. I didn't know you can ski.
___ OK 6. The first day was sunny, but after that it got cold.

Number wrong: ______	Number correct: ______	Checked by: ____________________

New English Firsthand

Units 7 & 8 - Quiz

Name: ______________________

Class: __________ No. __________

Part I. Write the missing words.

1. Does Peter ________ a college education? — Yes, he does.
2. _____ you type? — Yes, I'm good at typing.
3. How _____ going to a concert on Sunday? — Sorry, I can't. I have other plans.
4. What would you like to do tonight? — I feel _____ going to a movie.
5. What time _______ we meet? — Let's meet at 6:00.
6. Let's go see Batman II. — No, I ______ it last week.
7. Let's go to an art show. — I'm not really ________ in art shows.

Part II. Match the words or expressions.

1. _g_ Let's…	a. a person who repairs engines
2. ___ clerk	b. 4:45
3. ___ mechanic	c. don't like
4. ___ outgoing	d. What's on?
5. ___ a quarter to five	e. a quarter after eight
6. ___ not interested in	f. not reserved
7. ___ What's playing?	g. Why don't we…
8. ___ 8:30	h. 5:15
9. ___ Sounds good	i. OK
	j. engineer
	k. difficult but interesting
	l. worker in a store or office
	m. half past eight

Part III. Find the mistakes. Correct them.
If a sentence has no mistakes, check _√_ OK.

___ OK 1. That sounds like good.

___ OK 2. Can you typing?

___ OK 3. I like to books.

___ OK 4 What time is it start?

___ OK 5 It starts 7:30.

___ OK 6. I don't really like science fiction films.

Number wrong: ______ Number correct: ______ Checked by: ______________________

New English Firsthand

Units 9 & 10 - Quiz

Name: ____________________

Class: ________ No. _________

Part I. Write the missing words.

1. ________ are you going to do during winter vacation?	I'll probably visit my parents.
2. May I help you?	Yes, I'm ________ for a sweater.
3. How ______ is this one?	$30.00
4. Do you have anything ______ expensive?	Yes, this one in only $20.00.
5. ______ it's sunny, let's go to the beach.	That sounds good.
6. How ______ pages?	About 50.
7. I'd like a yellow one, please.	Sorry, we don't have _____yellow ones.

Part II. Match the words or expressions.

1. ___ predict
2. ___ plan to
3. ___ in 10 years
4. ___ I'm looking for…
5. ___ kind
6. ___ I'll probably
7. ___ three dollars and twenty-five cents

a. three and a quarter
b. 10 years ago
c. I want to buy…
d. I might...
e. (be) going to
f. three and a half
g. type
h. I'm almost sure I'll...
i. 10 years from now
k. say something will happen
l. Be sure to...

Part III. Find the mistakes. Correct them.
If a sentence has no mistakes, check _√_ OK.

___ OK 1. I plan to relax this weekend.

___ OK 2. The blue one is more cheaper than the red one.

___ OK 3. I'm not sure. Maybe I'll study.

___ OK 4. My most favorite department store is Sears.

___ OK 5. These are very cheaper than those.

___ OK 6. I'm going to visit the zoo and maybe I'll go to the beach.

Number wrong: ______	Number correct: ______	Checked by: ________________

New English Firsthand

Units 11 & 12 - Quiz

Name: ____________________

Class: __________ No. __________

Part I. Write the missing words.

1. Have you ________ Tom Cruise's new movie yet? Yeah, I saw it last week.
2. ________ did you like it? I thought it was boring.
3. What's the ______ interesting place you've visited? Hong Kong
4. What's the best book you've ________ read? I don't really have a favorite
5. How does this machine ________? It's easy. I'll show you.
6. Golf is really exciting. Oh, I don't __________ so.

Part II. Match the words or expressions.

1. ***b*** press	a. not really good or bad
2. ___ after that	b. push
3. ___ boring	c. cook in oil
4. ___ finally	d. frightened
5. ___ wallet	e. the opposite of exciting
6. ___ boil	f. the last thing
7. ___ fry	g. write information on a form
8. ___ peel	h. cook in water
9. ___ scared	i. then
10 ___ so-so	j. something to keep money in
	k. take off the skin
	l. cut into small pieces

Part III. Find the mistakes. Correct them.
If a sentence has no mistakes, check _√_ OK.

___ OK 1. Jazz is more interested than rock.

___ OK 2. She was disappointed because her team lost.

___ OK 3. He went into the wrong room because he was embarrassed.

___ OK 4. What is the most worst movie you have ever seen?

___ OK 5. Finally, take it out of the oven and bake it.

Number wrong: ______	Number correct: ______	Checked by: ____________________

Answer Key

Units 1 & 2 - Quiz

Part I. Write the missing words.

1. **Would** you like some coffee?
2. What do you **do**, Bill?
3. **How** do you know Mary?
4. **Where** are you from?
5. What does she look **like**?
6. What's she **wearing**?
7. What **color** is her hair?
8. **How** do you spell your name?

Part II. Match the words or expressions.

1. e — enjoy (e. like)
2. **k** — hometown (k. birthplace)
3. **g** — slim (g. not fat)
4. **i** — occupation (i. job)
5. **a** — cousin (a. your aunt's or uncle's child)
6. **d** — marital status (d. married or single)
7. **f** — nephew (f. your brother's or sister's son)
8. **b** — single (b. not married)

Part III. Find the mistakes.

1. Where ~~are~~ **do** you live?
2. **OK:** Is he married?
3. I live ~~in~~ **at** 5134 Astor in New York.
4. **OK:** He likes skiing.
5. She ~~is~~ **has** brown hair.

Units 3 & 4 - Quiz

Part I. Write the missing words.

1. **How** often do you go shopping?
2. What are you **doing?**
3. **They** are under the sink.
4. **Would** you like to go to a movie?
5. I usually **leave** for work at 8:00.
6. **Are** there any pictures?

Part II. Match the words or expressions.

1. ***b*** — won't (b. will not)
2. **e** — weekend (e. Saturday and Sunday)
3. **a** — Could you? (a. Would you....?)
4. **h** — The dot (•) is between A and B. (h. A • B)
5. **g** — The dot is to the left of A. (g. •A B)
6. **j** — The dot is under B. (j. A B)
7. **i** — The dot is next to B. (i. A B•)
8. **f** — always (f.100 %)
9. **c** — leaves for (c. goes to)

Part III. Find the mistakes.

1. I almost **always** get up at 7:00.
   OR: I usually get up at 7:00
   OR: I almost never get up at 7:00
2. I go to the movies every Saturday.
   I ~~never~~ **always** go to the movies (on Saturday).
   OR: I often go to the movies.
3. I go to bed at 9:00 on Monday, Tuesday and Wednesday nights.I ~~never~~ **sometimes** go to bed early.
4. **OK:** How often do you play tennis?
5. She usually goes to bed ~~until~~ **by** 11:30.
   OR: She usually goes to bed at 11:30.
6 **OK:** She likes to play volleyball.

Units 5 & 6 Quiz

Part I. Write the missing words.

1. **How** do I get to the art museum from here?
2. Is **there** a bookstore near here?
3. **It's** on the corner of Main Street and Third Street.
4. We moved here when I **was** 10.
5. **How** do you say that in English?

Part II. Write the missing words.

I **had** a bad day yesterday. I overslept and **got** up at 9:00. I didn't **have** time for breakfast so I **ate** an apple in the car. **On** my way to work, I hit another car. I finally **got** to the office at 10:30. During lunch I spilled coffee on my suit. Later, when I **was** fixing dinner, I burned it. I **fell** asleep watching TV. I finally **went** (OR: got) to bed at 10:30.

Part III. Find the mistakes.

1. How do I get ~~to~~ there?
2. **OK:** It's next to the hotel.
3. Last year, she ~~go~~ **went** to Los Angeles.
4. Turn left **at** the corner.
5. I didn't know you ~~can~~ **could** ski.
6. **OK:** The first day was sunny, but after that it got cold.

Units 7 & 8- Quiz

Part I. Write the missing words.

1. Does Peter **have** a college education?
2. **Can** you type?
3. How **about** going to a concert on Sunday?
4. I feel **like** going to a movie.
5. What time **shall** we meet?
6. No, I **saw** it last week.
7. I'm not really **interested** in art shows.

Part II. Match the words or expressions.

1. **g** Let's… (g. Why don't we...)
2. **l** clerk (l. worker in a store or office)
3. **a** mechanic (a. a person who repairs engines)
4. **f** outgoing (f. not reserved)
5. **b** a quarter to five (b. 4:45)
6. **c** not interested in (c. don't like)
7. **d** What's playing? (d. What's on?)
8. **m** 8:30 (m. half past eight)
9. **i** Sounds good. (i. OK)

Part III. Find the mistakes.

1. That sounds ~~like~~ good.
   OR: That sounds like fun.
2. Can you ~~typing~~ **type** ?
3. I like ~~to~~ books.
   OR: I like to read.
4. What time ~~is~~ **does** it start?
5. It starts **at** 7:30.
6. **OK:** I really don't like science fiction films.

Units 9 & 10 - Quiz

Part I. Write the missing words.

1. **What** are you going to do during winter vacation?
2. Yes, I'm **looking** for a sweater.
3. How **much** is this one?
4. Do you have anything **less** expensive?
5. **If** it's sunny, let's go to the beach.
6. How **many** pages?
7. Sorry, we don't have **any** yellow ones.

Part II. Match the words or expressions.

1. **k** predict (k. say something will happen)
2. **d** plan to (d. I might...)
3. **i** in 10 years (i. 10 years from now)
4. **c** I'm looking for (c. I want to buy…)
5. **g** kind (g. type)
6. **h** I'll probably (h. I'm almost sure. I'll...)
7. **a** three dollars and twenty-five cents (a. three and a quarter)

Part III. Find the mistakes.

1. **OK:** I plan to relax this weekend.
2. The blue one is ~~more~~ cheaper than the red one.
3. **OK:** I'm not sure. Maybe I'll study.
4. My ~~most~~ favorite department store is Sears.
5. These are ~~very~~ **much** cheaper than those.
6. **OK:** I'm going to visit the zoo and maybe I'll go to the beach.

Units 11 & 12 - Quiz

Part I. Write the missing words.

1. Have you **seen** Tom Cruise's new movie yet?
2. **How** did you like it?
3. What's the **most** interesting place you've visited?
4. What's the best book you've **ever** read?
5. How does this machine **work** ?
6. Oh, I don't **think** so.

Part II. Match the words or expressions.

1. **b** press (b. push)
2. **i** after that (i. then)
3. **e** boring (e. the opposite of exciting)
4. **f** finally (f. the last thing)
5. **j** wallet (j. something to keep money in)
6. **h** boil (h. cook in water)
7. **c** fry (c. cook in oil)
8. **k** peel (k. take off the skin)
9. **d** scared (d. frightened)
10. **a** so-so (a. not really good or bad)

Part III. Find the mistakes.

1. Jazz is more ~~interested~~ **interesting** than rock.
2. **OK:** She was disappointed because her team lost.
3. He was embarrassed because he went into the wrong room.
   (Clauses were in the wrong order.)
   OR: Because he went into the wrong room, he was embarrassed.
4. What is the ~~most~~ worst movie you have ever seen?
5. Finally, bake it and take it out of the oven. (Clauses were in the wrong order.)

Useful language for the classroom

What does ________ mean?
(it)

How do you say ________ in English?
(that)

How do you spell ________ ?
(it)

I don't understand.

I don't know.

Could you repeat that?

Excuse me?

____

____

____

____